Additional Praise for *Suzanne's Children*

"Immersive . . . By placing Spaak's singular story in the broader context of the occupation, *Suzanne's Children* vividly dramatizes the stakes of acting morally in a time of brutality. Ms. Nelson's exhaustive research reveals in chilling detail the gruesome methods with which the Nazis nearly succeeded in ridding France of its Jews and exposes the easy complicity with which too many French aided them in that goal. . . . [Suzanne Spaak's] is a legacy worth reading about."

—*The Wall Street Journal*

"At a time when we most need heroes, Anne Nelson gives us Suzanne Spaak, an undiscovered heroine of the French Resistance. Brave and enterprising, Suzanne defies Vichy and Nazi authorities and rescues hundreds of Jewish children. Impressively researched, *Suzanne's Children* is vivid proof that much more might have been done had others followed Spaak's mantra in the face of evil, '*il faut faire quelque chose*.'"

—Kati Marton, *New York Times* bestselling author of *True Believer* and *Enemies of the People*

"During the German occupation of France, Suzanne Spaak displayed almost superhuman courage, setting up an elaborate network to save Jewish children while working with numerous resistance groups. She knew full well the risks involved, but never let them slow her down. Anne Nelson has written an extraordinary book that finally does justice to Spaak's story of heroism and sacrifice."

—Andrew Nagorski, author of *The Nazi Hunters*

"One person of courage can make a difference. Anne Nelson tells the story of Suzanne Spaak, an elegant Belgian aristocrat who risked her life to save Jewish children in Nazi-occupied France. Her conscience told her someone had to do something. But, as Nelson's gripping book shows, doing the right thing can also come at a price."

—Alan Riding, author of *And the Show Went On: Cultural Life in Nazi-Occupied Paris*

"Largely forgotten over the years is the story of Suzanne Spaak, whose efforts resulted in the survival of Jewish children . . . [accomplished] through a network of like-minded individuals, including aid from her own young children . . . right under the noses of the Germans and French police. . . . In spite of the tragedy of this story, one must admire the fact that so many more lives were spared an unthinkable end . . . thanks to the humanity of just one individual. It is additional reinforcement of the idea that personal sacrifice should always be recognized and honored."

—*New York Journal of Books*

Suzanne's Children

A Daring Rescue in Nazi Paris

Anne Nelson

Simon & Schuster Paperbacks

New York   London   Toronto   Sydney   New Delhi

Simon & Schuster Paperbacks
An Imprint of Simon & Schuster, Inc.
1230 Avenue of the Americas
New York, NY 10020

First Simon & Schuster trade paperback edition October 2018

SIMON & SCHUSTER PAPERBACKS and colophon are registered trademarks
of Simon & Schuster, Inc.

For information about special discounts for bulk purchases,
please contact Simon & Schuster Special Sales at 1-866-506-1949
or business@simonandschuster.com.

The Simon & Schuster Speakers Bureau can bring authors to
your live event. For more information or to book an event,
contact the Simon & Schuster Speakers Bureau at 1-866-248-3049
or visit our website at www.simonspeakers.com.

Interior design by Lewelin Polanco

Manufactured in the United States of America

3 5 7 9 10 8 6 4 2

The Library of Congress has cataloged the hardcover edition as follows:

Names: Nelson, Anne, author.
Title: Suzanne's children : a daring rescue in Nazi Paris / Anne Nelson.
Description: New York : Simon & Schuster, [2017] |
Includes bibliographical references and index.
Identifiers: LCCN 2017008567 (print) | LCCN 2017010549 (ebook) | ISBN
9781501105326 (hardcover : alk. paper) | ISBN 9781501105333
(trade pbk. : alk. paper) | ISBN 9781501105340 (ebook)
Subjects: LCSH: Spaak, Suzanne. | Righteous Gentiles in
the Holocaust—France—Paris—Biography.
Classification: LCC D804.66.S68 N45 2017 (print) | LCC D804.66.S68
(ebook) | DDC 940.53/18092 [B]—dc23
LC record available at https://lccn.loc.gov/2017008567

ISBN 978-1-5011-0532-6
ISBN 978-1-5011-0533-3 (pbk)
ISBN 978-1-5011-0534-0 (ebook)

To Suzanne's Children:

Pilette and Bazou,
Larissa, Sami, and Jacques.

The children she cared for then,
The children she would care for now.

I end up wondering if I won't simply decide to split the world in two: the world of those who cannot understand (even if they know, even if I tell them . . .) and the world of those who can.

—Hélène Berr, Journal, October 19, 1943

contents

contents

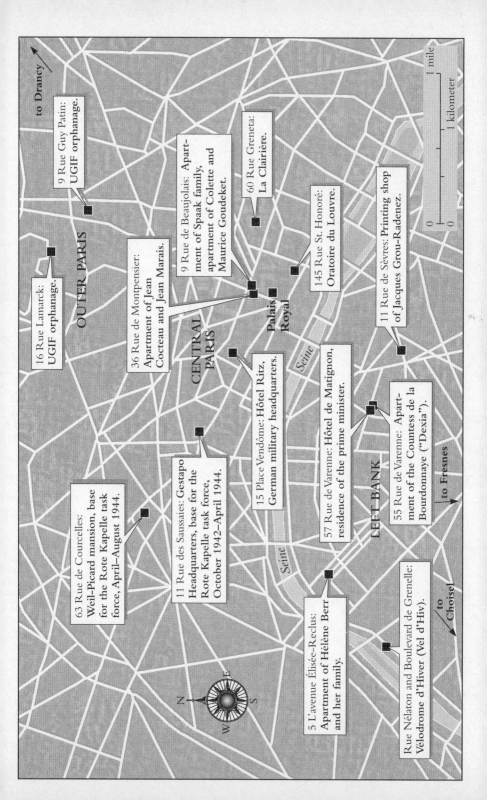

16 Rue Lamarck: UGIF orphanage.

9 Rue Guy Patin: UGIF orphanage.

to Drancy

OUTER PARIS

36 Rue de Montpensier: Apartment of Jean Cocteau and Jean Marais.

9 Rue de Beaujolais: Apartment of the Spaak family, apartment of Colette and Maurice Goudeket.

60 Rue Greneta: La Clairière.

CENTRAL PARIS

Palais Royal

145 Rue St. Honoré: Oratoire du Louvre.

11 Rue de Sèvres: Printing shop of Jacques Grou-Radenez.

Seine

15 Place Vendôme: Hôtel Ritz, German military headquarters.

57 Rue de Varenne: Hôtel de Matignon, residence of the prime minister.

63 Rue de Courcelles: Weil-Picard mansion, base for the Rote Kapelle task force, April–August 1944.

11 Rue des Saussaies: Gestapo Headquarters, base for the Rote Kapelle task force, October 1942–April 1944.

LEFT BANK

55 Rue de Varenne: Apartment of the Countess de la Bourdonnaye ("Dexia").

to Fresnes

Seine

5 L'avenue Élisée-Reclus: Apartment of Hélène Berr and her family.

Rue Nélaton and Boulevard de Grenelle: Vélodrome d'Hiver (Vel d'Hiv).

to Choisel

0   1 mile

0   1 kilometer

N E W S

dramatis personae

The Spaaks

Paul Spaak, writer; married to

Marie Janson Spaak, daughter of Belgian prime minister Paul Janson, sister to Prime Minister Paul-Émile Janson, and world's first female senator

Their Children

Paul-Henri Spaak, prime minister of Belgium; married Marguerite

Charles Spaak, screenwriter of *Grand Illusion* and numerous other films

Claude Spaak, playwright and art connoisseur; married Suzanne Lorge

Madeleine (Pichenette) Spaak Masson

The Lorges

Louis Lorge, financier; married to

Jeanne Bourson

dramatis personae

Their Children

Suzanne (Suzette) Lorge; married Claude Spaak
Alice (Bunny) Lorge; married Milo Happé
Angèle (Teddy) Lorge; married Maurice Fontaine

Claude and Suzanne Spaak's Children

Lucie (Pilette)
Paul-Louis (Bazou)

Ruth Peters, Suzanne Spaak's childhood friend and Claude
Spaak's mistress

Soviet Agents

Leopold Trepper, Polish Jewish Communist
Georgie de Winter, Trepper's young mistress
Hersch (Harry) and Miriam (Mira) Sokol, Jewish refugees turned
radio operators
Madame May, Trepper's elderly courier
Fernand Pauriol, French Communist who supported Trepper's
radio operations

The Jewish Underground

Leon Chertok, Jewish refugee doctor and a leader of the chil-
dren's rescue efforts
Sophie Schwartz Micnik, Polish trade unionist and women's leader
Charles Lederman, Polish-born French Jewish lawyer
Adam Rayski, Polish-born journalist and militant
Édouard (Arek) Kowalski, Jewish Communist military leader

Jewish Children Rescued by the Network

Larissa Gruszow
Sami Dassa

Jacques Alexandre

Simone and Armand Boruchowicz

The Doctors and the Ladies

Robert Debré, leading French Jewish pediatrician

Elisabeth de la Panouse, Countess de la Bourdonnaye, Debré's partner, known as "Dexia"

Fred Milhaud, French Jewish pediatrician working for the UGIF Jewish Council; married to

Denise Milhaud, president of the Entr'aide Temporaire relief organization

The Berrs (Raymond and Antoinette, their daughters Hélène and Denise; cousin Nicole Schneiderman; and Denise's sister-in-law, Nicole Job), activists with Entr'aide Temporaire

Marguerite "Peggy" Camplan, MNCR partner

The Protestants

Pastor Paul Vergara, pastor at the Oratoire; married to Marcelle Vergara

Sylvain Vergara, the Vergaras' teenage son

Eliane Vergara, the Vergaras' oldest daughter, married to

Jacques Bruston, a member of the Gaullist Resistance

Marcelle Guillemot, social worker at La Clairière church soup kitchen

Odette Béchard, a member of the Oratoire who joined Entr'aide Temporaire

Maurice-William Girardot, church deacon and courier for funds

The Gaullists

Jean Moulin, leader of the Gaullist resistance

Jacques Grou-Radenez, master printer who helped the student movement Défense de la France

Hugues Limonti, family friend of Marcelle Guillemot and
Gaullist agent in Paris

The Neighbors

Colette, considered France's greatest writer of her time, Palais
Royal resident with her Jewish husband, Maurice Goudeket
Jean Cocteau, prodigious French artist and writer, Palais Royal
resident with his lover, actor Jean Marais

The Germans

Theodor Dannecker, SS officer who organized deportations in
Paris from September 1940 to July 1942
Helmut Knochen, SS officer placed in charge of the Gestapo in
France in November 1940
Klaus Barbie, SS officer placed in charge of the Gestapo in Lyon
in November 1942
Alois Brunner, SS officer placed in charge of the camp at Drancy
in June 1943
Heinz Pannwitz, Gestapo officer in command of the Red
Orchestra task force (Sonderkommando Rote Kapelle),
charged with tracking down Leopold Trepper and his associates
Rudolf Rathke, Gestapo officer on the task force

The British

Benjamin Cowburn, agent of the Special Operations Executive
(SOE)
Johnny Barrett, radio operator for the SOE

1

strangers

S uzanne and Claude Spaak moved to Paris in 1937, bring-
ing their two children, a surrealist art collection, and a large
wicker trunk. They were a golden couple, attractive, affluent,
cultured; the move was designed to mend the fault lines. Claude
was frustrated in his writing career, and their marriage had faltered.
Maybe Paris would help.

Claude had outgrown Brussels, though the city had offered him
every advantage. He owed many of them to his wife. "Suzette" was the
oldest child of Louis Lorge, one of Belgium's leading financiers. A self-
made man, he spent his life pursuing wealth and social status. He had
married into a prominent family and employed German and English
governesses for his daughters. He provided his family with a mansion
in Brussels, a house in the country, and holidays on the French Riviera.

Louis doted on his firstborn, a petite blonde with long ringlets
and a Cupid's bow mouth. He decided that she should marry into
the aristocracy and sent her to finishing school to study embroidery,
piano, and household management. But she chafed at her father's
mercenary values and leaned toward literature and social reform.

Suzanne's Children

The summer she was fourteen, Suzanne fell in love with Claude Spaak, her fifteen-year-old neighbor at their country estate. A dreamy-eyed poet and a member of Belgium's leading political dynasty, he courted her on romantic boat rides, reciting French verse. The two became secretly engaged. Suzanne was also enamored of Claude's mother, Marie Spaak, a tiny dynamo who fought for women's suffrage, labor reforms, and immigrant rights. When Marie's father died in 1921, she was invited to take his place in the Belgian senate. According to family lore, "She refused the position and told her family. Her sons burst out laughing, and she was so insulted she changed her mind and accepted"—becoming the first female senator in the world.[1]

Louis Lorge strongly opposed Suzanne's choice of husband, but she stood firm. A last-minute complication arose. The couple's mothers discovered that there was a third party to the romance, a Canadian classmate of Suzanne's named Ruth Peters. The two girls shared everything, including an infatuation with Claude. The mothers sent Ruth home to Toronto, and Louis took measures to protect his daughter's fortune. Rather than disbursing her dowry in a lump sum, he would pay it in monthly installments to guarantee her a good living.

Claude Spaak was the youngest of three brothers, all of them tall and combative. Paul-Henri, the oldest, ran away as a teenager to enlist in the Belgian army in the First World War and ended up in a German prison camp. He returned to join the family's political enterprise, and it was said that he addressed the Belgian parliament as "*Monsieur le Président, Sénateurs, et Maman.*" The second son, Charles, was on the way to becoming a celebrated screenwriter in Paris. Claude struggled to emerge from his brothers' shadows. Little was heard of their sister, Madeleine, known as "Pichenette."

When the brothers joined the family at weekly lunches, they never made it to dessert; one was certain to have stormed out. They taunted Claude's young fiancée. When there was a lull, she stared at her plate until one demanded, "Suzette, do you hear the clock ticking?" and she would run to her room. As her father's favorite, Suzanne expected to be treated with respect, but Claude chose to see her take his place at the bottom of the stack.

The couple married in 1925. Within a year Suzanne was pregnant and miscarried, but the next year she gave birth to a healthy girl, Lucie. Claude sent the news to Ruth in Canada in an envelope bearing three horses, indicating her place in their relationship. The family nicknamed the child "Pilette" after a famous Belgian race car driver, whose garage sign caught her attention on her daily stroll.

Claude was appointed the first artistic director of Brussels' new Palais des Beaux-Arts, where his job was to organize exhibits and answer complaints. He dealt with the boredom by taking up the avant-garde. He was attracted to a struggling Belgian painter, René Magritte, a rough-hewn man from the coal-mining region west of Brussels, six years his senior. Magritte was eking out a living designing wallpaper and sheet music. He aspired to make a name as a surrealist painter, but he struggled with the complex wordplay of the Parisian intellectuals. Claude helped him along by suggesting ideas for paintings, then acquiring them for himself and the extended family (some of whom hid them in the attic). Curious canvases began to fill the Spaaks' walls. Other families displayed pictures of dead ancestors or bowls of fruit, but the Spaaks' Magrittes showed a tuba bursting into flame and leather boots sprouting toes.[2]

At home, all was far from well. Claude's temper drove Suzanne to tears, and there were other complications. Claude was smitten with an older woman, whom he followed to the South of France. She humored him for two weeks, then sent him packing back to Brussels, whereupon he began an affair with a coworker.

Divorce was legal but rare in Belgium, and Suzanne would be required to show cause, embarrassing the family. She wrote Ruth in Canada and asked her to come back. If Claude was going to have a mistress, it might as well be someone she liked. Ruth could calm

Claude's tantrums and intuit his wishes—and she could type. So she became his secretary, and Claude alternated between two beds.

In 1931 Suzanne gave birth to Paul-Louis, or "Bazou." On the way home from the hospital the taxi driver looked at him and exclaimed, "*Quel petit gros bazouf!*" ("What a big little fatso!"), and the nickname stuck. Claude and Ruth stood over his cradle and promised never to do anything that would hurt the children.

Pilette contracted polio at the age of two. After a long search, Suzanne found a Swedish doctor who helped her with a new procedure. The painful operation kept her in a cast for months, but it saved her leg. Suzanne then turned to social issues. The Depression had driven factory workers into the streets. In 1935 Paul-Henri was appointed to serve as Belgium's youngest cabinet minister. Though he advocated for the workers, Claude and Suzanne thought he was too cautious. Suzanne turned to the World Committee of Women against War and Fascism, a leftist coalition of feminists and pacifists.[3]

She took an interest in the plight of the Jewish immigrants she met there, a growing population invisible to most Belgians. Jews counted for less than 1 percent of Belgium's population of eight million, and only a small fraction were citizens. Most had fled hardship and pogroms in Eastern Europe, and the Nazis were adding thousands to their ranks. When Suzanne read some articles by a young Polish Jewish activist, Julia Pirotte, she encouraged her to take up photojournalism. She commandeered her sister Bunny's Leica Elmar III. "You never use it," she told her, and Bunny's Leica launched Pirotte's career as a world-class photographer.[4]

In 1936 Claude commissioned Magritte to paint family portraits. He began with a snapshot of Suzanne, placing her image on a page of a book opening to a patch of blue sky with white clouds. Then he did portraits of Claude and Ruth seated in front of surrealist backgrounds. Claude disliked them and cropped the paintings, leaving only the heads. The next year Magritte painted the children in front of a window open to a road strewn with surrealist icons. His final painting of Claude's family was *L'Ésprit de géométrie*, which depicted a mother with Bazou's childish head, holding an infant with Suzanne's adult head. It is both the most disturbing and successful of his Spaak portraits.*

By 1937 Claude decided that his career was stalled. Brussels was small, provincial, and dominated by his powerful family; his uncle was the current prime minister, and his brother Paul-Henri, the boy wonder of Belgian politics, was about to assume that position. In France, brother Charles had become one of the country's leading screenwriters, and his coattails would be useful. Claude submitted some plays to Paris producers. Several expressed interest, and he packed up the family.

It was, of course, Suzanne's inheritance that made the move possible. Claude rented a comfortable apartment in the suburb of Saint-Cloud, and the couple installed the children, unpacked their trunks, and hung their Magrittes. Claude mingled with theater and film folk, but Suzanne felt out of place. Parisians were defying the Great Depression with madcap pursuits. Le Hot Club de France had just launched its first jazz label. Hemlines were long, waists were narrow, and the collaboration between surrealists and couturiers sizzled. Elsa Schiaparelli and Salvador Dalí designed a hat that looked like a shoe and a "skeleton dress" with a protruding rib cage.

In July 1937 Suzanne's father died, leaving her a sizable inheritance, and the couple bought a farmhouse in the bucolic village of Choisel, thirty miles south of Paris. They renovated it top to bottom and set aside a room for Ruth. Suzanne thought the country would be good for the children. Bazou was thrilled to be reunited with his German shepherd, Wotan, who had been left behind in

---

* The painting was acquired by the Tate Collection in London.

Brussels, but Suzanne now found herself stranded in a hamlet of flinty French farmers and weekenders.

Magritte, still struggling, wrote to patrons pleading for a stipend. When they turned him down, Suzanne offered him one thousand francs a month (roughly the salary of a secretary) in exchange for a series of paintings. The Spaaks amassed an extraordinary collection of forty-four works that would one day grace the world's leading museums.

The Spaaks had moved to France for art's sake, but there was no escaping politics. Over the mid-1930s Paris was rocked by street violence, and the country was polarized. The Left formed a coalition of Socialists, Communists, and trade unions, which won the 1936 elections. Léon Blum became France's first Socialist and first Jewish prime minister. The Right responded with rage, echoing the Nazi diatribes against immigrant "Jewish agitators" and the "international Jewish banking conspiracy."

France was still officially at peace, but war was in the air. Edith Piaf sang "Mon Legionnaire," and there was a new vogue for war movies. One of them was *La Grande Illusion*, written by Charles Spaak. The 1937 masterpiece, directed by Jean Renoir, was based in part on Paul-Henri's experiences as a German prisoner of war. It became an international sensation, but Paul-Henri, Belgium's foreign minister, banned it in that country for fear it would enflame anti-German sentiment.*

In Spain, Fascist forces battled the democratically elected Republican government, and French newspapers warned there was worse to come. In April 1937 German and Italian planes bombed the town of Guernica, killing hundreds of civilians. Tens of thousands of refugees poured across the border into France. Suzanne

---

* Nazi propaganda minister Joseph Goebbels also banned it in Germany, while in the US, Eleanor Roosevelt screened it at the White House.

helped those she could, including a girl named Carmen, who taught the children to dance the *jota*. Suzanne sewed Spanish costumes, and she and Claude took them to neighboring towns with the family gramophone. Locals gathered in the town square to watch them perform. Suzanne unfurled a banner—"Open the borders to Spain!"—as Bazou passed the hat. A photo shows Suzanne and her entourage raising their fists in a *"No Pasarán!"* salute.

The French public tended to regard the conflict as a Spanish problem. They were convinced that a broader war was unlikely and that their army and defenses shielded them. But the November 5, 1938, edition of *Le Figaro* challenged their complacency:

Monsieur von Rath [*sic*], third secretary of the German embassy [in Paris], was grievously wounded in his office. The aggressor is a young refugee of Polish origin who is not authorized to reside in France.

Le Figaro concluded that the attack was a tragic consequence of France's lax immigration policies.

France's ongoing excessive tolerance creates a battleground for those who are not interested in serving our country's interests, only in undermining them.

The teenaged Jewish gunman, Herschel Grynszpan, was a magnet for French anti-immigrant sentiment. He had acted in response to an immigration dispute between Poland and Germany that had left his elderly parents stranded in a refugee camp on the border. He walked into the German embassy and randomly chose his victim, who died three days later. On November 9 the Nazis unleashed *Kristallnacht* in Germany, burning synagogues, murdering dozens, and sending more than thirty thousand Jewish men to concentration camps. Some families ransomed their relatives and sent them abroad, driving another wave of Jewish refugees into France.

On November 11, *Le Figaro* expressed shock at the German violence:

> A kind of madness seized the German population, and the hatred of the Israelite race today reached its paroxysm.

The paper included a response from the *Berliner Lokal-Anzeiger* calling on the French government to expel the foreign trouble-makers who "make their nest in Paris" and urging it "to begin with those who bear arms for Jewish Bolshevism." France's "excessive tolerance" toward Jewish refugees was now under internal attack.

Suzanne had sympathized with the Jewish exiles in Brussels, among them Miriam Sokol. One day in 1938 she and her husband, Hersch, appeared on the Spaaks' doorstep in France. The tiny, raven-haired Mira had met Suzanne through her women's committee. Born in Vilnius, she had earned a PhD in social science in Brussels, where she met "Harry" Sokol, a young physician from a prosperous Jewish family in Bialystock.

The Sokols, like many of France's immigrant Jews, came from the tumultuous zone that spanned the Russian-German divide, where it was possible to live in three different countries over thirty years without moving house. They had been born in Czarist Russia, grew up under German occupation, and came of age in the newly reconstituted Poland. Each disruption brought more travails for the Jews. It was not uncommon for Jewish families to send their children as far away as possible, praying they would never come back.

Harry Sokol was a short, slight man with alert brown eyes and a puckish smile. He had studied and worked in England, South Africa, and Switzerland, and spoke English, French, and German. When he met Mira in Brussels he was completing his medical studies, but his immigration status made it impossible for him to practice. They attempted to emigrate to Russia, but the Soviets turned them down with the excuse of a housing shortage in Moscow. They applied again in 1935 with the same result.[5]

Mira found a job working for a Socialist member of the Belgian parliament, and Harry became a traveling medical supplies salesman who gave Marxist lectures on the side. This violated Belgium's rules barring aliens from political activity, and they were expelled in 1938.[6] They made their way to France with little more than Suzanne Spaak's address.

Suzanne was glad to see Mira. The two women shared interests and social concerns, as well as their outsider status. The salons of Paris had little to offer a shy Belgian housewife with a bookish turn of mind. Things were far worse for Mira, a penniless Jewish émigrée. Her husband's medical degree and her doctorate meant nothing in France.

Suzanne helped the Sokols find a place to live, and Mira visited her frequently. Years later Claude recalled, "My wife and I belonged to a group of left-wing intellectuals, which is why our assistance was sought. . . . My wife was very fond of [the Sokols]. For my part, I found their sectarianism a little excessive and rather oppressive, but I admired their idealism, the absolute purity of their convictions."[7] Claude found Harry strident and doctrinaire. The Spaaks' young son, Bazou, called him "*Monsieur je-sais-tout,*" or "Mr. Know-it-all." Pilette agreed. Harry was a "cold fish," but Mira was "soft, loving, a true friend."

When the Sokols arrived in France, Stalin's purges were imprisoning and murdering tens of millions of Soviet citizens. Still, in Harry's eyes Stalin could do no wrong. The Spaaks' circle of friends included Communist Party members, but they considered Stalin and Hitler both to be monsters who had to be stopped. Suzanne was willing to help Communist refugees, but she had no interest in joining the party.

Mira was Jewish? A *litwak*? A Communist? For Suzanne, these labels were of no interest. She could talk to Mira about family and literature. They discussed politics, but they were more concerned with humanitarian issues than ideology. For Suzanne, Mira's Jewish identity was a subject of interest, not prejudice.

Jews had lived in France since Roman times. The Revolution granted the country's Jews full rights of citizenship, as it did France's other persecuted minority, the Protestants. Most traditional French Jews had roots in the Alsace-Lorraine, the territory that straddled the French-German frontier. They began moving to Paris in the early nineteenth century, and soon gained entrée into elite schools, professions, and neighborhoods.

In the late nineteenth century, assimilation was tested by Jewish migration from Central and Eastern Europe. Between 1880 and 1925, 3.5 million Jews left the region, 2.5 million of them for the United States.[8] But in 1924 the US Congress passed severely restrictive immigration laws whose stated goal was "to preserve the ideal of American homogeneity."[9] Within a year, France overtook the United States as a destination, largely because it needed immigrant labor to compensate for its disastrous losses in the First World War and the Spanish flu epidemic. In 1927 the French parliament passed a law allowing fifty thousand Jewish and other immigrants to obtain French citizenship, inspiring more Eastern European Jews to "*Lebn vi Got in Frankraykh*" (Live like God in France).[10]

Then came the crash of 1929. The appetite for immigrant labor vanished, but Jewish immigrants continued to arrive, spurred by the 1933 Nazi takeover of Germany. Between 1914 and 1939, the Jewish population of Paris doubled, and over 90,000 of the city's 150,000 Jews were foreign-born. The newcomers were highly visible, expanding the Jewish quarter of the Marais and spilling over into Belleville and Montmartre.

France was also straining to cope with refugees from Spain. The Spanish Republican government collapsed in March 1939, and Fascist forces took control of the entire country. Refugees crossed the Pyrenees into France until their numbers approached half a million. The French government's response was wretchedly inadequate. Some ten thousand Spanish refugees perished of cold, hunger, and disease.

The Spaaks completed their handsome renovation of the house in Choisel, and it stood blanketed in blossoms and tranquility. But history was intruding, as Europe headed for war. In the summer of 1939 Suzanne suffered what her daughter later described as a breakdown. As the children played with the dog in the garden, Suzanne watched immobile from the chaise. Why did their mother look so sad? the children wondered. Something had gone terribly wrong. Suzanne, who didn't drive, was trapped in Choisel. At thirty-five, she had no control over her life. Claude was pulling further and further away. Her marriage was a failure, but she couldn't bring herself to leave him while the children were young. She was cut off from her friends and family in Brussels, as well as the activist circles that gave her purpose. She feared an impending war that threatened to destroy everything she loved.

On August 23, 1939, Germany and the Soviet Union announced a mutual nonaggression pact. In political terms, this was impossible to grasp: the Nazis and the Bolsheviks were blood enemies. It made sense only in that both countries wanted something, and they needed to cooperate in order to get it. What they wanted was Poland, a country glued back together from the fragments of Russian- and German-speaking empires twenty years earlier. Stalin and Hitler denied Poland's right to exist. Germany claimed the port city of Gdansk, formerly Danzig, and the western territories that had previously been East Prussia and expanses of the Austro-Hungarian Empire. The Soviets coveted western Ukraine and the Baltic regions.

Suzanne's Children

Since 1918, Poland's government had been run by a series of generals and dictators. Anti-Semitism was rife, and the political system was corrupt. Nonetheless, France and England had signed mutual defense treaties with Poland. For three years they had stood by as Hitler grabbed the Rhineland, Austria, and Czechoslovakia in violation of international law, but Poland was where they drew the line.

The French Communist Party, subservient to Moscow, was trapped in contradiction. Many of its members were Jews and Communists who had fled the Nazis. Now they were expected to support their persecutors as allies against the "Western Imperialists" in Britain and France.

As the war approached, Ruth Peters returned to Europe and joined the Spaaks in Choisel. France was in disarray. Léon Blum, the Socialist Party leader, begged the French Communist Party to renounce its allegiance to Moscow. When it refused, the French government dissolved the party, and it went underground. Mira and Harry Sokol's situation was more precarious than ever. They risked arrest or deportation as undocumented immigrants, and the Soviet Union was the only imaginable avenue for escape.

The Sokols might have paused had they known more. Stalin's purges had decimated his army officer corps and the intelligence service, and he had extended his accusations to the international Communist movement. Within a few years he slaughtered hundreds of members within his reach, including most of the Central Committee of the Polish Communist Party (many of them Jewish). Following the pact with Hitler, he ordered his agents to round up six hundred German Communists who had sought refuge in the Soviet Union (many of them Jewish) and deliver them to the Gestapo.

The Sokols' failure to emigrate may have prolonged their lives, but their prospects were dim. They were stranded in France, jobless, homeless, stateless, and friendless—except for Suzanne and Claude Spaak.

2

the real war

On September 2, 1939, the morning papers reported that Germany had invaded Poland, though *Le Figaro* still found room for a list of *sportives* at the Grand Prix in Deauville. Two days later, France and Britain declared war on Germany. The French army quickly mobilized five million men, but there was little panic. The French had built costly fortifications on the border, known as the Maginot Line, and the government assured the public that the country was safe.

On September 17 the Soviets attacked Poland from the east. Poland's last defenders were crushed. They surrendered on October 6, leaving the victors to divide the spoils.

Neither France nor Britain had a strategy in place. The French made a few incursions into Germany and withdrew. The Royal Air Force dropped leaflets on the German naval base at Kiel, warning, "You cannot win this war." Then the Germans paused. The *drôle de guerre*, or "Phony War," had begun.

A French officer expressed his country's misplaced optimism in his diary:

Suzanne's Children

We know that our land is safe from invasion, thanks to the Maginot Line; no one has the least desire to fight for Czechoslovakia or for Poland, of which ninety-five Frenchmen out of every hundred are completely ignorant and unable to find on a map. We have no belief that Hitler will hurl himself on us after having swallowed up the little nations, one by one. We tell ourselves that having obtained what he wants, he will leave us in peace.[1]

The governments in London and Paris distributed gas masks and evacuation plans, but civilians grew weary of waiting on permanent alert and went back to their business. Members of the Spaaks' circle, including Claude, Charles, and Harry Sokol, weighed their sense of duty against their family obligations. Millions of conscripted Frenchmen lined up to get their hair cropped and mustaches trimmed, but once they reached the "front" they spent their days drilling, drinking, and mugging for the cameras.

Immigrants were eager to enlist. For Spanish Republicans, military service was an instant ticket out of the camps, even if these soldiers' informal style came as a shock to their French officers. (One startled young lieutenant reported that his jolly Spaniards greeted him every morning with "*Buenos días, Papá!*"[2])

Some thirty thousand Jewish immigrants enlisted, making up almost a third of the foreign recruits.[3] But here, too, anti-Semitism persisted. Jews had no chance of becoming pilots, and seasoned soldiers found themselves reporting to French officers their juniors in age and experience. They were relegated to "special units" in the French Foreign Legion, described as "poorly equipped, poorly trained, and poorly armed."[4]

One day Bazou Spaak accompanied Suzanne to Paris to visit the Sokols, who had moved into a small flat near the École Militaire. Bazou asked Harry, "Who's going to win the war?" Harry answered, "France, of course!" and signed up for the French Foreign

Legion not long after. Harry's national origin temporarily worked in his favor. Had he been German or Austrian, he would have been designated an enemy alien. The French arrested some eight thousand Germans and Austrians, three thousand of whom were Jews and other political exiles.*

The Spaaks were technically immigrants, but their circumstances were more favorable. France welcomed Claude as an artist, and his family's independent income was another advantage. He had a minor heart condition that exempted him from military service, freeing him to concentrate on theater. His producers had rented the Théâtre des Mathurins, a playhouse just north of the Madeleine. They needed a comedy and hoped that Claude could fill the bill. The production team settled on a new adaptation of the Restoration comedy *The School for Scandal*.

It was a family affair. Claude trimmed superfluous characters and streamlined the action. He asked Suzanne and Ruth Peters to collaborate on a new translation, for which he took credit. The play, which had premiered in London in 1777, seemed an odd choice for Paris in 1939, but it turned out to be perfect. The producers reckoned that Parisians needed to laugh, and the social machinations of Lady Sneerwell and Sir Benjamin Backbite offered a welcome break from their diet of dread. The cast was fresh and lively and the costumes scintillating. The producers gambled on a little-known thirty-five-year-old designer named Christian Dior, who had been mobilized for farmwork but allowed to return on leave. The unlikely soldier sat in the back of the theater, a slight man with soft features, already starting to bald. A friend described his costumes as "almost caricatures. His hats were exaggeratedly large

---

* Britain interned nearly thirty thousand Jewish exiles, though in better conditions. The United States interned smaller numbers in Tennessee, Georgia, and upstate New York.

with upturned brims, and his use of color was quite novel, bright as those acid drops the English are so famous for." The bold black and pink stripes on one gown inspired the audience to break into spontaneous applause. The play made Dior the talk of the town.[5]

The playbill was illustrated by Claude's friend Jean Cocteau, who was launching his own play next door. Cocteau had recently been convicted of drug trafficking, a consequence of his long-standing opium addiction, and he was worried about his handsome young lover, Jean Marais, who had just been called up for military service. When he wasn't appearing in court, undergoing rehab, or shadowing his lover, Cocteau dashed off a torrent of poems, plays, and illustrations.

L'École de la médisance opened in February 1940. It was an instant hit, and the company settled in for a long run. At the theater, Suzanne stood quietly in the background with Bazou and Pilette as Claude accepted the accolades. But Claude was surprisingly ambivalent. He spurned evening attire, hated curtain calls, and often fled before the end of the performance. But he avidly consumed the reviews and called the theater every night from Choisel to check on the box office receipts. He finally decided to stop—at which point the operator, who had been eavesdropping, called and asked, "Monsieur, don't you want to hear how the box office did tonight?" As the play approached its hundredth performance, it seemed as though Claude's writing career had finally taken off.

In April the Germans invaded Norway and Denmark to wrest control of matériel and supply lines. Then they turned westward, and, as in past wars, the path to Paris ran through Belgium.

Occupying center stage was Claude's brother Paul-Henri, who labored for peace where none was at hand. He was just past forty and had recently rotated from the post of prime minister to foreign minister. As a youth he had returned from prison camp to a blasted homeland and a starving population. Why, he asked, should the Belgians offer up their country as a battlefield when they had nothing to gain?

Paul-Henri served as the cabinet's intermediary to the Belgian king, a foppish young man who looked down on plebeian politicians. Paul-Henri, his occasional golfing buddy, was the only minister he liked. As a hereditary German prince, Leopold III hoped to ingratiate himself with the Nazis and preserve his dynasty. The Germans had pressured the Belgians again and again to prove their submissiveness, and they complied. Spaak's uncle, Paul-Émile Janson, the minister of justice, drew up a list of "suspect Belgians and foreigners"—including Jewish refugees—who would be arrested when it "proved necessary."[6]

On May 10 the Germans attacked Belgium, the Netherlands, and France. The German ambassador arrived in Paul-Henri's office to make the formal declaration. Paul-Henri interrupted him, acting "very, very emotional, [his] heart beating at an appalling rate, extremely indignant." He pulled out a text and read aloud: "For the second time in twenty-five years . . . Germany is committing a criminal aggression against a neutral and honest Belgium."[7]

Later that day, the "suspect Belgians and foreigners" were rounded up, loaded onto sealed train cars, and deported to France. One Jewish survivor reported that townspeople along the way accused them of being German parachute agents.[8]

Brussels fell on May 18. By the time the German troops reached the Royal Palace, most of the ministers had escaped to France. Paul-Henri dispatched their families to his brother in Choisel along with his own wife and three children. The parade of black Packards stood in a long row outside the house like a funeral cortege gone astray. Claude sent them to a nearby hotel.

On May 25, Paul-Henri fled to Dunkirk. Hundreds of thousands of French and British troops had been driven to the sea and were awaiting evacuation. Paul-Henri and two other ministers went to the head of the line, and their small torpedo boat arrived in London by nightfall. Belgium surrendered two days later. A quarter of the country's eight million people fled to France, along with a quarter of its nine-hundred-thousand-man armed forces.[9]

Suzanne's Children

One of the refugees was René Magritte, who had been living in Brussels on Suzanne's monthly stipend. Five days after the German invasion he fled with some friends, leaving his wife, Georgette, behind. Magritte told a friend she stayed to recover from appendicitis, but she actually refused to abandon a lover.[10] Magritte believed with some reason that the Nazis might target him for arrest. He was a sometime member of the Communist Party, and the Nazis condemned surrealists as "degenerate." He had given a public lecture in 1938 in which he called Hitler a "pain in the ass" and his followers a "fistful of fanatics."[11] Magritte and his companions left Brussels under a hail of German bombs, traveling by train, streetcar, taxi, and on foot—any conveyance that still functioned. Magritte planned to hole up outside Carcassonne in the southwest with some other painters, but he needed money. He stopped off at the Spaaks' home in Choisel asking to "borrow back" some paintings.

"There's a rich American who's sailing for New York, and she's buying art to take along," Magritte told Claude. "I think I can sell her something. Don't worry, I'll replace it later." The painter scurried off, clutching a shiny green portfolio filled with a dozen paintings. A few days later he tracked down Peggy Guggenheim at a framer's shop in Montparnasse.[12] He conveniently happened to be carrying *La voix des airs*, an oil he had "borrowed" from the Spaaks. She bought it from him then and there.*

Claude, Suzanne, and Ruth spent the following days gathered around the radio, listening to the news and reviewing their options. Paul-Henri had quietly advised his family to move money out of Europe and make contingency plans. The previous year, Claude had deposited $10,000 of Suzanne's fortune in a Manhattan bank under

---

* After the war, Claude spotted the painting, depicting three bells floating in space, in the Guggenheim Museum in Venice.

the names of "Monsieur and Madame Spaak." He transferred more funds to a bank in England, and stored a third sum in gold coins at home in a sturdy leather bag.

Now they should leave, Claude decided, with New York as their ultimate destination. If the Germans continued to advance, there would be mass panic. They should get on the road before the crush. Claude loaded the bag of gold into the car. Suzanne was worried about those under her care. What would happen to Mira? Would the Germans bomb Paris to rubble, as they had Warsaw? What about the Spanish refugees trapped at the border? Bazou wanted to know if his dog, Wotan, would be safe. There was no time to answer.

Claude bundled Suzanne, Ruth, and the children into the black Citroën, squeezing them in amid luggage and provisions, and headed south through a landscape glowing with yellow fields of rapeseed. They sheltered in a farmhouse along the way.

France surrendered on June 17, but some areas of the country were still untouched. Claude decided to strike out for the coast in hopes of sailing to North America. But first they made a stop at the grand château where Claude's mother, the Belgian senator, had found refuge. They found her resting in queenly fashion in a satin-canopied bed beneath an opulent ceiling covered with clouds and cherubs. They stayed for a week, until the château's population swelled to nearly a hundred. Claude decided to head south and buy passage to New York, hoping to make it ahead of the German troops.

The Spaaks left on a sultry Sunday morning that would be torrid by nightfall. The road was empty as far as the eye could see, both ahead and behind them, a perfect allée that stretched between two sentinel rows of trees. No one talked. From her window Pilette could see a dejected Belgian soldier sitting by the side of the road in his red-tasseled cap, chewing on a blade of grass. Later she realized that if the soldier had walked a kilometer west, he could have made it back to Belgium. But he stayed put, suggesting he would spend the next four years as a prisoner of war.

At one point Claude's hands gripped the steering wheel. "Don't turn around; act normally," he said tensely. Two German soldiers on motorcycles had appeared in his rearview mirror. They sped up and passed the car. A few hours later the family pulled up at a railroad crossing and saw townspeople crowded at their windows. Pilette was taken aback to see how excited they were, "as though they were waiting for a bullfight," watching the two German motorcyclists, who had stopped at the barrier. The Spaaks learned that Bordeaux would be occupied the next day. They would not be going to America.

Instead, Claude veered east to Carcassonne. The overloaded Citroën kept blowing out tires. He found a room for the women and children and went to see Magritte, who was staying outside town. Claude invited Magritte to join them, but Magritte preferred to sulk. He wrote to a friend, "I wish I could drop dead very soon."[13]

The next day Claude drove the family to Sainte-Maxime, a small town on the French Riviera, where he found a villa to rent. The children thought it was paradise, with a garden of mimosa and fig trees and a terrace overlooking Saint-Tropez across the bay. The rooms were cool, bright, and serene. Claude settled into an office on the second floor, where he wrote and tutored his daughter.

Bazou pined for his Wotan, and his mother decided to take the train north to fetch him. Suzanne spent the first night in Marseille in a bedbug-infested hotel, where she filled a large bucket with water and slept in a chair placed in the bucket. But she accomplished her mission and returned with the dog.

At this point the children thought they were "happy and complete," but Suzanne knew otherwise. Claude went back to his writing and Ruth withdrew to her room, but Suzanne spent much of her time in tears, worrying about her Spanish refugees and her friend Mira. She besieged Claude with a constant refrain: "I want to do something." Europe was in flames, her refugees were in crisis, and here she was, trapped at a beach resort. Finally, in September, he relented.

Claude obtained a laissez-passer that authorized the family to return to the Occupied Zone, and the Spaaks, Ruth, and Wotan piled back into the Citroën. As they approached the border of occupied France, Claude scanned the horizon, fearing he might be arrested and sent to Germany. At the checkpoint, he handed the pass to the soldier on duty, who put it in a pile to process. Claude turned to his family and said, "Let's let Wotan pee one more time in the free world."

He walked the dog and returned for the pass. The sergeant stared at him in dismay, then looked down the road. He had mistakenly given it to another driver, now long gone. The family could get another permit, but it would take weeks. Claude installed them in an inn and set to work getting a new pass. A recently demobilized French officer named André Mercier helped, and Claude offered him a ride back to Paris in return. The additional passenger made the squeeze even tighter; Wotan's food, a huge bag of rice, hung precariously from the antenna. The Spaaks later learned that Mercier had hidden his revolver in his luggage. If the Germans had found it at a checkpoint, it would have endangered them all.

The Spaaks made their way back to Choisel through a new landscape. Roads bore signposts in German; clocks were set an hour forward to Berlin time. German soldiers guarded each junction. The Spaaks' house appeared unscathed, but when they entered the salon they found two uniformed German officers seated in the armchairs. They greeted the Spaaks politely. "We're veterinary officers from the Wehrmacht," one of them announced. "We'll be staying for three days." Assigned to care for army horses, they stated their presence as a fact.

The Spaaks had traversed the country, witnessing defeated soldiers, throngs of refugees, and country folk greeting German troops.

They had imagined another existence in New York, where Claude might open an art gallery on Fifty-Seventh Street, Suzanne could knit stockings for the Red Cross, and the children would go to the zoo in Central Park—a place where the Nazis were a distant headline in the *New York Times*. That future was not to be.

The invasion had altered the demographic map of France. The casualties were never accurately recorded, but it is believed that between fifty thousand and ninety thousand French soldiers were killed, and nearly two million taken prisoner.[14] Eight million people had fled, six million of them French, and the rest refugees from Belgium and neighboring countries.[15]

Claude's associates returned to the theater, and Suzanne's refugees went to ground. Hard times were coming, but the Spaaks were buffered by wealth and privilege. They could lie low until it was over. They had the ability to choose, and the sensible choice seemed obvious.[16] Nonetheless, events were transpiring that would complicate that choice.

On June 14, the same day that Paris surrendered, twenty uniformed Gestapo officers checked into the Hôtel du Louvre. The next morning one appeared at the Prefecture of Police to demand the French dossiers on left-wing opponents: Communists and Freemasons, in addition to the interned German and Austrian exiles, many of whom were Jews.

The French police had the files ready and handed them over without objection. The exiles who had been rounded up by the French as suspected German agents were now subject to arrest as enemies of the Reich.[17]

The French government was paralyzed. Winston Churchill urged its leadership to set up a government in exile in London like the Belgians' and fight on with their troops overseas. But the

French were beaten and ready to cut their losses. On June 16 a new French government was formed by men who were prepared to negotiate a surrender.

On the seventeenth the Spaaks, like millions of others, heard Marshal Philippe Pétain deliver his first broadcast as chief of state. "It is with a breaking heart that I tell you today that we must stop fighting," he announced.[18] His message was met with both sorrow and relief by an audience that was haunted by newsreels of Warsaw in ruins and that still grieved for the last war's casualties. Pétain, the heroic field marshal of the First World War, promised them survival with a modicum of dignity.

The next day, the Spaaks gathered at the radio to hear Charles de Gaulle's broadcast from London contesting Pétain's message. "It is absurd to consider the fight to be lost," he said. "The flame of French resistance is not extinguished, and must not be extinguished." Few Frenchmen heard this broadcast; the BBC had to repeat a similar version of the address four days later.

What did it mean? The "flame of French resistance" was invisible, and the officer purporting to fan it was an unlikely leader. At six feet five inches, de Gaulle was almost a foot taller than the frail Pétain and the pudgy Churchill, with beady eyes, a double chin, and a beaked nose. His green uniform's taut shoulders and billowing breeches exaggerated his awkward build. They called him "the great asparagus." His voice was high and reedy, and he spoke with fussy precision. But he was prepared to lead. Although de Gaulle lacked the authority to establish a government in exile, he announced that he was organizing a Free French army in London. Suzanne and Claude heard the news with interest, although Suzanne had reservations about him as a conservative military man.

The dust began to settle. Most of the one hundred thousand French soldiers who were evacuated at Dunkirk returned to France voluntarily within a week, including many Jews. Only a few thousand remained in Britain with de Gaulle.

On June 1, 1940, as the fighting continued, Adolf Hitler made a surprise trip to Belgium to confer with his generals and revisit his old stomping grounds from the First World War. Family lore held that Hitler stayed at the home of Suzanne's sister Bunny after the Germans requisitioned it. Three weeks later he arrived in Paris to inspect his next conquest. He had never traveled beyond German-speaking territories and knew Paris only through pictures. He roamed the empty streets at dawn in an open staff car crammed with four underlings, bypassing the city's most exquisite sights in favor of its monuments to grandiosity.

Life changed for the Spaaks at Choisel. As a British citizen, Ruth faced internment, so she departed to the Free Zone, and Magritte returned to Brussels. The Spaaks prepared for a long haul. Suzanne went to the yarn shop and bought up the available stock, then purchased four pairs of shoes for each family member, the children's in four different sizes. "Four pairs for four years, to last the war," she said. Within weeks the shoe stores were empty, but her family was shod.

The Germans were commandeering French vehicles and gasoline, so Claude reluctantly parked the black Citroën in the garage and covered it with straw. Now getting to Paris meant a three-mile walk or bicycle ride to the train station for an hour-long trip. A *Life* correspondent wrote that the absence of traffic left Paris "weirdly silent," like a "lost city discovered by archaeologists."[19] Claude had to fiddle with the radio dial for illegal BBC transmissions to find out what was going on in the world; the French newspapers and broadcasters had been taken over by Vichy propagandists and Nazi censors.

Two million Parisians had fled, and half had not returned by September. If the decision was difficult for most Parisians, it was harder for Jews. They were aware of the Nazis' abuses elsewhere, but French Jews believed that their citizenship would protect them. Leaving France required money, visas, and a perilous journey, as well as the willingness to abandon family and property.[20] Only five thousand Jews left the country between June 10 and 25, and another fifteen thousand by the end of the summer, barely 5 percent of the Jewish population.[21]

Many of the initial German occupiers were young, handsome, and correct. When they commandeered a dwelling they usually apologized, and there were reports of them offering their seats on the Métro to elderly Jewish ladies. German troops helped refugees return to their homes and distributed food to their families. "Poor French people," one leaflet stated. "See how your government and its prefects have abandoned you, how they have lied to you and presented us as barbarians. . . . But since they are not doing anything for you, the German army will come to your aid."[22]

The illusion of civility would not last, and the early warning signs came from the French. In July, roving bands of young thugs appeared wearing the pale blue shirts of the French Fascist party. They began by putting up anti-Semitic posters along the thoroughfares and moved on to smashing the windows of Jewish shops on the Champs-Élysées.[23]

The Germans took over the administration of the northern Occupied Zone, headquartered in Paris, while Pétain and his government installed themselves in the southern spa town of Vichy, chosen for its extensive hotel accommodations. The democratic French République was no more, replaced by the authoritarian État Français. Laws made in Vichy applied to both zones, but the Germans could overrule or amend them. Pétain urged his countrymen to turn away from the divisive democratic politics of the past—namely, the Popular Front of Léon Blum—and instead embrace the authoritarian values of "*travail, famille, patrie*" ("work, family, and fatherland") in a spirit of submission and resignation. Pétain's portrait hung in every church and school. Every morning, Pilette and

Bazou stood to attention with their classmates to sing the new anthem, "*Maréchal, nous voilà!*" ("Marshal, We Are Here!")

Pétain promoted a vision of "France for the French": a nation that was white, French born, French speaking, and Catholic (although Pétain himself was lapsed). Over the next six months, his government began to rid the country of immigrants—many, but not all, of whom were Jewish.* In July 1940 his interior minister sealed the French borders "so that foreigners cannot trouble public order."[24] The following month, the government decided to revoke the citizenship of those it deemed "unable to assimilate into French society."[25] Over fifteen thousand individuals were affected, 40 percent of them Jews.[26] Another law restricted the practice of medicine and law to those born of French fathers. These restrictions affected Polish, Italian, and Spanish Catholics, as well as Jewish immigrants.[27]

But the next phase targeted the Jews, under the direction of SS captain Theodor Dannecker, the Paris representative of the Nazi Office of Jewish Affairs (Judenreferat). Dannecker was the paragon of a Nazi storm trooper: stone-faced, brutal, and corrupt. The twenty-seven-year-old officer combined anti-Semitism with fierce efficiency, a violent temper, and a taste for the louche life. He was responsible for coordinating operations with the French police and reported directly to Adolf Eichmann, the SS colonel in charge of eradicating the Jewish populations of conquered lands. Dannecker's mission was to eliminate the Jews of France without upsetting the political equilibrium.

Dannecker began by ordering a census in the Occupied Zone to register "all those who belong, or used to belong, to the Jewish

---

* As of 1939, only about 0.35 percent—that is, one-third of 1 percent—of the total population of France were Jewish immigrants. Less than 1 percent was Jewish, and Jews made up only 6 percent of its total foreign population.

religion, or have more than two grandparents who are Jewish."
French police were instructed to collect the records.[28] Nearly
150,000 Jews complied, including 60,000 immigrants. The French
police typed the information on small index cards in accordance
with Gestapo guidelines, which required them to be:

> Subdivided alphabetically, with Jews of French nationality and
> foreign Jews having files of different colors. The files should
> also be classified according to profession, nationality and street.

This marked the first time a French census had recorded religious
affiliation since 1872.

The rules grew more ominous. An October decree declared
that "aliens of the Jewish race" could be held in special camps or
under house arrest at the discretion of the local police forces. Adult
male immigrants could be arrested for being "superfluous to the
national economy." The arrests mounted.

Some of the new measures, such as the October law barring
Jews from the professions, applied to all Jews, not just foreigners.
Exemptions were possible but rare. In November Jacques Helbron-
ner, a prominent Jewish lawyer and Pétain supporter, proposed a bill
to limit the anti-Semitic measures to immigrants, but the government ignored him.[29]

As the foreign Jews of Paris felt the net tightening, they turned
to trusted associations from the past and looked for ways to fortify
them. In November 1940 some Polish Jews from the Communist-
backed Yiddish-MOI (Main d'oeuvre immigrée) labor union met
in Montmartre and founded an umbrella organization uniting some
fifty preexisting groups. They called it Solidarité.[30]

3

paris by night

| JANUARY–DECEMBER 1941 |

Anxious and isolated, Suzanne absorbed the unrelenting bad news. Many around her had resigned themselves to the German domination of Europe, and at this point it was hard to imagine another outcome. The Nazis controlled nearly every country on the Continent. The few exceptions, such as Hungary and Spain, remained neutral or actively served Nazi interests. That left Great Britain, embattled and alone. The prevailing expectation in France was, in the words of the historian Robert Paxton, of a "short war, British defeat, danger of revolution, imminent peace."[1]

Mira and Harry Sokol moved to a different part of Paris hoping to be less conspicuous, but now that the Germans had arrived, it was impossible to feel safe. After Harry was demobilized, the couple filed a third appeal for repatriation to the Soviet Union. This time they acted on the advice of a minor embassy official, who suggested that the Soviets were more interested in technicians than doctors and social scientists. The couple's new application, describing them as radio experts, attracted the attention of Ivan Susloparov, the Soviet attaché who oversaw military intelligence operations in France. He made the Sokols an offer: if they consented to work for Soviet intelligence, he would provide them with money, housing, and forged papers. The couple underwent training in radio operations and waited to be activated.[2] From their seclusion in Paris, they had little to offer their friend in Choisel.

One day in early 1941, Suzanne Spaak stood with her daughter at the foot of the Eiffel Tower and pointed out Mira and Harry's new apartment: the first building to the left of the Trocadero, on the top floor under the mansard. Suzanne never took the children to visit them these days; the Sokols were too nervous.

One day Mira rushed to Choisel with a plea. "Harry's been arrested. He's been sent to the camp at Pithiviers, and you're the only ones who can help."

Harry's detention may have taken place amid the first mass arrest of Jews in 1941. Over the second week of May, French police officers had gone door-to-door in the immigrant Jewish neighborhoods delivering *billets verts*—green slips. The printed form was headed *Préfecture de Police*, the blanks filled in with neatly handwritten entries: Jewish names and addresses that had been provided by the recipients themselves in the German-mandated census the previous fall. The forms politely stated:

> Monsieur [name, birthdate, address] is invited to present himself, in person, accompanied by a family member or friend, on May [————], 1941, at 7 am, to [address] to examine his status. Please bring identification. Anyone who does not report at the specified day and time will be subject to the most severe sanctions.

The slip was signed the *Commissaire de Police*.

The green slips reached 6,694 Jewish households, and 3,710

Jewish men (most of them Polish, some Austrian and Czech) reported to the listed sites, expecting to simply present their papers for review. The majority had valid resident permits, but all were immediately taken into custody, while the accompanying family member or friend was sent home to fetch a few belongings. A few days later the detainees, suitcases in hand, were taken by train to camps outside Pithiviers and Beaune-la-Rolande, two small towns some fifty miles south of Paris. Their money and identification papers were confiscated and they were herded into crude wooden barracks surrounded by barbed wire and patrolled by French gendarmes.[3]

Pithiviers's 1,700 prisoners included Jewish men of every persuasion, among them members of the Yiddish-MOI and its new offshoot, Solidarité.[4] Harry was named barracks chief and took his place among the eight directors of the camp's Resistance Committee, alongside leading activists from the two organizations.

The internees established a library of over 1,800 books and a lecture series on topics ranging from Yiddish literature to mechanical engineering. Harry was assigned to work in the camp infirmary along with thirteen other doctors, who held office hours twice a day.

At least one witness expressed outrage. A local Red Cross volunteer named Madeleine Rolland protested that these were innocent men, not the black market scoundrels depicted in *Le Petit Parisien* and *Paris-Soir*—but her appeal went unheard.[5] On May 15 a pro-Vichy newspaper rejoiced, "Five thousand Jews are gone. . . . That makes five thousand fewer of the parasites that had infected greater Paris with a fatal disease."[6]

Harry and the other prisoners were allowed to send and receive one letter per week, but their family members were prohibited from visiting or staying in the town outside the camp. There was little that Mira could do to help her husband. Solidarité and other Jewish groups made up packages for the prisoners, offered support to their families, and tried to publicize the arrests, but this action was impossible in the censored press. The activists wrote out their texts in Yiddish on stencils (or typed them, if they could lay hands on a typewriter), then ran them through small, mimeograph-like machines called *roneos*. The resulting leaflets, called tracts, were usually slipped under doors or circulated hand to hand.

At the end of May, Solidarité published a new appeal denouncing the arrests in the name of the Groupe des femmes et enfants juifs (Group of Jewish Women and Children):

> People of France! On Wednesday May 14, before noon, hundreds of Parisians witnessed the expulsion of masses of Jews towards an unknown destination, monitored by police . . .
>
> It is with a heavy heart that we resort to these "illegal" means to inform you of the suffering we have been subjected to. We well know the misfortune that has come to the French people and we take our share of them. But we cannot allow the beastly lies to pass in silence, with which we are stricken by people without conscience, who present us as those responsible for the woes of France.
>
> We appeal to you in the name of your glorious past, in the name of the "Declaration of the Rights of Man and of the Citizen" . . . to join us on our protest arising from the 5000 innocent victims, the 5000 ruined homes, the thousands of children exposed to hunger and misery.[7]

The pamphlet represented a major departure for its Communist, Yiddish-speaking authors. It was the first to appear in French, directed to the French public, and the first to draw the line between barbarism and civilization instead of capitalism and socialism. It portrayed the anti-Semitic measures as a threat in themselves, a departure from the French Communist Party's depiction of them as a ploy to divide the working class.[8]

Still, the new strategy was unlikely to yield quick results. Harry Sokol, trapped behind the barbed wire, realized that the Soviets were his best hope for freedom, but he had to compete for their attention. More than two hundred other prisoners had also appealed to the Soviet embassy, begging the officials to recognize their citizenship and arrange their release.[9] This was feasible given the nonaggression pact, under which the Germans exempted Jews who could prove they had been born in what was now Soviet territory. But the Soviets were in no rush to help Jewish immigrants. Harry, the Soviets' newly trained radio operator, knew he might receive special consideration. However, a daunting challenge remained: securing the necessary documentation and delivering it to the proper French authorities. This fell to his wife.

Mira went to the Soviet embassy in Paris and obtained a certificate to confirm that Harry's birthplace lay within Soviet territory. The officials warned her that under no circumstances would they issue a second copy. It was this certificate that she entrusted to Claude Spaak. "Promise me, on the heads of your children, that you will deliver this to Harry," she begged. Claude overcame his dislike for Harry and agreed to help.

The distance from Choisel to Pithiviers was only fifty miles, but the towns were worlds apart. Claude's journey took the better part of a day; when he finally arrived, the only available lodging turned out to be a brothel. The next morning, he set out on foot for the camp.

Unknown to Claude, Solidarité had put out more flyers, this time in Yiddish, directed to the families of the arrested men, summoning them to a protest led by a feisty organizer named Sophie Schwartz. The group rallied dozens of Jewish women to march on the barbed wire enclosure, demanding the right to see their husbands and send them provisions.[10] Claude found himself amid a phalanx of wives and mothers flanked by a testy police escort. By the time the protesters reached the camp, Claude thought the scene resembled Dante's *Inferno*:

> The poor devils were behaving like lunatics. Messages were being screamed back and forth, hands were helplessly reaching out parcels, the women were sobbing and wailing. . . . Police were walking up and down between the cages, quite indifferent to what was going on.[11]

Claude, a tall, commanding figure, walked up to a French policeman and confidently asked for his assistance. He showed him Harry's certificate and asked him to deliver it. "You realize it's his life you hold in your hands," Claude told him.

The policeman responded respectfully. "I give you my word of honor I will deliver it to him." He refused, however, to take the parcel Claude had brought, because, Claude believed, it would have caused further commotion among the women. Half an hour later the policeman returned and handed Claude a page torn out of a notebook. It bore a handwritten message: "Thanks—Harry."[12] Harry was freed.

Suzanne Spaak found her way to Solidarité soon after, perhaps through Harry's committee in Pithiviers. The activists were reluctant to accept a non-Jewish member, and their initial reaction was not promising. One recalled:

> We received an offer from a certain Madame Suzanne Spaak to help with the resistance work. We quickly learned, against all of the rules of clandestinity, that Madame S. Spaak was the sister-in-law of Foreign Minister Spaak and the daughter of a major Belgian banker.
>
> We weren't very optimistic regarding the productivity of our new collaborator. On that point we were mistaken. . . . When she came to us, she said, "Tell me what I can do, I'm

ready to take on any task as long as I can serve in the fight against Nazism."[13]

Suzanne may have been impressed by her new colleagues' colorful histories and outsized personalities. One cofounder was Adam Rayski, a twenty-seven-year-old journalist from Bialystock, a compact man with fierce black eyebrows who sported natty suits and a black fedora. He had written fiery editorials for the *Naïe Presse*, the Yiddish Communist daily, until it was closed under the occupation. Now he lived in Paris semiclandestinely with his wife, Jeanne, and their toddler, Benoît. Another principal was the distinguished Communist lawyer Charles Lederman. Lederman had been born in Warsaw but had lived in France since infancy. Both he and Rayski had enlisted to fight the Germans, and both had made daring escapes as prisoners of war. But there were marked differences: Rayski was dark and querulous, with a strong Polish accent. Lederman was blond and tactful, and spoke perfect French.

A third partner was a relative newcomer named Dr. Léon Chertok. Rayski first heard about *le Docteur Alex* (his nom de guerre) as someone who could help the Yiddish-MOI recruit "Aryans" to support their movement.[14] Lederman later wrote that Chertok introduced Suzanne Spaak to their group, and Chertok wrote that it was Lederman, which suggests that Suzanne met the two men around the same time.

Chertok was born to a well-to-do Jewish family from a small town outside Vilnius. Rayski considered the doctor's background bourgeois and his politics feeble, but he reluctantly admitted that Chertok, "though he wasn't a Communist, was providential for us. He had the telephone directory of the city of Paris in his head at a time when we were confined to our social and geographical ghetto."[15]

The young doctor exuded charm, with a winning smile and wavy black hair. In the spring of 1939, Chertok had fled the

German invasion of Prague, where he had been studying medicine. He arrived at Luxembourg station and took a taxi to his lodgings instead of trudging from the Gare du Nord to the Marais like other Jewish immigrants. He shunned the grimy bistros around the Place de la République, installing himself at the Café de Flore in Saint-Germain, where Picasso and Jean-Paul Sartre held court. When war broke out, Chertok joined the Polish regiment in France, despite his qualms about Polish anti-Semitism. He was informed that he didn't qualify for a weapon or a uniform; they were in short supply and Jews were the last in line. Soon France's war and Chertok's military career were over.

In May 1941, Chertok was among the thousands who received a *billet vert*. Rather than reporting to the French police, he went underground. But for Chertok, "underground" did not mean "out of sight"; there were always females willing to assist him—in this case, two friends from the Café de Flore, the Catala sisters. Not only did they help him move to new quarters, they also gave him the birth certificate of their brother Yves, who had been killed in the war. Chertok added a baptism certificate and a medical certificate documenting an operation for a foreskin abnormality to explain his circumcision. With these, he noted, "I was all set."[16] He faced one last problem: in Prague, Chertok had purchased a set of "superb poplin shirts" with his monogram over the pocket. He obtained another set of false papers with initials to match the shirts.

Reinvented as "Yves Catala," Chertok returned to his cafés on the Left Bank, but he was shocked at the way other Jews had been lured into captivity, and he decided to join the Jewish resistance. If the Communists had the most effective organizations, he would work with them. He chose Solidarité. It provided him with a monthly stipend and a list of *planques*, or hideouts, warning him not to sleep in the same one two nights in a row.

Solidarité needed to find more financial resources and broader public support, and its Communist roots worked against it. The group had to transcend its insularity and intolerance regarding non-Communists, and overcome its distrust of French Christians, traditional French Jews, and France's economic elite. Its founders needed to convert their former "class enemies" into allies— rendering unconventional recruits like Léon Chertok and Suzanne Spaak essential.

On November 1, 1940, SS officer Helmut Knochen arrived to take charge of the Gestapo in France, setting up shop at 72 Avenue Foch, a few blocks from the Arc de Triomphe. His mandate was "the Jewish question," with a special emphasis on resistance activities. His specialty was *Verschärfte Vernehmung*, or "enhanced interrogation," a term the Nazis invented in 1937. It was said that he put in an order for special equipment:

50 coffins to be added to present supply
150 handcuffs requested by the Reich Main Security Office
    (RSHA)
thick curtains for vans taking persons to execution
2000 liters of fuel oil for burning the corpses of the executed in
    the Père-Lachaise crematorium
refreshments (whisky, wine, snacks) for the execution squads,
    preferably to be served in their barracks*[17]

SS captain Theodor Dannecker technically answered to Knochen's command, though Eichmann's man in Paris had his own agenda. In January 1941 Dannecker distributed a memorandum to his staff concerning his "gigantic" mission. Its "success can be assured only by the most meticulous preparations." Its end was

----

* Even if the list is apocryphal, it reflects the activities his bureau would conduct.

described as "the carefully implemented complete deportation of the Jews prior to a colonization action in a yet to be determined territory."[18]

Dannecker pressed for the creation of two new organizations. One was the Coordination Committee of Jewish Relief Organizations, made up of both French and immigrant Jews, to promote compliance with Dannecker's measures.* The second was the General Commissariat for Jewish Affairs (CGQJ),† a Vichy government body to administer anti-Semitic restrictions and liquidate Jewish property, under the direction of the anti-Semitic French politician Xavier Vallat.

In April 1941 Dannecker launched a new publication, *Informations juives*, which described itself as the organ of the Coordination Committee of Jewish Relief Organizations. In reality its editorial director was Dannecker himself, working through his Jewish "technical adviser," Israel Israelowicz. The newsletter urged its readers to prove they were "good citizens" by complying with the anti-Semitic decrees. The first issue, sent to sixty thousand addresses in Paris, advised that it was designed "to give advice or provide aid only to those who openly belong to the Jewish community of Greater Paris"—in other words, those who had registered with the police.

Those same households received a second mailing, this one anonymous, warning, "Jews, beware!"—*Informations juives* was part of a trap. Someone in the Coordination Committee office had smuggled out the mailing list and given it to the Jewish underground.[19] Distrust of the Coordination Committee grew.

That summer, France was stunned by the news of the German invasion of the USSR. On June 22, 3.5 million German and Axis troops, representing the largest military operation in history,

---

* Comité de coordination des oeuvres de bienfaisance du Grand Paris.

† Commissariat général aux questions juives.

launched a surprise attack at dawn, overwhelming defenses and pressing rapidly into Soviet territory.

The invasion helped unmask the Nazis' intentions concerning the Jews of Europe. In July SS general Reinhard Heydrich asked German vice chancellor Hermann Göring to authorize the preparation of a plan for a "final solution." An important step took place on August 1, when the SS Cavalry Brigade in Soviet Byelorussia received the orders, "All Jews must be shot. Drive the female Jews into the swamps."[20] Within weeks, the measures to wipe out Bolsheviks and to eliminate Jews became fully conflated. In Paris, the public myths were maintained; it was difficult for anyone there—beyond officers in the highest reaches of the SS—to grasp what was happening.

The invasion of the USSR altered the dynamics of French resistance. For the Sokols, it erased any possibility of emigrating. Harry had been lucky to get out of the camp when he did. The invasion freed Jewish Communists from the French Communist Party's adherence to the nonaggression pact, and paved the way to action. In late June the Communist Party newspaper *L'Humanité* called for attacks on factories, German installations, and German troops. French Communists opened a new dialogue with the Gaullist resistance. In a heartbeat, the Soviets were transformed from the scourge of the Western democracies to their ally. Three weeks after the invasion, the British signed a mutual defense treaty with the Soviets.

The French Communist Party's leadership was torn. Party elders considered sabotage and bombings the tools of anarchists, and the initial response fell to the hotheaded youth of the party. The *bataillons de la jeunesse*, or "youth battalions," launched minor attacks and protests, most of them impulsive and inconsequential. But the Germans seized the opportunity to link the events to their war against the Jews and launched a series of roundups and executions, culminating with the August arrest of over four thousand Jewish men. A German report noted that the measure took place "following a demonstration that was led by Jews, and to intimidate the whole Jewish community. . . . The collaboration of the French police [around 2,500 officers] was good."[21] On August 21, forty Jewish lawyers from the Paris bar were arrested, including French-born members of the profession, dashing any hope for redress through the legal system. The *bataillons de la jeunesse* escalated their attacks on German servicemen, often chosen at random, and the Germans retaliated by executing French hostages, a disproportionate number of them Jewish.

The Jewish communities were thrown into confusion. Who was safe and who should go underground? Which of the rumors could be trusted? Sometimes uncertainty led to paralysis. Adam Rayski noted that Jewish men who went into hiding experienced "major psychological problems. It was not without difficulty that they left their family circle and went to live in complete secrecy. . . . At that moment, the awareness of danger wasn't very clear. Not even the most sophisticated believed in the threat of extermination."[22]

In September 1941 the Spaaks decided to move to Paris. It wasn't difficult to find housing. Stripped bare by the occupation, Paris offered prospective renters an abundance of desirable options. Claude had some friends who told him about an apartment in the Palais Royal. The immediate explanation for the move was Pilette's education; there was no high school in Choisel.

But Suzanne also needed to be closer to the action. Her early involvement in Solidarité was limited to low-level activities as she introduced herself to the members and earned their trust, but she was eager to do more. Her first order of business was to help with the tracts; if she wanted evidence of the power of propaganda, she didn't need to look far. That fall the Germans opened an exhibit called "Le Juif et la France," which offered a "scientific guide to recognizing a Jew." Giant posters depicted Jewish writers and artists who had "taken over" French literature and cinema. The catalog's cover showed a spider crouching on a Star of David imposed on a map of France. The exhibit ran for six months in Paris, where attendance exceeded 150,000. It opened on the Rue Sainte-Anne, a ten-minute walk from the Palais Royal.

The Spaaks' new apartment overlooked an expanse of gardens rimmed by shops nestled under graceful arcades. It came furnished, but the family brought some household items from Choisel, including a large selection of paintings by Magritte and another Spaak protégé, Paul Delvaux. The apartment included a maid's room and came with the services of an elderly widow named Madame Lacour, a retired cabaret singer. Madame was too frail to work, but Suzanne welcomed her to the family table, where she amused the children with tales of her colorful past.

Suzanne didn't discuss her role with Solidarité with the family, but they could see she was up to something. She employed a succession of unlikely "maids" with strange accents who did little housework, muttered anti-Nazi sentiments, then disappeared—once they received their forged papers from Suzanne's network.

The Palais Royal had been constructed in the early seventeenth century as a residence for Cardinal Richelieu, the consigliere to King Louis XIII. It faced the once royal residence in the Louvre, not far from the royal chapel, the Oratoire du Louvre. After Richelieu's death, the palace passed into the possession of the king and was renamed the Palais Royal. For the next 150 years French monarchs used it to house discarded queens, dissolute princes, and scheming courtiers, and its gardens served as a playground for the future Louis XIV.

The French Revolution transformed the Palais Royal into a hotbed of political ferment. Rabid mobs seized its royal residents and hauled them to the guillotine, while revolutionaries made incendiary speeches from the balconies. The apartments were converted into gambling dens, and its arcades became showcases for courtesans. Patrons could consult a twenty-four-page *Liste complète des plus belles femmes publiques et des plus saines du palais de Paris* offering the names and addresses of the Palais Royal's "prettiest and healthiest" prostitutes. The Marquis de Sade opened a bookstore to sell his pornography, and another shop sold Charlotte Corday the kitchen knife she used to stab Marat. A few decades later the Bourbon monarchy was restored, and the dignity of the Palais Royal along with it. A young librarian named Alexandre Dumas gazed into the garden and found the inspiration to write a series of romances set in the palace.

By the time the Spaaks arrived, the Palais Royal was more eccentric than grand, but it was still a coveted address for writers and artists. There were a dozen theaters within walking distance, including the Théâtre du Palais Royal (a tawdry vaudeville house) and the Comédie Française. Under the occupation, the revered classical theater was obliged to present the Berlin Schiller Theater's production of *Kabale und Liebe* for the benefit of the German troops.[23]

Claude and his colleagues puzzled over the proper response of the artist under occupation. Claude continued to write, but he chose to boycott opportunities to produce his work so long as the Germans ruled Paris. He made one exception: as the hardships of occupation grew, his actors begged him for permission to remount *The School for Scandal* as a benefit for indigent performers. He relented, on the condition that his name would not appear on the program or the posters. Claude settled for attending the theater frequently, often with wife and children in tow, and spending time with his movie and theater friends.

These included Jean Cocteau, who lived just around the corner. Cocteau had moved into the Palais Royal in the fall of 1939. When war was declared, his first question was reportedly "But how will I get my opium?"[24] He flirted with Fascism and saw no reason why the occupation should deprive the public of his genius, or his genius of its revenues. He frequented fashionable salons that welcomed German officials, and praised Arno Breker, Hitler's favorite sculptor. His lover, Jean Marais, paid a price. When he tried to join the French Resistance he was turned away because his partner was considered untrustworthy. But Cocteau may have had a motive beyond ideology. The persecution of homosexuals was less draconian in occupied France than in Nazi Germany, but as public figures, Cocteau and his lover were vulnerable. Ingratiating himself with the authorities may have been a tactic for survival.

Cocteau loved the "spell that the Palais Royal works on certain spirits . . . of the ghosts of the *révolutionnaires* who haunt it," a sentiment shared by the Spaaks.[25] One evening the family joined him at a restaurant across the street and he accidently spilled some red wine on the table. The children watched with delight as he idly sketched the dark liquid into fantastic designs. Pilette was aware of Cocteau's fame, but it was the handsome Jean Marais who caught her eye, and she wasn't alone. Jean Cocteau had written a series of scripts to showcase Marais, and the teenage girls of Paris went crazy, hiding in the stairwells of the Palais Royal to catch sight of their idol.

After her isolation in the countryside, Suzanne found that the Palais Royal's "small town within a city" suited her very well. She performed her tasks for Solidarité invisibly while taking family matters briskly in hand. The country house in Choisel compensated for food rationing and shortages: she converted the garden into a potager, planting half the lawn with potatoes, and fitted Wotan's kennel with rabbit cages and chicken pens. On Saturdays she or Pilette would take the train out and load up a bicycle with baskets of vegetables, meat, and eggs, then push the bicycle three miles back to the train station.

Suzanne enrolled Pilette, fourteen, in the École Alsacienne, a progressive school founded by French Protestants near the Luxembourg Gardens, hoping she could make some new friends. Bazou, ten, studied at the prestigious Lycée Henri-IV, whose graduates included Guy de Maupassant, Jean-Paul Sartre, and the former prime minister Léon Blum.

Suzanne's Children

Soon after the family moved into their new home, Claude received a visit from the maid in the apartment downstairs, bearing a note. "Those little feet make too much noise. Please get your children some felt slippers." Quiet was a necessity for the Spaaks' downstairs neighbor, who was widely recognized as France's greatest living writer. Colette was famously particular about her writing conditions. The walls of her room were covered in red silk. She wrote on a lap desk from her daybed overlooking the garden, surrounded by her vast collection of millefiori paperweights. She composed on blue paper—always with a Parker pen—in light cast by blue-tinted bulbs, wearing her special dressing gown and in her bare feet.[26] Every detail was carefully maintained by her formidable maid, Pauline Tissandier. Colette had tried to relocate to the countryside, but she always came back to the Palais Royal, saying, "*Les pierres de Paris me tiennent*" ("The stones of Paris hold me fast").[27] Her neighbors, described by her biographer Judith Thurman, would become the Spaaks'.

> Everyone recognized her: the bookseller in the arcade, the friendly hookers, the man who sold crêpes on the corner, the neighbors who shouted greetings from their open windows. . . . The concierge was a deaf erotomane prematurely wasted by her passionate exertions, which had recently driven her husband to his grave.[28]

But Colette's good friend and neighbor Jean Cocteau noted trouble in paradise. A juvenile gang roamed the garden, and ten-year-old Bazou joined with gusto. Cocteau described their encounters:

> Children are playing police and burglar games in the garden. A queen disturbs their tumultuous adventures. She is Madame Colette, a hat on her shrubby hair, a scarf around the neck, naked feet in her sandals and a cane in her hand. Like those of

a lioness, her magnificent eyes severely observe those games of war, police and crime.[29]

The Spaaks' relations with their famous neighbor were cordial nonetheless. Suzanne and the children often found Colette seated in her favorite chair under the leafy allée of chestnut trees. As the two women chatted, Bazou tried not to stare at the writer's gnarled toes, the red lacquered nails emerging from the sandals she wore even in winter. Another favorite perch was the large fountain outside her window, but, much to her annoyance, it had been drained, along with the rest of the city's fountains. British bomber pilots used the reflection to guide their nighttime navigation, so the authorities reduced the flow to a trickle, just enough to keep the pipe from freezing.

At sixty-eight, Colette was a living legend. Her appearance was as remarkable as her habits, with enormous eyes rimmed in kohl, a sharp nose, and a pointed chin. She often posed with her cats to highlight her feline traits. After a tumultuous love life, she had finally found contentment with her third husband, Maurice Goudeket. Sixteen years her junior, Goudeket was of Jewish extraction, a slender man whom Colette rapturously described as "a chic type with satin skin." He had been a pearl broker until his business failed with the Depression, then turned his hand to other ventures, all of which ended with the 1940 anti-Semitic regulations.

Colette became his full-time occupation. Goudeket flirted with her, fussed over her, and offered her every attention an aging siren could desire. She adored him in return. Her need for him grew as her condition worsened; her sandals and cane were the result of a crippling case of rheumatoid arthritis. As she became less mobile, the gossip in the garden became an important source of research. She pressed Pilette for her opinions of the boys in school and how it felt to hover on the verge of womanhood. She was researching a new novel about a fifteen-year-old girl called Gigi.

Suzanne's Children

Colette and Goudeket had fled the invasion like everyone else, but returned to the Palais Royal after a few months. To the eyes of the world, Colette, if not exactly a collaborator, was surely an accommodationist. She published articles in *Le Petit Parisien*, a mouthpiece of the regime, as well as in the virulently Fascist *Gringoire*. Like Cocteau, she moved in circles that welcomed the German and Vichy elite.

Colette's early conversations with Suzanne Spaak skirted sensitive matters as they took each other's measure. They soon learned they had much in common: They both cared deeply for individuals who suffered under the anti-Jewish statutes. They also shared expertise in the advanced art of coping, which Colette wrote about in detail. There was no gas for cars, no leather for shoes, no fabric for clothes. Growing children went to school dressed in made-over tablecloths, and French women, inspired by Scarlett O'Hara, cut up their curtains for dresses. Young ladies expressed their style through increasingly fanciful hats.[30] At the great fashion houses, affronted saleswomen watched their clientele shift from the grandes dames of Paris to the wives and mistresses of the German occupiers. Other offensive new customers were the plebian "BOFs," or "Butter-Egg-Cheese" women, who made fortunes selling food on the black market. As the available cotton, wool, and silk was shipped off to Germany, resourceful French designers introduced fabrics made of cellulose and platform shoes fashioned of wood with flexible ribbed soles. One startling newsreel showed the sweepings from barbershops being spun into gloves and sweaters made from human hair.

Suzanne Spaak joined the legions of other Parisian women on bicycles, implements that transformed female apparel. Women adopted culottes, and Elsa Schiaparelli reinvented underwear, substituting drip-dry synthetics for silk, and elastic for buttons.[31] Suzanne's practicality infuriated her daughter. Pilette noticed that Ruth Peters and Suzanne's sisters spent serious money on clothes, somehow obtaining scarce silk stockings, but Suzanne wore thick cotton hose. One day, on the way to the theater, Pilette confronted her mother about her dowdy appearance. "Your maid wears nicer stockings than you do!" Suzanne, stung, crossed the street and marched off without her—but she didn't change her ways.

There was little Suzanne could do to help Mira and Harry, who were increasingly cut off from her visits, friendship, and assistance. She could only channel her concern through her work with Solidarité. Sustenance for the Jews of Paris had become a complex matter. They were now barred from many workplaces, and their families limited to starvation rations. Officially, the French State oversaw Jewish charities. In actuality, the official charities functioned as extortion rackets run on an industrial scale, and the authorities were always trying to improve their efficiency.

In November 1941 the Germans reconfigured the Jewish Coordination Committee into the General Union of French Jews, or UGIF.* Every legal Jewish charity was consolidated under this union, and any that remained outside were dissolved. The UGIF has gone down in history as one of the most controversial institutions of the occupation. The directors were given the impossible task of administering relief to Jewish families at the same time as they implemented Nazi policies. Self-interest played a major role in their participation. For much of the occupation, the UGIF council offered its members and their families immunity from arrest and deportation. Jews were required to pay dues to the UGIF, effectively compensating the regime for depriving them of their rights, their property, and their safety.

Among the institutions placed under the UGIF's direction were the Rothschild charities. Before the occupation these were showcases of modern philanthropy, but now they struggled with inadequate staff and scant supplies. UGIF orphanages became warehouses

_____

* Union générale des israélites de France.

for Jewish children who had been left behind by the arrests. By the end of 1941 the number of children had grown to fifty, and they became a critical concern for Solidarité and Suzanne Spaak.

That winter was the coldest in memory, compounded by a dire fuel shortage. Parisians packed into the Métro stations to keep warm. Some spread their meager possessions out on blankets to sell, employing a code—"22-22"—to say "Pack up, the Germans are coming!"

Violence mounted as young Communist militants stepped up their attacks. One of them was Maurice "Fifi" Feferman, a teenage fellow prisoner of Harry Sokol's who had escaped Pithiviers. Feferman began his campaign by leading a raid for twenty-five kilograms of dynamite. In November he firebombed the display window of a collaborationist bookstore near the Sorbonne. Over an eight-week period he helped to assassinate a German officer, bombed the Imperator Hotel, exchanged fire at a French fascist rally, and bombed a theater that was showing the anti-Semitic film *Jud Süss*.[32]

The Nazis responded to the attacks by executing hundreds of hostages over the following year, terrorizing the population and crippling the underground Communist Party. Red-bordered posters appeared on walls and lampposts across Paris announcing the latest victims. The average life span for a youth battalion recruit was seven months.[33]

The ground shifted again in December, when the Japanese attacked Pearl Harbor and Hitler declared war on the United States. Pilette was the first in the family to hear, and she rushed home from school to wake up her father. Claude was electrified; with the United States in the fight, the Allies' chances improved immeasurably. A few days later—some said as a reprisal against the United States—the Gestapo arrested 1,098 prominent French Jews, known as the "Notables." One of them was Colette's husband, Maurice Goudeket.

The Gestapo came for him at the Palais Royal before sunrise on December 12. Colette helped him pack a bag and hobbled to the stairwell, struggling to maintain her composure. Goudeket was interned with other Notables, housed thirty-six to a hut in freezing, lice-infested quarters with scant rations. One of his bunkmates called it *le camp de la mort lente* ("the camp of slow death"). They passed time trading lectures and writing accounts of their ordeal.[34] Goudeket managed to get some requests smuggled out to his wife—for food, books, and old neckties—and she arranged to get the items smuggled in.

Colette was sleepless and frantic with worry. She vowed to do anything in her power to win her husband's release, including prostrating herself to those responsible for his detention. Goudeket understood her desperation. "There was no negotiation she wasn't ready to try, no humiliation she wouldn't face. She saw collaborators, she saw Germans. And who can blame her for it? I would have, I hope, done as much."[35]

Her dilemma was hardly visible to the public; the arrest of the Notables went uncovered in the paper she wrote for, *Le Petit Parisien*, as did the woes of the Jewish prisoners and their stranded children. When the paper issued a call for humanitarian action, it was on behalf of French children in range of British bombs.[36]

Colette understood that her husband's only hope lay with his persecutors. One obvious but unappealing option was the German ambassador, Otto Abetz. In April 1941, Abetz had met with the Vichy official Xavier Vallat and informed him that "the Germans are interested in progressively ridding Europe of Jewry." The measures in France would begin, he said, by interning several thousand foreign Jews, plus "Jews with French nationality who are particularly dangerous or undesirable."[37]

But Abetz, an unctuous blond aesthete, had a weakness for writers and artists, and his French wife was a passionate fan of Colette's. Eight weeks after Goudeket's arrest he was released, apparently on the ambassador's orders. Colette sent Madame Abetz a bouquet, and a few weeks later, Colette and her Jewish husband were invited for tea at the German embassy.

Goudeket moved back into the Palais Royal, but he immediately began to look for hiding places in case of another emergency. (It was said that admiring maids offered him refuge in their beds upstairs.) He acquired forged papers and decamped to the Free Zone, but a few months later he was back at the Palais Royal. He stayed out of sight for the rest of the occupation, moving among Colette's apartment and attic rooms.

Colette continued to publish in *Le Petit Parisien*. Her essays were studiously apolitical: mostly delicate, closely observed pieces about life at the Palais Royal. The Nazis were mentioned only obliquely, and the hardships of occupation were handled with stoicism and even humor. Few individuals were identified, but she wrote of anonymous neighbors who may well have included the Spaaks. Many judged Colette harshly, but their verdict was mistaken; the writer was using her journalism as a smoke screen. Not only was she protecting the life of her beloved Jewish husband, she was also taking a growing interest in the activities of her upstairs neighbor, Suzanne Spaak.

4

la plaque tournante

The Spaaks' life in the Palais Royal had settled into a new rhythm; their broken marriage had achieved a truce: Claude and Ruth were effectively a couple, Suzanne was the silent partner, and the children were left in the dark. To avoid internment as an enemy alien, Ruth had decamped to the Free Zone; first to Nice, then to a small hotel in the town of Lancey outside Grenoble. Claude stayed with her for long stretches at a time, hiring a guide to take him across the frontier illegally.

The children adored Claude, who, despite his bluster, was also brilliant, seductive, and larger-than-life. "I didn't believe in God," Pilette recalled, "I believed in him." Suzanne still cared for her husband. She told Pilette she was glad to see him come, and glad to see him go. He continued to make Suzanne's life miserable. "When father came back to town, he would come to the Palais Royal, but then they'd start fighting," Pilette recalled. "He'd tell her the children were left alone too much. She wasn't there enough. She spent too much money. What she was doing was too dangerous. Then he'd go to the hotel next door so he could get some sleep and Bazou went with him. This happened repeatedly."

Nor did Pilette escape his wrath. "If you came early, he got angry. If you came late, he got angry. If you didn't come, he got angry. Whatever you did, he got angry." One evening when Suzanne was out, Claude decided that their large white kitchen was dirty and asked Pilette to scour it with him—walls, floors, and ceiling—from eight o'clock until well after midnight.

In the spring of 1942, the family was shaken by a revelation. Claude and Bazou had gone to stay with Ruth in the Free Zone, and Suzanne decided to take Pilette there for Easter. Suzanne determined that if she wasn't allowed to cross over, Pilette should go on without her, but she was worried about what she would find there. One day Suzanne asked Pilette to join her for lunch, and explained that Claude and Ruth were lovers. "I wanted you to hear it from me." The fourteen-year-old was scandalized. "Are you going to get a divorce?" she demanded. "Not until Bazou is old enough to understand," her mother answered. A few days later Suzanne was turned back, and Pilette traveled on to Ruth's hotel in Lancey. She cringed at the sight of Claude and Ruth together, and her relationship with her father never recovered.

Suzanne was increasingly elsewhere, involved in her mysterious activities, and Bazou felt her absence keenly. As a shy boy of ten, he would come home from school in the afternoon in dread of putting his key in the lock. If it turned once, it meant that his darling *maman* was home to welcome him with hugs and encouragement. If it turned twice, it meant he was facing another long afternoon on his own. More and more often, the key turned twice.

Managing the household was becoming more difficult. Paris grew darker and drearier. The fuel shortage meant little hot water and fewer baths. Women of fashion carefully made up their faces, but their necks were grimy and they wore turbans to hide their unwashed hair. Suzanne's charwoman and Pilette had to stand in line for hours for rationed food. The rules were complex. To buy fish, Suzanne had to sign up at a fish market—the one near the Madeleine was the best—where she received a numbered slip. This qualified her to claim her fish with the family's coupons when the number was called. She was dismayed to see that hers was above 18,000. Weeks passed, and she returned to the market only to learn that her number had been called and she'd missed her chance.

In the old days, Suzanne welcomed the children home with skinny *ficelle* baguettes smeared with *boudin noir*, but sausage had disappeared. The Parisians' beloved boulangeries now used crude mined salt instead of delicate *sel de mer*, and the children had to pick small stones out of their baguettes before they could eat them. There was plenty of wine, but no coffee; an acrid acorn brew served as a poor substitute.

The family was fortunate to have chicken and rabbit from Choisel. Suzanne still had to bicycle from the village to the train station in the neighboring town of Saint-Rémy-lès-Chevreuse. Claude worried about the trip and told her, "I forbid you to go down the hill on the bicycle; it's too steep." One day in November she set out for the city with a friend, with bags hanging from her handlebars and a hatbox tied on the back. She skidded on a turn and stopped just short of a concrete pole; any farther and she might have been killed. Her friend called an ambulance, which took her to the American Hospital in Neuilly. Pilette reached her father, who was sitting in the Marignan café, helping his brother Charles with a screenplay.

The surgeon feared she had fractured her skull. Fortunately, she had escaped a serious head injury, but her arched "Bourbon" nose was embedded with gravel. When the doctor informed her that the detritus had to be removed, Suzanne, the least vain of women, asked him to combine the procedure with a rhinoplasty. Her "Bourbon" nose could be mistaken for a "Jewish" nose, she said. If she was going to devote herself to helping Jews, it would be better if her nose didn't make her look like one. The surgeon narrowed it and smoothed the arch.

Now Suzanne became the most theatrical member of the family, transforming herself for a new role. As Pilette put it, "Mother disguised herself as a lady," turning herself into the image of the wealthy woman of fashion the world expected her to be. For years she had worn her hair unfashionably long, twisted into a figure eight at the nape. Now she had it cut and styled. She bought a new burgundy suit (from the sale rack at Lanvin, Pilette thought), finished with velvet pockets. She added an ochre blouse to complete the ensemble. She had always been slender; now, under the occupation, her collarbones began to show, making her as svelte as a mannequin. Claude bought her a coat made of shining beaver fur. She purchased two new hats, one brown and one black with a pink rose, which she wore at a rakish tilt. She completed the look with fine leather gloves from a shop on the Avenue de l'Opéra. She had taken good care of her brown Bally flats, which was fortunate; replacing them now would be impossible.

Suzanne was photographed in her new suit. She now wore a winning smile rather than the glum expression she had offered Magritte four years earlier. Even her movements were transformed. Two years earlier she had sat immobilized for hours in a lawn chair. Now she walked quickly, her children noted, "always eager."

Suzanne was grooming herself to be the public face of Solidarité. The group's members could be arrested at any moment for the crime of being Jewish, further compromised by their acts of forgery, smuggling, and money laundering. She could move freely aboveground. Over time, a Solidarité activist wrote, Suzanne proved that she could "play the role of the *grande dame* in the 'best society'" when necessary. She was equally content to serve as "a simple office worker, a typist, a distributor of flyers."

Suzanne had repeatedly asked her friend Mira "What can I do?" and her friend had put her off, even after Claude helped extract her husband from Pithiviers. Finally, perhaps when Claude was away with Ruth in the South, Suzanne was told, "You can type."

The fact was, she couldn't. Her finishing-school education had focused on domestic arts, not secretarial skills. But she managed to lay hands on a little burgundy portable Olivetti, perhaps one that Ruth had left behind. Pilette often heard her pecking at the keys into the night. The Jewish resistance needed more tracts: to alert the community, to rouse the French, to spread the news from the BBC and Radio Moscow, to counter despair. Suzanne typed double-sided copies, rolling eight blue carbons through the platen at a time. A typographical error was a disaster when so many copies had to be corrected. Suzanne read the texts as she typed, every line increasing her sense of urgency.

In the winter of 1941 Suzanne Spaak joined a new organization, an offshoot of Solidarité. It was called the National Movement Against Racism, or MNCR. In this case, "racism" signified "anti-Semitism." If the Nazis and the Vichy government were going to impose "racial" laws to harm the Jews, this group would oppose them. Unlike Solidarité, the MNCR was designed to reach across religious and political divisions. Charles Lederman, Adam Rayski, and Léon Chertok were involved, but as an illegal organization, its membership was fluid and its activities took place in the shadows. Suzanne worked with each of the three men, but it appears that she was closest to Léon Chertok.

Suzanne's center of gravity shifted. After years as the neglected wife of an irritable husband, she was surrounded by new friends who found her kind, generous—and essential. She was, after all, a vibrant woman. Antoinette, Paul-Henri's daughter, saw her as the most charismatic member of a difficult family: "She was adorable, gay, the only one who was affectionate with me. Suzanne loved people—she was full of kindness and generosity, luminous. And she was *grande bourgeoisie*" (a member of the gentry who could marry into aristocracy). Antoinette's mother, the former first lady of Belgium, paled in comparison. "My own mother was provincial."[1]

The activists from Solidarité saw her in a similar light: a dazzling creature who had wandered into their grim circle from an alien world of wealth and ease. Charles Lederman described Suzanne as "a small blond woman, with very clear blue eyes, with a charm born of intelligence, delicacy, and simplicity." That said, some of her traits puzzled him.

> She lived in a superb apartment looking out on the gardens of the Palais Royal that I visited a number of times. The Spaaks owned a collection of important paintings, among which was a Magritte that she was fond of, that intrigued me. My personal taste didn't incline me towards this genre of painting. I never told her. Why spoil a pleasure?[2]

One of Suzanne's attractions was her radio, a massive receiver made of blond wood placed at the entry of her apartment. Deprived of their radios, Jews considered foreign broadcasts a crucial link to the outside world. Every day, Suzanne and the children gathered for the thirty-minute BBC broadcast *Les Français parlent aux Français* (*The French Speak to the French*). The Nazis tried to jam the signal, and merely listening to the broadcast could bring a six-month prison sentence, but Suzanne was undeterred. She didn't even bother to turn down the sound; the stone walls of the Palais Royal were built to guard a cardinal's secrets. And, recalled Pilette, "No one else was around to hear it." But they did turn the dial to a different station after the broadcast.

Suzanne and the children listened intently to the opening timpani beats—"tam-tam-tam *tam*"—the cadence of Beethoven's Fifth, representing the Morse signal *V* for "Victory." Then the announcer intoned, "*Ici—Londres*," and another world opened up, beyond Nazi censorship and Vichy propaganda. One regular jingle mocked Vichy's propaganda outlet, sung to the tune of "La Cucaracha": "*Radio Paris ment, Radio Paris ment! Radio Paris est allemand"* ("Radio Paris lies, Radio Paris lies! Radio Paris is German"). The broadcasts included thrilling *"messages personnels,"* London's coded instructions to the Resistance: "The gardener's dog is crying." "The library is on fire."[3]

French listeners used these phrases to conjure images of espionage, airdrops, and rescues carried out by legions of gallant *résistants*—even if, in that frozen winter, resistance forces were thin on the ground.

In some respects the news was disappointing. At this point neither the BBC's French service nor Radio Moscow considered the plight of France's immigrant Jews worthy of notice.[4] Nonetheless, the foreign broadcasts offered an alternative to the Vichy press's menu of despair, in which every German war crime was an act of self-defense, every battle a German victory, and a world ruled by Nazis a matter of time. The BBC provided much-needed news of Allied victories and outrage at Nazi crimes, making it possible to imagine a future without mass arrests and swastikas. For members of the Jewish underground, moving from cellar to attic to avoid arrest, Suzanne's receiver was a lifeline to the outside world, extended to their community through their tracts.

News gathering was a major challenge. Beyond the banned foreign broadcasts, the activists scraped together rumors and whispered reports from sympathizers, many of them Communists who worked for the police and other government agencies. Every step was perilous. The sound of a radio or the clatter of a typewriter from a Jewish residence could attract the police. Anyone looking to buy paper in quantity without authorization came under suspicion. *Roneos*, or mimeographs, required malodorous chemicals and a cumbersome apparatus that had to be moved frequently to avoid detection. The tracts were often hand delivered, and the possession of one was a serious crime. Each step in the operation invited a tip-off to the Gestapo from a hostile neighbor or concierge.

Suzanne's Children

The Jewish underground rose to the challenge by setting up various copying and forgery shops and procuring supplies in outlying cities and towns. Suzanne was a natural choice as a courier. She could travel without fear, since neither the Vichy nor the German authorities had reason to suspect her. Her legal identity papers, fixed abode, and access to food and money made her a rare treasure.

The winter and spring of 1942 marked a new phase in the Nazis' war against the Jews. Once again, the policy was concealed by Vichy censorship, Nazi propaganda, and outright lies. Forced labor lay at the heart of the deception.

France was reluctantly on the move, as workers across the country boarded trains bound for Germany. At first they signed up in desperate response to France's massive unemployment; an April 1942 report estimated that a total of 157,000 French workers had voluntarily gone to Germany to date and 96,000 were still there.[5] But the German war machine had an insatiable appetite, and as the campaign on the eastern front dragged on, more French workers were needed for German farms and factories.

The Vichy government explained the detention of immigrant Jewish males within the context of labor requirements, and most of the public, including the Jewish community, bought the explanation. Furthermore, the number of detained men was relatively small. France's immigrant Jews numbered 150,000 individuals; people were far more concerned about the nearly two million French prisoners of war.

The Jewish arrests were erratic and therefore confusing. Initially, only immigrant Jewish males were detained, and in some cases they were released. Then the Jewish arrests were expanded to include male French citizens, including professionals and military veterans, who had been treated with deference in the past. Even so, there was cause for optimism. In the fall of 1941, a German military commission visited a detention camp and denounced its abject conditions; about 750 of the sickest prisoners were freed. The prisoners reasoned they were unlikely to be arrested again, but they were wrong.

January 1942 was the turning point, though this would not be immediately apparent. On January 20, fifteen Nazi officials gathered in a gracious villa on a lake in the Berlin suburb of Wannsee to plan the extermination of the European Jews. The Nazi hierarchy had discussed a number of options, including shipping them to the island of Madagascar or creating a new Jewish homeland on the Russian-Polish border, but these were discarded.

The "Holocaust by bullets" had already begun on the eastern front. Now the officials laid the groundwork for the next stage. It wasn't feasible to murder Jews en masse, in situ in Western Europe; the local populations were more likely to protest and the news would travel quickly to the Allies. Those Jews who were not murdered locally under other pretenses (as resisters or hostages) would be deported to a new network of camps in Poland under the guise of conveying the prisoners to perform forced labor like millions of other Europeans. However, unlike the other slave laborers, Jews would be deported whether or not they were suitable for work, with the goal of murdering all of them on an industrial scale. The Wannsee Conference approved the administrative apparatus to make the machinery of genocide run smoothly. The meeting was over in ninety minutes.

Its protocol evaluated the political conditions in each occupied country and estimated the number of Jews each one was expected to yield. France was assigned to "Category A": occupied and compliant. The Nazis' estimate for its Jewish population was wildly mistaken: 165,000 for the Occupied Zone and 700,000 for the Free Zone, when the total for both zones never exceeded 330,000.

The officials took pains to shroud their proceedings in secrecy. No one who was not directly involved in the implementation of the killings was to know about them, whether citizen or soldier, and those who came close enough to learn of them were sworn to silence on pain of death. It is believed that only thirty copies of the Wannsee minutes were made.

The Germans constructed gas chambers in the camps in late 1941 and soon dispatched their first victims, Soviet prisoners of war and Polish political prisoners. The mass gassing of Jews would not begin until after the Wannsee Conference a few months later. Polish villagers living near the camps could see evidence of the murders, but for most of 1942, the terrible secret was kept from the world. Jews were not the only target. In May 1940, the Germans had launched a program to execute tens of thousands of Polish teachers, engineers, priests, and even Boy Scouts in an effort to obliterate the country's leadership. The Nazis targeted tens of thousands of Roma and millions of "racially inferior" Slavs as well.*[6]

These crimes were committed far from France, and the French public received little information from the East. Polish Jewish immigrants tended to be better informed than their French counterparts, via networks of family and friends. Yet even these reports were difficult to evaluate, having passed through countless links in a terrifying game of telephone. The news was so dire that it was hard to believe. Many French officials and businessmen simply weren't interested; they were making good money through collaboration. But by the spring of 1942, they had reason to reconsider. The entry of the United States reinvigorated the Allies, and Germany's campaign on the eastern front had bogged down. Suddenly the feasibility of the Final Solution was in doubt. The Nazis reacted by accelerating

---

* The estimates for non-Jewish Poles murdered by the Nazis range from two to three million, compared to three million Polish Jews. In northern Russia, the Nazis implemented the murderous *Hungerplan*, diverting agricultural produce to the German army and leaving four to seven million Soviet civilians to starve over the course of the war.

it. The next year would prove decisive. As the historian Christopher Browning wrote:

> In mid-March of 1942, some 75 to 80 percent of all victims of the Holocaust were still alive, while 20 to 25 percent had perished. In mid-February 1943, the percentages were exactly the reverse. At the core of the Holocaust was a short, intense wave of mass murder. The center of this mass murder was Poland.[7]

Thousands of Jewish men languished in a tenement complex at Drancy, a working-class suburb of Paris, as well as other camps in Compiègne, Beaune-la-Rolande, and Pithiviers. Malnutrition and foul sanitary conditions were killing inmates by the score, but the prisoners still hoped for release.

On the afternoon of March 27, 1942, four thousand Jewish prisoners at Drancy were ordered to assemble in the sunny courtyard. A German officer read a list of 545 names. The men, mostly working-class immigrants from the eleventh arrondissement, stepped forward and were taken to the train station a few blocks away. There they boarded third-class passenger cars, buzzing with the rumor that they were being sent to the Ardennes to cut lumber. "We thought we were going to leave a place we considered hell, but in reality it was just the antechamber," one recalled.

Their first stop was Compiègne, where the train took on another 547 men, most of them French Jews who had been arrested along with Colette's husband the previous December. They included Léon Blum's younger brother, a ballet impresario who had chosen to return from New York after the invasion, as well as a senator, a colonel, and a number of prominent lawyers. French policemen guarded the train up to the German border. The prisoners were told that if anyone escaped, the occupants of the car would be shot. One prisoner did escape, but the retaliation did not take place. The rest arrived at Auschwitz-Birkenau.[8]

All were selected for labor. No one from the first convoy was gassed upon arrival, but only twenty-two of them survived until the end of the war.

Over the next few months the convoys rolled quickly, some at two-week intervals, some every two days. Subsequent trains used cattle cars instead of passenger compartments, and prisoners were crammed into the dark, airless spaces. The rumors of labor details persisted, now more tentatively.

On May 12, 1942, the German military command in France circulated a notice forbidding the terms "deportation" and "toward the East" in internal communications. The permissible phrase was "sent to hard labor."[9]

The Germans and the Vichy government continued to link the Jewish deportations to the attacks carried out by young Communists, even though the *bataillons de la jeunesse* were by no means exclusively Jewish. Pierre Georges, the youth who shot a German naval cadet in the Barbès Métro, was the non-Jewish son of a Paris baker, and his squad included an Italian, a Haitian Creole, and a German Communist, as well as a Russian Jew and a Greek Jew.*

The youth battalions' casualties continued to mount, and Solidarité's Adam Rayski decided they needed help. He had been one of the first advocates for armed struggle, and in early 1942 he helped found a new, predominantly Jewish urban guerrilla movement connected to the Yiddish-MOI labor organization called the FTP-MOI (Franc-tireurs et partisans, or Sharpshooters and Partisans). Rayski and his friends recruited Jewish survivors of the youth battalions and stepped up the production of counterfeit documents for their use.

They also launched a search for illegal arms and explosives. It was a maddening pursuit, starting with antique weapons stashed

---

* Georges came to be known as "Colonel Fabien." A Métro stop in Paris is named after him.

away in Jewish junk shops in Saint-Ouen, a northern suburb of Paris. "Antiquated pistols didn't always come with the corresponding bullets," Rayski wrote, "so we had to consider switching to explosive devices."[10] His group set up its first bomb factory in a student apartment on the Left Bank facing the Jardin des Plantes, manned by Salek Bot, a twenty-year-old violinist, and Hersz Zimmerman, a thirty-two-year-old chemist. It was a disaster. On April 25, the two were constructing a bomb intended for a German barracks when it exploded, killing both. The police arrested six Jewish Communists, who were executed by firing squad at Mont-Valérien.

After each arrest, the survivors conducted an internal investigation to determine how the suspects had been identified. It was often found to have been through the efforts of the Brigade Spéciale, a new unit made up of several hundred French agents assigned to investigate Communists and "domestic enemies." One common tactic was the *filature*, in which agents tailed individuals who led them from one contact to another, then swept in and made multiple arrests. Rayski noted that it was possible to develop a "certain psychosis and believe you're being followed when you aren't. But it was also dangerous to be too confident."[11]

Rayski and the FTP-MOI opened a second laboratory on Rue Saint-Charles on the Left Bank, but its amateur bomb maker set off another accidental explosion, severely burning his face. It was impossible to take him to an emergency room, since the hospitals were under orders to report wounded suspects: police were looking for a man who had been pulled out of the flames with an overcoat over his head. The FTP-MOI turned to Léon Chertok. The doctor placed the burn victim, who was almost blinded, in a bicycle taxi and conveyed him to a private clinic, where he spent six months recovering.[12]

Rayski's recruits were an unlikely assortment of students, artists, and blue-collar workers, most of whom had no experience with the mechanics of war. The exceptions were Jewish veterans of the Spanish Civil War, but even they lacked matériel. Léon Chertok was impatient with his medical role and longed to see action in the armed resistance. But Rayski and his group squelched that idea; Chertok was too valuable as a medic. Chertok became the FTP-MOI's emergency room physician without an emergency room, treating an ever-growing number of wounded militants and forging ties with the legal medical community for supplies and support.[13]

Printing operations were another priority, and an equal challenge. Rayski and Lederman had recruited Rudolf Zeiler, a Communist printer from Bohemia who was willing to help, but Zeiler was arrested and executed by firing squad in December 1941. Then the two set up small makeshift print shops, eventually operating four or five in Paris and more in the Free Zone. These weren't proper businesses but rather apartments or rooms rented under false names with front offices, usually in immigrant neighborhoods such as Belleville. The underground journalists smuggled in *roneo* machines and paper, dashed off their work, and vacated the premises, hoping to stay a step ahead of the police.[14]

Forged documents were a critical part of the operation. Rayski used one of his forgeries to illegally cross into the Free Zone, where he established a Jewish resistance network and an edition of his Yiddish underground newspaper in Marseille. The forgeries were also distributed to Solidarité's membership, which rose to over a hundred. These papers allowed them to register with the police under false addresses. Since the arrests had been limited to adult males, the men rented garrets and maid's rooms in "bourgeois districts," while their wives and children remained at home.[15]

The Jewish underground had to alter its message. It had previously concentrated on warning the Jewish population about anti-Semitic measures and supporting the prisoners' families. Until now, the internees had assumed they should bide their time in hopes of release. Now they were urged to escape at the first opportunity.

In April 1942, the MNCR launched a new clandestine publication called *J'Accuse*, with the participation of Suzanne Spaak.* Its editor, Mounie Nadler, had served on the resistance committee at Pithiviers with Harry Sokol the previous year. Nadler was arrested following the April 25 explosives disaster a few weeks after the newsletter's debut, and died among the six Jewish Communists shot at Mont-Valérien—but the newsletter continued to publish.

J'Accuse marked a transition from the Jewish insularity of Solidarité to the broader mission of the MNCR. This was the first time the group called on non-Jewish intellectuals to rally the broader French public.[16]

J'Accuse may have been the first publication to convey a sense of terror regarding the Jewish deportations, and it hit home. Over April and May, a record seventy-three Jewish escapees succeeded in fleeing the camps.[17]

It soon became clear that a larger operation was under way. On May 29, 1942, the authorities announced that all Jews in the Occupied Zone over the age of six would be required to wear yellow stars on their garments. Yellow stars had been imposed on Jews in medieval England, Spain, and France, as well as in Nazi Germany, and the Nazis had already instituted the stars in occupied Poland, Czechoslovakia, and Romania. It came as a shock to France.

The French expressed no enthusiasm for the order but implemented it. Textile workers produced four hundred thousand yellow stars from specially ordered cloth, and fashioned celluloid stars for butchers and members of other "messier professions."[18]

There were a few reports of insults on the streets, especially among schoolchildren taunting classmates who were suddenly "different." But most passersby responded with mute embarrassment or

---

* The publication was named after Émile Zola's condemnation of the Dreyfus Affair in 1898.

expressions of sympathy. Clusters of young Parisians appeared bearing hand-lettered stars that read, "Goy," "Swing," or "*Catholique*." Others sported stars with the letters "JUIF"—for *jeunesse universitaire intellectuelle française* ("French university intellectual youth").

French police officers arrested about forty of the protesters and sent them to Drancy, where Dannecker ordered them to wear white armbands with the words "Friend of the Jews" and a yellow star. They embraced detention as a gesture of solidarity, and deplored the camp's meager provisions and squalid conditions. But the "friends of the Jews" were released in late August on Dannecker's orders, while the Jewish prisoners were not. Many "friends" joined the Resistance.

Suzanne Spaak never declared herself a "friend of the Jews" by wearing a yellow star, and her friends in Solidarité would have been appalled if she had. She was far too valuable to consign to Drancy for a symbolic act.

At the clandestine meetings she hosted, the Jewish activists arrived one by one, careful not to attract attention, and climbed the grand stairway to the Spaaks' apartment. There they sat, sharing news of arrests and planning their strategy in the luxury of a home that wasn't under surveillance. Their attention would wander to the Magrittes on the wall and they would puzzle once more at their hostess's peculiar taste in art.

Suzanne was careful to schedule the meetings for times when Claude was away and the children were elsewhere. She hid clandestine materials—tracts and memos, addresses of contacts—between the pages of volumes stored in the large bookcase in the entryway. These were time bombs should they ever fall into the wrong hands. When Pilette and Bazou arrived home from school, there was no evidence a meeting had ever taken place.

5

monsieur henri

One day in June 1942, Leopold Trepper appeared unannounced at the Palais Royal. The Soviet agent was prone to fidgeting, and on this occasion he was even more nervous than usual. His operations, as well as his life, generally depended on the kindness of strangers, and this time his fate lay in the hands of Suzanne and Claude Spaak. He knew that the Sokols trusted them, but they were close friends, while he was unknown to them. One word to the police or slip to a neighbor and he was finished. Claude opened the door. Trepper introduced himself as "Monsieur Henri," then delivered the bad news. "The Sokols have been arrested."

Claude summoned Suzanne, and Trepper was struck by how calmly the couple received the information. They seemed certain that, even under Gestapo interrogation, the Sokols would not implicate them. Looking around the apartment filled with books and paintings, Trepper could see that the Spaaks were people of wealth and privilege.

"I've got the gold coins Mira left with us," Claude told him. "Do you want them now?"

"No," Trepper answered. "When I do, I'll send someone to collect them."

Claude took to Trepper immediately. Years later he described him to the French journalist Gilles Perrault: "He seemed thoroughly humane and inspired total trust; his eyes shone with goodness."[1] Claude found Trepper's urbanity a welcome contrast to Harry's belligerence.

This, at least, was Claude's version of his first encounter with Leopold Trepper—the story he offered to Perrault, his children, and anyone else who asked until the day he died. It coincided with Leopold Trepper's own account in his memoir, *The Great Game* (first published in 1975, eight years after Perrault's book *The Red Orchestra*).* In the future, a different version would emerge, although it, too, was riddled with uncertainty. This is not entirely surprising. After all, both Claude, a dramatist, and Trepper, a spy, told tales for a living.

Harry and Mira Sokol had been introduced to Trepper in the spring of 1941, courtesy of the Soviet military attaché. "I told [Mira] that the job involved 'special work' that wasn't directly tied to the Communist Party, and would require them to keep their distance from various people, especially known Communists," Trepper recounted later. "Based on our meetings, I was convinced that she was a discreet and intelligent woman. I proposed to her that she learn Morse code . . . and the husband and wife learned together. They received money for subsistence."[2]

Harry and Mira Sokol began their transmissions in February 1942 from a house Trepper provided for them in Maisons-Laffitte, a town northwest of Paris. They sent the coded messages to the Soviet embassy in London, which relayed them to Moscow. Desperate

---

* That is, the first publication of the French editions, *Le Grand jeu* and *L'Orchestre rouge*, respectively.

for information, Moscow pushed them to the limit in their transmission, and the Sokols realized that their lengthy sessions were inviting detection.

In June 1942—a scant four months after they began—a roaming German police van picked up their signal in a suburb northwest of Paris. The vehicle returned accompanied by a Gestapo officer and two black Mercedes full of agents. They re-located the signal and homed in on the source, a nondescript house in a residential neighborhood.

The Gestapo stormed the building and raced up to the attic, where they caught Harry bent over his keyboard in the act of sending a transmission. Mira, clutching a batch of encoded messages, bolted from the back window, but the agents seized her in the garden. The Germans shoved the couple into one of the Mercedes and took them to their headquarters on the Rue des Saussaies. Thus began their season in hell.

According to Wilhelm Flicke, a German officer who observed the interrogations, Harry was taken to a tiled room, stripped, and seated by a metal bathtub. Three Gestapo agents drenched him in ice-cold water and administered electric shocks. "I've told you everything I know," Harry protested. "I have no idea who gave me instructions or where he lives." The torment continued until Harry's face and hands turned blue and he began to convulse.

They brought Mira in for the next round. She had dressed for the hot summer day in shorts and a light blouse, and shivered in the dank chamber. Flicke reported that she tried to stall.

"What's the name of the head of your organization?"

"He's called—I—I don't know."

An agent thrust a gun to Harry's head.

"Do you want your husband to be—"

Mira faltered. "His name is— Oh, I don't know his name; they call him Gilbert."

"And where does he live?"

"They say he lives in Brussels, but I think he's here in Paris."[3]

The interrogation continued for several months, with ever-increasing brutality. After their initial questioning the Sokols were transferred to Fresnes, the forbidding prison outside Paris. It still held common criminals, but they were joined by growing numbers of Allied flight crews and French *résistants*.

The Gestapo was uncertain where the Sokols fit into the picture. Because their transmitter was too weak to reach Moscow, they initially assumed they were working for the French Resistance under London's direction. But once the captured messages were analyzed, it was clear they matched the earlier transmissions to Moscow the Germans had intercepted from Trepper's operations in Brussels. In September the Gestapo transferred the Sokols to the SS prison in Belgium, the base for their new investigation.

Fort Breendonk was a stone citadel surrounded by a moat filled with cold gray water where no living thing could survive. Constructed in 1906, it had been converted by the Nazis into one of their most fearsome prison camps. The commandant was a corrupt, sadistic SS officer named Philipp Schmitt, the master of a vicious German shepherd named Lump that he deployed in his interrogations. Some prisoners held that Breendonk was worse than the industrial-scale prison camps, because its small population allowed the SS officers to know their individual prisoners and tailor their torture accordingly.

One of the Sokols' fellow prisoners was Betty Depelsenaire, a Belgian Communist lawyer who had been a member of Suzanne and Mira's women's group in Brussels before the war. Depelsenaire had also been arrested for supporting Soviet intelligence efforts and was held in Breendonk from September until Christmas 1942.

Depelsenaire described Mira's arrival on a sunny morning in September.[4] (Harry Sokol was delivered to the fort separately.) A frail woman of thirty-three, Mira stumbled down the chilly corridors still dressed in her summer shorts and blouse. She had already heard of Breendonk and its horrors.[5] The SS officers who ran the prison boasted they would make short work of her interrogation and identify everyone involved in the radio operation. She was handcuffed, placed in a chilly cell, and put on starvation rations.

Mira was desperate to contact the outside world. Communicating through the pipes, she asked for help from the other political prisoners, who managed to smuggle a pencil and some cigarette paper into her cell. Mira placed it on her table and contorted her body until she could write.

> Dear All: I'm in Breendonk. They have threatened to whip me since it's impossible for me to furnish the information they demand. I have my hands tied behind my back. I'm holding on, but I think of you all a lot. Help me if you can. I know that you will do everything in your power to get me out of this.[6]

It is not known if anyone outside the prison walls ever received that message. Leopold Trepper was silent on the subject. But another message somehow reached Suzanne Spaak in Paris via her sister-in-law Pichenette. "Mira's in Brussels," she wrote. "She's very cold." Suzanne sent Mira Pilette's blue-and-white dressing gown made of warm quilted cotton.

One day Mira received a visit from Commandant Schmitt, accompanied by his German shepherd. Betty Depelsenaire wrote, "All of the hatred of his master was expressed in the movements of the animal's muscular body, always ready to attack." The creature growled and bared his teeth, terrifying Mira, who was still in chains. He leaped at her and knocked her over. The commandant watched in amusement, leaning against a table with a cigarette dangling from his lips.

Then he pressed her for names. Who recruited them? Who hid them? Who helped them? Who ran the operation? Mira maintained ignorance.

"You pretend you don't know him?" he mocked her. "*Ma petite,* I pity you. Breendonk is not a pleasant place for a young woman." The dog snuffled through a box of Mira's belongings, then urinated on her clothes. The commandant smiled and departed with his pet.

It got worse. Once Mira's interrogators were convinced that she had no intention of being "reasonable," they dragged her by the hair to a torture chamber, where she was tormented with whips, then hoisted by her handcuffs. Mira screamed and lost consciousness, but she did not talk. She was transferred to a hut where Harry was being held following a similar ordeal. The couple was held in separate cells, but at least they could occasionally shout to each other over a ceiling partition.

The torture sessions continued for four months, but the couple held fast. The Gestapo realized that their greatest vulnerability was their concern for each other.

Deprived of nutrition and subjected to constant abuse, the prisoners wasted away. Betty Depelsenaire recorded an exchange in the prison clinic:

Everyone who was tortured had to go for a medical check-up today. This wasn't to diagnose or cure illnesses, but rather to let the camp authorities collect statistics and eventually isolate the incurable. Everyone had to get weighed. The results are catastrophic.

"How much do you weigh, George?"

"119 pounds! I weighed 171 two months ago."

"And you?"

"I lost 44 pounds."

"And you, Mira?"

"I lost 33 pounds."

"And you, Robert?"

He hesitated to answer.

"Don't be afraid, dear."

"83 pounds."

Mira was choking, but she found the strength to joke, "At least you're staying slim."[7]

After six months in detention, Harry's face, once round and puckish, was hollow-cheeked and empty-eyed, and his weight dropped to eighty pounds. The camp doctor was overheard to exclaim, "My God, he's not dead yet! He's a tough one. It's amazing how long the human organism can hold out."

Harry died in January 1943, hanging by his wrists, whipped and beaten by guards, and mauled by the commandant's dog. Four months later Mira was sent to a concentration camp in Germany and was not heard from again.[8]

The Sokols possessed all the information necessary to destroy Trepper and his operation. They could describe the man and his habits, and they knew the Soviet radio code. They could have identified Trepper's second in command and offered other information leading to Trepper himself. They did not.

The loss of the Sokols was the first of the many disasters to afflict Leopold Trepper over 1942. Shortly after the June arrest, the Gestapo created a unit called the Sonderkommando Rote Kapelle (Red Orchestra Task Force) to coordinate the various threads of the Trepper investigation.

It proceeded efficiently. At the end of June the Gestapo arrested Trepper's only remaining radio operator in Brussels, and his entire network in the Netherlands was rounded up. In July, German army analysts succeeded in cracking the Soviet code with the help of material they had captured with Trepper's team the previous year in Brussels.

In late August, the Gestapo used its breakthrough to obliterate Trepper's Berlin contacts and their associates, who made up one of the most extensive and effective anti-Nazi resistance networks in Germany. Based in Berlin, it consisted of dozens of small affinity groups whose only shared characteristic was their abhorrence of Hitler and his crimes. Beginning in the mid-1930s, its members infiltrated the Nazi regime in order to undermine it from within. They sent extensive intelligence to the Allies, first through the US embassy, then through Trepper's network and other conduits.

The Gestapo investigators grouped the Germans together with Trepper's operation under the rubric of the Rote Kapelle ("Red Orchestra"), even though none of them had ever heard the term or met Trepper.* The Germans included artists, academics, and government officials—in addition to a few paid Soviet agents. Their resistance work included activities that were strictly forbidden to actual Soviet intelligence operatives, including publishing anti-Nazi flyers and sheltering persecuted Jews.

The German resistance group was crushed as a result of Soviet bungling. In October 1941, Trepper received a message from Moscow instructing him to send an agent to Berlin to set up radio communications. The transmission included the Germans' names and home addresses. "I was startled by their recklessness," Trepper wrote later. "I knew that no code, however skilled, was unbreakable."[9] Once the code was broken, the Gestapo placed the group under surveillance and widened the list of suspects. Over the fall of 1942 they arrested over 150 people, almost half of them women. Over fifty were executed by the Nazis. Women and minor figures died at the guillotine. The alleged ringleaders were subjected to a new method approved by Hitler himself: slow strangulation from meat hooks. The Berliners' resistance work and their Jewish rescue operations died with them.

Now the Gestapo task force concentrated on Trepper and every individual he knew, no matter how slight the connection. The

---

* The Germans called a transmitter a *Klavier*, or "keyboard," and a network a *Kapelle*, or "chamber orchestra." *Rote*, or "red," signified a Soviet connection.

Sonderkommando regarded all of them as "agents" of the Rote Kapelle and Leopold Trepper as the mastermind. The Sokols were an important link in the chain.

Trepper learned of the Sokols' arrest from Fernand Pauriol, the young French Communist who had cobbled together their transmitter. Pauriol had been monitoring Harry's transmission when it suddenly stopped. Trepper sent a messenger to the Sokols' safe house in Maisons-Laffitte to confirm their arrest, then dispatched a crew of "house cleaners" to their apartment on Rue Chevert to remove any evidence.[10]

Trepper went into hiding, consoled by his young mistress Georgie de Winter. But his network was shattered and his transmitters were no more. The Gestapo had closed him down in Brussels, Amsterdam, Berlin, and Marseille. Dozens of his agents were undergoing Gestapo interrogations across Europe, and some of them would turn, begging to work for the Germans in return for their lives. Trepper had only a shadowy idea of what was transpiring in the Gestapo cells and had no choice but to lie low, knowing it was only a matter of time before someone gave him away. The astonishing thing was how many didn't.

In his book on the Rote Kapelle, Gilles Perrault described the difference between the professional and the amateur intelligence agent. The professional, he wrote, regards an interrogation as a game of chess, recognizing that it is sometimes necessary to sacrifice pawns, and considering himself a prime asset. Both sides understand that they may benefit more from a sophisticated exchange of information than a crude confession extracted under torture.

The amateur, on the other hand, is often motivated by idealism, which can include an idealized sense of self. The interrogator can expect an "all-or-nothing" set of behaviors: the amateur will either impart nothing or, giving way, spill everything he knows and even offer to assist his captors.

By this measure, Trepper's radio team in Brussels and the Sokols were amateurs of the idealistic, unbending sort, while Leopold Trepper was a consummate professional.

Mira and Harry Sokol disappeared into historical limbo. Harry's story was consigned to the murky annals of Soviet espionage, while Mira was recorded in Jerusalem's Yad Vashem as a victim of the Holocaust. Her scant file there states mistakenly that she spent the war in Belgium and adds, probably accurately, that she was murdered in a concentration camp in Germany in April 1943.

For the Soviets, the Sokols were two pawns on the chessboard. For Suzanne Spaak, the loss was immeasurable. Furthermore, she had reason to believe that even though Mira had implicated her by hiding Trepper's money in her home, she had never, throughout her long ordeal, uttered her name.

6

spring wind, winter stadium

Mira Sokol's arrest was a terrible blow, but Suzanne Spaak had little time to absorb the impact. Scarcely a month later an event occurred in the heart of Paris that would shake her world to its foundations. It had been clear for a while that something was in the works, but it was impossible to tell what. In March the convoys began heading east from Drancy, each carrying about one thousand Jewish men, and little was heard from them afterward. At the end of May the imposition of the yellow star was announced—but to what end? These questions haunted a brilliant Sorbonne student named Hélène Berr, whose mission would soon intersect with Suzanne Spaak's.

Hélène was the daughter of Raymond Berr, a prominent businessman with impeccable credentials. The son of a judge from an Alsatian Jewish background, he had been wounded and decorated for valor in the First World War; his twin brother was killed in action. Berr rose to the position of managing director of Établissements Kuhlmann, one of France's leading chemical manufacturers. Kuhlmann was considered vital to the German war effort, and Berr's expertise won him a privileged position. His wife, Antoinette, like many women of her class, devoted herself to her five children and charity work. The Berrs had close ties to other members of the French Jewish elite, including the eminent physician Robert Debré. Hélène was good friends with Debré's son Olivier, an art student, and one of her sisters was married to his nephew Daniel Schwartz.

Initially Hélène felt no compunction to "do something." A student of literature and a talented violinist, she embraced life with a twenty-one-year-old's passion and expressed little interest in either Judaism or politics. But it was impossible for her to ignore what was happening around her. In 1941 Hélène and her mother joined a private charity, Entr'aide Temporaire (Temporary Assistance), which dated from the First World War. Its founder, Lucie Chevalley, was a distinguished Protestant lawyer who took up the cause of refugees and enlisted the wives of wealthy businessmen and professionals, Protestant, Catholic, and Jewish. With the occupation, Entr'aide concentrated its philanthropy on immigrant Jews.

Between 1942 and 1944 Hélène Berr kept a journal. It began as a college girl's musings on her studies and her latest crush, but as conditions deteriorated it became a testimony to Jewish life in Paris under the occupation. The journal was hidden away for over fifty years, but when it was finally published in 2008, it became a classic work of Holocaust literature, earning its author the title of "the French Anne Frank." Anne Frank may have resembled Berr, a striking young woman with a cloud of dark hair, had she been allowed to reach the age of twenty. Hélène Berr would not live to be much older. The publishers of Hélène's journal were unable to identify some of the names and events she mentioned. It is only by placing Hélène Berr within the context of Suzanne Spaak's network that these coded references become clear.

The Berrs moved comfortably among Jewish and non-Jewish elites, but they had little contact with Jewish immigrants beyond their charity work. Hélène played Mozart in her string quartet; it's doubtful she ever heard a klezmer band. The Berrs spoke exquisite French; Yiddish was an alien tongue.

On June 8, 1942, Hélène described the glorious summer morning, but added:

> It's also the first day I'm going to wear the yellow star. Those are the two sides of how life is now: youth, beauty, and freshness, all contained in this limpid morning; barbarity and evil, represented by this yellow star.[1]

The next day she learned that the stars would be used to segregate Jews into the last cars in the Métro. The German ordinance also banned Jews from restaurants, theaters, swimming pools, parks, racetracks, museums, and libraries.[2]

A few weeks later, Hélène's father was arrested on the grounds that his yellow star was stapled to his clothing, not sewn on according to regulation. Raymond Berr was sent to Drancy. His colleagues at Kuhlmann launched a campaign for his release, a process that dragged on for three months until he was allowed to go free.

Suzanne Spaak and the MNCR viewed the yellow star as a warning of worse things to come. They had received disturbing news from one of their sources at police headquarters. In early June they learned that the police were planning a roundup of Jews on an unprecedented scale.

The group was worried about the Jewish children. Over the spring of 1942, French police officers had started to arrest Jewish women, leaving their children behind. Some were entrusted to neighbors and relatives who had no means to support them; others were left to fend for themselves on the street. The Vichy government instructed the UGIF to deal with the problem by registering and housing the children in the shelters and orphanages under its direction.

The core members of the MNCR, including Suzanne Spaak, Léon Chertok, and Charles Lederman, raced to expand alliances beyond Jewish enclaves and the Communist Party. Léon Chertok's friends from the Left Bank cafés were vital, as were Suzanne Spaak's connections.

The group was determined to save Jews from deportation to concentration camps and contest the premise of Nazi ideology. Nazi anti-Semitism was grounded in the pseudoscientific argument that "inferior races" created social blight. This theory conflicted with France's traditional legal definition, which considered Judaism, like the two other state religions, Catholicism and Protestantism, a matter of personal choice. Before the occupation, French Jews were not only granted freedom of religion, they could become Christians upon baptism or conversion. Under the new laws, birth was destiny. To win French support for the immigrant Jews, it was essential to combat the Nazi concept of race.

The leaders divided their tasks along accustomed lines. Adam Rayski worked on tracts, Charles Lederman ran his network in the South, and Léon Chertok appealed to the medical profession and his female admirers. Suzanne Spaak became banker, business manager, and ambassador to the elite non-Jewish world.

Four convoys leaving Drancy in June had emptied the camps, suggesting there would be another round of arrests. By July, they had assembled the names of some two hundred Protestant and Catholic institutions that might be willing to shelter Jews.[3]

The tip-offs from the police source lacked an important detail: the date when the mass arrests were to take place. Nonetheless, Solidarité published a Yiddish tract headlined "The Enemy Is Preparing an Unheard-of Crime against the Jewish Population," offering what the group had learned so far:

Brothers and sisters . . . according to the information we have received from a reliable source, the Germans are going to organize a massive round-up and deportation of Jews. . . . The danger is great! . . . The question before every Jew is: what can you do to avoid falling into the hands of the SS bandits? What can you do to hasten their end and your liberation? . . .

1. Don't wait at home for the bandits. Take every measure to hide yourself and your children with the help of the sympathetic French population.

2. After assuring your own freedom, join a patriotic combat organization to fight the bloody enemy and avenge their crimes.

3. If you fall into the hands of the bandits, resist in every way, barricade the doors, call for help. You have nothing to lose. It may work and save your life. Try tirelessly to flee. Every free and living Jew is a victory over our enemy, who must not and will not succeed in our extermination.[4]

Suzanne Spaak joined the teams of Jewish activists who went door-to-door alerting the residents of immigrant Jewish neighborhoods, working alongside members of Zionist and Communist youth groups. They slipped flyers under doors and handed them to worried tenants, asking everyone to pass along the information.

Adam Rayski fumed over the denial encountered by Suzanne and her fellow canvassers:

The MNCR activists hit a wall of incomprehension everywhere they went. Non-Jews reproached them for over-dramatizing the situation. Among the Jewish families—where they were trying to convince mothers to send the children to the countryside, or to entrust them to be sent to a safe place—they met with nothing but astonishment and refusal. This situation led me to launch this appeal, in a tract for Jewish mothers:

> "Today, the danger is such that your maternal instinct
> must oblige you to separate from your children, and
> not, as usual, hold them close."[5]

Jewish men, spurred by the previous arrests, took heed, usually acting on their own. Up to that point, the arrests had swept up able-bodied men who were candidates for forced labor, and they had no reason to think this raid would be different. Thousands of husbands and fathers went into hiding in garrets and cellars, believing that their wives and children would be safe at home.

Solidarité was not the only Jewish organization to receive advance word of the July roundup—but it was the only one to publish a warning. The UGIF remained silent.

The UGIF's decision was made by its vice president, André Baur, the son of a prominent banker, a nephew of the chief rabbi of Paris, and a member of the Berrs' social circle. On July 1, an official from the Vichy agency for Jewish affairs (CGQJ) sent a letter to Baur ordering him to take up a collection of shoes and clothing from the Jewish community sufficient for seven thousand people, in preparation for another deportation. The letter came from Pierre Galien, a notorious French anti-Semite who had ingratiated himself with SS officer Theodor Dannecker, reportedly by shepherding him to bars and brothels.[6]

Baur was distressed by the request, but he also believed the information should be withheld from the immigrant community. He cautiously replied:

> It seems particularly dangerous to us to let the Jewish popula-
> tion know that it may expect a vast new deportation initiative.
> It is not our role to sow panic by giving it even partial fore-
> knowledge of your letter.[7]

The French police would call the operation Vent Printanier ("Spring Wind"), but it went down in history as the "Vel d'Hiv."* It had been months in the making. The previous March, over a thousand Jewish prisoners had boarded passenger cars confident that they were en route to farms and factories. Several months passed without additional convoys while the Germans assembled the necessary railway cars.

The next round was set in motion on May 6, when Reinhard Heydrich, a leading architect of the Holocaust, came to Paris to meet with René Bousquet, the head of the French police in the Occupied Zone.[8] Heydrich told him that he expected the French to fully execute the mechanics of the arrests and deportations.

The pace accelerated in June. A convoy departed on June 5, and three more in a single week at the end of the month, each bearing around a thousand people, including women. These prisoners boarded cattle cars, and they were far from confident.

Still, Berlin was unhappy. The Nazis viewed the French deportations as shoddy and inefficient, nothing resembling the industrial process laid out at the Wannsee Conference six months earlier. In order to meet Berlin's demands, every step had to run smoothly. The French police, responsible for the supply, needed to arrest enough Jews to meet the quotas when the trains became available. The French and German railways had to provide trains and railway personnel on a dependable basis. This complex coordination— replicated across occupied Europe—required energetic, competent administrators committed to the task.

A new series of parleys took place in early summer between René Bousquet and SS general Carl Oberg. Oberg, a pudgy, bespectacled veteran of the First World War, had run a tobacco stand

---

* Named after the Vélodrome d'Hiver, the winter bicycle-racing stadium where the prisoners would be taken.

in Hamburg before he joined the SS in 1932.[9] SS officer Dannecker, charged with making the trains run on time, was party to the talks. It was not going well. If the Final Solution was designed as an industrial operation, Oberg and Dannecker were responsible for the first link in the supply chain. They found the obstacles maddening—not just the shortage of the rolling stock, but also the endless dithering of the Vichy officials.

It wasn't a question of the Vichy regime opposing the deportations. Prime Minister Pierre Laval had described the Jewish immigrants as *déchets*, or "dross." He told a US diplomat that "these foreign Jews had always been a problem in France and that the French government was glad that a change in German attitude towards them gave France an opportunity to get rid of them."[10]

Vichy officials viewed the deportations as a solution for the violence erupting on the streets of Paris. Following the execution of French hostages, Vichy secretary of state Fernand de Brinon blamed the "Jewish authors" of the attacks rather than the Germans' policy of blind retribution. He informed Göring that he and "the entire French people" deplored "the actions of criminals incited daily by radio broadcasts of Jewish *émigrés* in the pay of the British government and the Bolshevik plutocrats."[11]

Brinon's own circumstance illustrated the fault line between French and immigrant Jews. His wife, Lisette, was the daughter of a Jewish banker and a Catholic convert who lived through the occupation as an "honorary Aryan."[12] Brinon negotiated desperately with the Germans to halt the executions of French hostages as reprisals for attacks on German personnel. In exchange, the French agreed to step up their efforts against "terrorism, anarchism and communism."

In mid-June the Germans presented the French with a new list of demands. Berlin wanted forty thousand Jews, male and female, between the ages of sixteen and forty. This demographic would support the explanation of work details. The arrests were to include thirty thousand adults from the Occupied Zone and ten thousand from the Free Zone. Sixteen thousand were to be French Jews.

The Vichy officials objected. It was unacceptable to include sixteen thousand French citizens. Laval called for a new census in the Free Zone to distinguish between French Jews and "the trash sent by the Germans themselves"—Jews deported to France from other Nazi-occupied territories.[13] The parties began to bargain. If the Germans expected the French police to carry out the arrests, the arrests should apply only to foreign Jews. The Germans acquiesced. They had little choice. The SS officers knew that they could not succeed without the support of the French police. As of 1942, there were fewer than three thousand German policemen in all of France, a country of forty million. In contrast, the French police numbered over thirty thousand in Paris alone.[14]

Under the revised plan, the July roundup would arrest 22,000 foreign Jews, as identified by the French police's color-coded index cards. It would target Jews from Germany, Austria, Poland, Czechoslovakia, the USSR, and those of "unknown origin." It would include both males and females between the ages of sixteen and fifty (instead of forty). Pregnant and nursing women would be exempted, as would some of the sick and the elderly, but the "sorting" would take place after the arrests.

Children under the age of sixteen were to be placed in the care of the UGIF and distributed among Jewish orphanages. Dannecker, outlining what he called the "transplantation" of the Jews, mentioned "the possibility of later sending the children under 16 years of age who have been left behind."[15]

The Paris police force would make the arrests and convey the prisoners to the stadium on the Left Bank known as the Vel d'Hiv. From there they would be transferred to Drancy and other camps to await deportation to the East.

By July 2, rumors were swirling through the Jewish neighborhoods of Paris, even penetrating elite households that had never heard of Solidarité. In her diary, Hélène Berr agonized over whether her family should flee the country, still barely possible via the Free Zone, or stay and resist. Leaving would mean sacrificing her sense of dignity and "that sense of heroism and struggle that you feel here. There is also giving up the feeling of equality in resistance, if I agree to stand apart from the struggle of other Frenchmen." That evening a friend of her mother's burst into their home with the news of an "order for July 15 to lock up all Jews in concentration camps."[16] If her eminent father could be arrested on spurious charges, no one was safe.

Now she decided it was time to take action. Entr'aide Temporaire was well and good, but she would go a step further. On July 6, Hélène, her sister Denise, and Denise's sister-in-law Nicole Job arrived at the UGIF headquarters on the Rue de Téhéran in a state of nervous excitement. The reception was less than enthusiastic: the secretary-general shouted, "You've no business here! If I have one piece of advice to give you, it's: Get out!" But the three young women were determined.

The Berr women understood that the UGIF was an instrument of the occupation, but it also offered the means to support immigrant Jewish families. The young women received UGIF certificates that exempted them and their families from arrest, though Hélène found them "distasteful." She regarded working for the UGIF as "a sacrifice, because I detest all those more or less Zionist movements that unwittingly play into the Germans' hands; and in addition it's going to take up a lot of our time. Life has become very peculiar."[17]

The plan for the July arrests, known as the *Grande Rafle*, stuttered again. The Germans wanted the arrests to take place over Bastille Day, but the Vichy officials insisted this was out of the question. Parisians traditionally celebrated the holiday with protests and demonstrations, and they wanted to avoid trouble. The Nazis agreed to postpone the arrests by two days.

Now the question of the children resurfaced. Pierre Laval was disturbed by the vision of thousands of Jewish children left behind. Who would be responsible for them—if not his own government? Dannecker sent Adolf Eichmann a telex asking for instructions:

Urgent, for immediate distribution.
Re: Jewish deportation from France.

Negotiations with the French Government have led to following result: all stateless Jews of the occupied and unoccupied zones are to be made available for deportation. LAVAL has proposed that Jewish families from the unoccupied territory bring along children under the age of 16.

The question of Jewish children remaining in the occupied territory does not interest him.

I therefore urgently request a decision as to whether, starting with the 15th Jewish transport from France, children under 16 can also be included.

Finally, it should be noted that in order to get the action fully underway, for the time being only stateless Jews, or rather foreign Jews, are under discussion.

In the 2nd phase Jews who were naturalized after 1919 or after 1922 are approached.[18]

Four days later, Dannecker sent Eichmann another telex. He expected the raids to produce about four thousand children. There were good reasons for deporting them, he said: one was to prevent "promiscuous" interactions between them and the non-Jewish children in care. The UGIF facilities could hold only four hundred children at a time, and the others would have to go somewhere, presumably to non-Jewish institutions.[19]

Serge Klarsfeld, the leading historian of the Holocaust in France, has argued that the French had additional reasons for requesting the children's deportation. First, they expected the raids to fall short of the German quotas. Every immigrant Jewish child on the train would fill a spot that might otherwise be assigned to a French Jew. Second, the feeding and housing of four thousand children would represent a major financial burden for the French government. Finally, if the children accompanied their parents to the camps, the public would not witness terrible scenes of separation.[20] The four hundred UGIF beds would be filled, but thousands of other children would go to the detention facilities along with their families.

On July 14 the UGIF's André Baur extended limited protection to the organization's staff members. His social workers were assembled to make four hundred labels for the children who would be lodged in UGIF facilities following the arrests. The next day, the Vichy official Pierre Galien ordered Baur to "abstain from communicating any biased information or any commentary whatsoever" to the Jewish community about the impending action.

The *Grande Rafle* commenced at 4:00 a.m. on July 16. It was a massive operation. A small army of French police officers—according to some accounts, over 8,000 men organized into 888 teams—fanned out across the immigrant Jewish neighborhoods of Paris carrying 27,000 colored index cards bearing the names and addresses of Jewish families.[21] They were instructed to arrest men, women, and children—including those who obviously had no place working on a farm or factory floor.

Parisians were shocked to see French policemen shoving their Jewish neighbors down stairwells and herding them into green and cream-colored city buses. A nurse on her way to work witnessed a scene outside the town hall: "A poor woman was dragging her little boy. His suitcase fell open and all of his things spilled on the ground, and the cop was shouting, 'Go! Go! There's no time, there's no time, hurry up!' He stopped her from picking up the things and was pulling her by the hair. . . . It was awful."[22]

Children didn't know whether to cling to their parents or obey their instructions to hide. Parents were uncertain whether to hold fast to their infants or thrust them into the arms of strangers. There were multiple suicides: one woman in the Marais threw her two young children from a fifth-floor window and leaped after them. All three died.[23]

Parisians had witnessed the deportations of POWs, the capture of *résistants*, and the mass arrests of Jewish men, but no one ever had seen anything like this.

The procedures were far from uniform. Some policemen, especially those operating singly, gave Jewish families advance notice, hoping to find their apartments empty on their return. Some officers allowed children to slip into neighbors' homes, and others refused to take French-born children. But many more executed their orders with chilly efficiency, and even hostility.

The MNCR, unaware of the date for the action, was caught by surprise. Suzanne Spaak had delivered advance warnings, but now she was out of commission. School had let out on the thirteenth, and the next day she had taken the children to the country house in Choisel for the summer. She was cut off with no access to information from Paris. Claude was in the Free Zone with Ruth. There was no possibility of using the car, and the railroad station was over three miles away. Her friends from Solidarité were scattered across Paris, all potential targets of the raid.

Adam Rayski had been staying in a rented maid's room near the Eiffel Tower, apart from the home of his wife, Jeanne, and their four-year-old son, Benoît, in Belleville. He thought his family was safe, and he was especially pleased at having procured a "genuine fake" baptismal certificate for his son.

On the morning of the *Grande Rafle*, Rayski had scheduled a meeting at the Passy Métro station, just across the bridge from his rented room. As he was descending the stairs to the quay he saw a bus pulling away. The rear platform held a policeman surrounded by suitcases and bundles. "My God!" Rayski exclaimed. "It's Jewish bedding!" The bus was piled high with the eiderdown quilts and comforters that Eastern European Jews had carried to their successive stations of exile. He knew they "always brought a pillow along so they would have a familiar place to lay their heads."

The bus slowed as it approached the bridge, and Rayski could see the expressions of those inside. The man he was meeting confirmed his fears: "Yes, it's a monstrous *rafle*."

Now all he could think of was his wife and child. It is striking that Rayski had helped produce a flyer warning about the *rafle* without taking precautions for his family. He had to reach them. Jeanne knew about some of his meetings and he hoped she would find him, but when he arrived at his appointments no one was there. He went to his aunt's home. Jeanne and the child had stopped by, she reported, then left for a small hotel. He went to the hotel, but the owner swore he hadn't seen them.

The couple had a fallback plan to meet at the Tuileries garden, but he was sure all was lost. As he approached the park he saw a little boy playing in a sandbox under the benevolent gaze of some German soldiers. Fearful it was an illusion, Rayski drew near. It was his son, filling and emptying his sand bucket, as Jeanne and a friend chatted quietly on a bench nearby. "Are children born with a natural instinct for clandestine life?" he wondered.

The previous night, Jeanne had arrived home at curfew to find her neighbors huddled in the yard. The concierge, whose husband was a policeman, had told them the raid was imminent, but, given the curfew, they didn't know what to do. Would the police just take the men? Then it would be better to put the children to bed. Would they take women and children too? How could they find hiding places in time? It might be better to keep their families together.

Jeanne didn't wait for the end of the debate. She ran to her apartment and threw some belongings into a bag. As she rushed out the door, she caught sight of the yellow star on her jacket. She ripped it off, but the fabric beneath still showed the outline. She clutched her toddler over her left side to cover it.

She convinced a hotelier to let them stay the night. He wouldn't allow her to pay for the room. "Keep your money," he said. "It's shameful to see this. Be careful."

Jeanne hoped her husband would keep their date in the Tuileries. Until then, she stayed in the Métro as long as she could, trying to comfort her hungry child with a piece of a baguette she had taken from the kitchen.

After she told her husband what had happened, Jeanne burst into sobs. Rayski waited for her reproaches but they never came. Jeanne left Benoît with a teacher nearby, and the couple spent the night together in Rayski's room. From time to time she trembled in her sleep, and he put his hand over her mouth to keep her from crying out.

The next morning they conferred. "Benoît will be safer in the country," she said. "Then I'll be free, and I can be a courier." They sought out Léon Chertok, who seemed to know everyone. Rayski had frowned on Chertok's bourgeois background and indifference to the Communist Party. Now these were the qualities that could save his son's life. Chertok had Protestant friends in a tiny hamlet in Deux-Sèvres called Noirvault. They would hide Benoît.[24]

Chertok had experienced his own ordeal. He had spent the previous night at the home of the Catala sisters, the friends who had lent him their late brother's identity. When he went out that morning, he found "an atrocious drama, because they had taken the children, and because it was the French police who had done the 'job.'"[25]

The French police were instructed to take families with children between the ages of two and twelve to the Vel d'Hiv bicycle stadium. Others, including teenagers, individual adults, and childless couples, were routed to Drancy pending deportation. Outside the stadium, city buses disgorged thousands of confused passengers clutching their suitcases and blankets. The police processed their papers as they entered, keeping meticulous records. Rayski joined Chertok outside, not daring to approach the building. But they had to know what was going on inside, and Rayski asked Chertok to find a non-Jewish friend to breach the premises and report on conditions. Once again, he turned to the Catala sisters, who had acquired forged credentials as social workers.

It was said that the early hours were calm; adults talked quietly as children scampered around the bicycle track. But by the time the Catala sisters arrived, it was pandemonium. Over the course of the first day 11,363 Jews had been arrested, and the second day brought another 1,521. By the end, the police had arrested 12,884 people, only 3,031 of whom were grown men.[26]

The Catala sisters found the environment "horrible, demoniacal, something that grabs you by the throat and keeps you from screaming." The overcrowded glass-roofed stadium had become an inferno in the July sun. Toilets were blocked and overflowing. Children and adults received scant rations of food and water, and hysteria set in. The sisters heard people screaming "Kill us, but don't leave us here!" and "I beg you, give me a lethal injection!"

The authorities admitted three doctors and a few nurses to attend to over twelve thousand people, including sick children, typhoid patients, and pregnant women.[27] "The medical staff didn't know where to turn," the sisters reported.

> The lack of water paralyzed us completely, and obliged us to totally neglect hygiene. We feared an epidemic. Not a single German! They were right. They would have been torn to pieces. What cowards to let the French do their dirty work![28]

Not every uniformed Frenchman behaved shamefully. Captain Henri Pierret, chief of the Paris Fire Department, was ordered to report to the Vel d'Hiv. He was surprised to find the site cordoned off by legions of French police officers and plainclothesmen. When he entered he encountered thousands of people without water for drinking or washing, and he told his men to turn on their hoses. A police lieutenant tried to countermand his orders but Pierret faced him down.

Pierret learned that the detainees had handed his firefighters thousands of messages for their families. He gave his men a day's leave along with Métro tickets to mail the letters a safe distance outside the city. He sent a warning to an off-duty Jewish firefighter named Ovadia Ruben not to return to the fire station. As a result, Ruben and his wife were able to escape to Spain.

Pierret returned home, where his son was impatiently waiting to celebrate his twelfth birthday. Muted and pale, the fire officer could only say, "I've been at the Vel d'Hiv. What I have seen and heard transcends the limits of horror and human cruelty. Thousands of people, many of them children, piled up for hours, crying, screaming, begging for something to drink. . . . I opened the hydrants and gave them water."[29]

The French police had done their utmost to obscure the event by closing the windows of the buses, limiting access to the stadium, and prohibiting photos. As a result, the Catala sisters could offer one of the few firsthand accounts. Rayski and Chertok published their story a few weeks later. It closed with:

> They would like us to be silent about this appalling crime. But no, we cannot permit ourselves. People have to know. Everyone needs to know about what happened here.

Described as "extracts of a letter written by a young social worker to her father," the tract was distributed widely, and Rayski believed it made a major impact.

The official news outlets focused their attention elsewhere. Movie houses showed mandatory newsreels; that week's roundup featured a bicycle race and a forest fire. *Le Figaro* publicized the regime's new *relève* program to recruit skilled French workers: for every three workers who went to Germany, one French prisoner of war could come home.[30] In other words, the only deportations that were covered in the official French press were voluntary.

One photograph did reach *Paris-Midi*, where Serge Klarsfeld found it in the archives in 1990. The photo showed five city buses outside the Vel d'Hiv and detainees lined up at the door.* On the back was a handwritten label: "*Juifs.*" The typed caption stated, "Early yesterday morning, foreign Jews were requested by police forces to board the bus. They are leaving for a new destination to work, no doubt." The photo and text were cleared with a Gestapo censor's stamp but they were apparently never published.[31]

Once again, Solidarité's fly-by-night reportage achieved what the official press would not. It was far from exemplary journalism. The Catala sisters were, by necessity, anonymous sources. The tract was typed in secrecy by a volunteer and distributed by hand or through furtive mailings. But it was the closest thing to contemporary news coverage the event would receive.

The UGIF's André Baur entered the stadium late on July 16 and recorded his distress at what he found: "One gets the impression that there are only children and sick people. The nurses have tears in their eyes, the policemen are heartsick. There is no trace of even the slightest organization, no direction, no chief or too many of them."[32]

When Baur appeared, the internees heckled him. Many of them knew that he and his colleagues possessed UGIF cards exempting them and their families from arrest. In contrast, the UGIF had sent the internees notices urging them to comply with the authorities' instructions. As the internees saw it, the UGIF had traded them for their own safety.

---

* The photo from the files of *Paris-Midi* is the only known photo of the event.

The police allowed UGIF doctors to enter the stadium in rotating teams of two, and they received a warmer welcome than Baur. One of them was Fred Milhaud, a brilliant young pediatrician and junior colleague of Robert Debré's who had also been dismissed under the Jewish ordinances.* His wife, Denise, had joined Entr'aide Temporaire in 1941, and, like the Berrs, she and her husband had joined the UGIF as a way to help stricken immigrant families. Soon the couple established a clandestine underground operation within the UGIF in concert with Hélène and the other Berr women. These privileged French Jews forged a link between the UGIF and Entr'aide to conduct acts of humanitarian sabotage that would soon connect to Suzanne Spaak's initiatives.

At the Vel d'Hiv Fred Milhaud and his colleagues could do little for the detainees beyond making hospital referrals for certain extreme ailments, such as "life-threatening hemorrhaging" and "contagious epidemic illnesses." Milhaud spent the night shift issuing (and often inventing) such diagnoses for detainees in an attempt to get them out—diagnoses he later described as "*farfelus*" ("wacky").[33] The handful of doctors, nurses, and social workers worked in shifts around the clock.

The children remained a pressing concern. A third of the nearly thirteen thousand detainees were minors, of whom roughly eight hundred were under the age of six. The Vichy government and the Gestapo had reached an agreement about deporting children from the Southern Zone, but the fate of the children in Paris was unresolved.

---

* Milhaud was a cousin of the composer Darius Milhaud, who had fled to the United States in 1940.

7

the ragged network

The first Jewish minor to be deported from France rode the initial convoy on March 27, 1942—the only one to use passenger cars. Israël Knaster was a rosy-cheeked seventeen-year-old from Warsaw who had been swept up in one of the early roundups. He arrived in Auschwitz on April 2 and died there two weeks later. There was a fifteen-year-old boy on the second convoy on June 5, and a seventeen-year-old on the third one three weeks later.[1]

Someone watching the trains depart may have imagined the boys assigned to a work detail, and it was still just possible to maintain that fiction. The subsequent convoys carried growing numbers of Jewish teenagers; sixteen were loaded on the fifth one, on June 28.

The plans concerning the children shifted, and shifted again. On July 17 Vichy's director of Jewish affairs, Darquier de Pellepoix, raised new objections to sending children to the camps, arguing for placing them in UGIF children's homes around Paris, disregarding the problem of capacity. That same day, Convoy 6 left Pithiviers, including twenty-two Jewish teens, while thousands still sweltered in the Vel d'Hiv.[2]

But the mass arrest of small children had irreparably cracked the facade. French police officials insisted on delivering them to the camps at Pithiviers and Beaune-la-Rolande.[3] Over July 19, 20, and 21, they shuttled the Jewish families from the Vel d'Hiv to the nearby Gare d'Austerlitz, roughly a thousand at a time. From there, the trains delivered them to the two outlying camps.

Jewish activists and their few non-Jewish partners faced a new crisis. Until now, they had divided their energies across many different areas: issuing underground publications, harassing the German military, gathering and sharing intelligence. Now some were compelled to focus exclusively on the deportations. For Parisians, the arrest of four thousand children made no sense. Both Jewish and non-Jewish parties were forced to reassess the official logic of the deportations, but there was no alternate explanation to take its place. After the war, Jewish prisoners who escaped from the death camps testified that none of them had known where the convoys were going or what would happen when they arrived. There is no record of such information reaching France before October 1942.[4] But the harsh absurdity of arresting children created a new sense of urgency among the Jews and their supporters, and a change in broader public opinion.

The MNCR took this opportunity to reach across political and social boundaries. Léon Chertok's most important new ally was the renowned Jewish physician Robert Debré. The son of an Alsatian rabbi, Debré still clung to his privileged position; Pétain himself had signed his exemption from the anti-Semitic law. One of Debré's relations explained that he was allowed to maintain his practice "because the Germans took their own children to him. He was the best."[5]

Debré, a widower, had met the elegant Elisabeth de la Panouse, Countess de la Bourdonnaye, while serving as pediatrician to her children. She had no use for her husband, the count, a Pétain supporter. She and Debré became a couple, who would unite in their determination to resist the occupiers. The countess, known as "Dexia," had joined the Musée de l'Homme circle, one of the first resistance groups, and was arrested along with them in 1941. She was released after six months in prison at Fresnes; other members of the group were deported or shot. Debré and Dexia continued their work for the Gaullist resistance, but with greater caution.[6]

Chertok enlisted Debré as adviser for his new medical group attached to the MNCR, Combat Médical, which united French and immigrant Jewish doctors to "denounce crimes and racist pseudo-scientists" and to "aid adult and child victims" of the occupation.[7]

Chertok's clandestine medical practice was growing rapidly. Many of Rayski's new FTP-MOI partisans were earnest young students ill prepared for amateur bomb factories or shoot-outs with the police. Chertok had to treat the wounded on the fly with whatever supplies he could find, working from hiding places around the city. He often stayed at the home of the ever-obliging Catala sisters at 74 Rue de Sèvres on the Left Bank, a five-minute walk from Robert Debré's clinic at the Hôpital Necker.

The thousands held captive in the Vel d'Hiv were lost to them. Chertok had achieved the near impossible by infiltrating the Catala sisters into the stadium. Now the doctors, Suzanne Spaak, and their associates concentrated on rousing the conscience of the French public.

One of their prime objectives was the Catholic Church. France was an overwhelmingly Catholic country, and Pétain relied on the Church to legitimize his government. Of the early members of the MNCR, only Suzanne Spaak had a Catholic background, and she had been a resolute atheist throughout her adult life. Nonetheless, just as she was willing to play the socialite, she was ready to revisit Catholicism.

To outward appearances, Suzanne was just another mother with children on school holiday; Pilette remembers her spending the summer reading, knitting, and taking occasional trips into Paris. The MNCR left a very different account, recording that Suzanne "knocked on the doors of cardinals and demanded that they take a position in the face of the persecutions" as part of a broader MNCR offensive.[8]

Days after the July roundup, Léon Chertok organized a visit of a non-Jewish delegation to Emmanuel Suhard, the Catholic cardinal of Paris, to plead the cause of the Jewish children. The group included the formidable Dexia, Countess de la Bourdonnaye, as well as Chertok's colleague Louis Pasteur Vallery-Radot, the grandson of Louis Pasteur. The delegation sought "to express the revolt of the French conscience against such acts of barbarism."[9]

Their efforts may have had an effect. On July 21 Suhard met with the French Assembly of Cardinals and Archbishops (ACA) and sent a letter to Pétain on the assembly's behalf, echoing the delegation's case:

> We are deeply concerned by the reports that have reached us concerning the mass arrests of Israelites last week and the harsh treatment they experienced, above all in the Vélodrome d'Hiver, and we cannot suppress our cries of conscience.
>
> In the name of Mankind and Christian principles we raise our voices in a protest, asserting the sanctity of Human Rights. This is also an anguished appeal to compassion in the face of the immeasurable great suffering, that above all so many mothers and children encounter. We request you, Marshal, to see that the principles of the law and charity are upheld.[10]

The letter was an important statement, but the churchmen limited its impact by voting not to make it public. Suhard himself was known as an accommodator, and he extended this approach to his relations with Vichy. In August he pleased the Germans and irked the Resistance by attending a service for French volunteers who

had died fighting alongside the Germans on the eastern front. Suhard rebuked two priests for providing false baptism certificates to
Jews, and invested his energies in opposing communism.[11]

But the MNCR found other, more promising Church contacts,
sometimes through unexpected avenues. Some appeared in the Free
Zone, where the MNCR's Charles Lederman pursued a parallel
course. Lederman's goals were similar to those of the northern resistance group: infiltrating the detention centers, documenting their
horrific conditions, and lobbying the non-Jewish elite. Lederman
lacked the social connections of Debré, Chertok, and Spaak, but he
had a secret weapon: Abbé Alexandre Glasberg, the Jewish village
priest. Lederman described him as

> of Polish-Russian origin, a converted Jew from Zhytomyr,
> where a long-established Jewish community maintained a
> well-known Yiddish culture.* He became a priest. Quite ro-
> tund, equally myopic, and a gourmand, this man had great
> heart and great courage, and was full of initiative. He revealed
> a talent for organization.[12]

The abbé was forty but looked older in his broad-brimmed sat-
urno and Coke-bottle glasses. His quaint, reassuring image helped
build a clandestine network of concerned Catholics and Jews called
L'Amitié Chrétienne ("Christian Friendship"). The group conducted rescues, lobbied the Catholic leadership, and published calls
to action.

On August 15, 1942, a month after the *Grande Rafle*, Lederman
obtained an appointment with Archbishop Saliège of Toulouse.
Saliège was crippled by a stroke and a poison gas attack he had suffered as a chaplain in the First World War. His fortitude was badly

---

* Glasberg's birth place is now in northwestern Ukraine.

needed. Various individuals could act with courage, Lederman observed, but "the representatives of the Catholic Church were the only ones who could express themselves publicly."

Lederman approached the door of the bishop's palace with trepidation. A nun admitted him and led him through the silent hallways to the presence of an old man sitting behind an enormous desk, wearing a black cassock, scarlet skullcap, and large gold cross.

Lederman told the archbishop everything he knew about the fate of the Jews in Paris: the yellow stars, the arrests, the deportations, and the terrifying rumors of camps in the East. He described the suffering of the children in the Vel d'Hiv, news that had not traveled to the public beyond Paris. "We expect you, if you agree, to make all of this known to the French people, and for you to appeal to Christians to help the persecuted."

The archbishop listened silently. When Lederman finished, he asked, "Can you assure me of everything you have told me? If so, next Sunday we will require all of the churches in my diocese to read a pastoral letter." Lederman contacted members of the Jewish resistance network: the MOI labor coalition, the MNCR, and the militant FTP-MOI. He asked Italian and Spanish members of the network to send someone to every church in the diocese the following Sunday.

On August 23, parish priests read Saliège's letter verbatim and without commentary from the pulpits of four hundred churches at once.[13] Saliège's words spread the MNCR's message to thousands of French Catholics and imbued it with the Church's moral imperative:

> Women and children, fathers and mothers treated like cattle, members of a family separated from one another and dispatched to an unknown destination—it has been reserved for our own time to see such a spectacle. Why does the right of sanctuary no longer exist in our churches? Why are we defeated? The Jews are real men and women. . . . They are our brothers like so many others.[14]

The pastoral letter, Lederman wrote, was a powerful catalyst. The MNCR's tracts could reach only a few hundred readers at a time, fearful recipients who debated whether to share them or destroy them. The archbishop's message reached French Catholics in their public place of worship and sowed the ground for a vast, complex effort to aid the persecuted Jews, especially the children.

The continuing disasters in the Northern Zone had created a new crisis in the South. Following the Vel d'Hiv arrests, thousands of Jews fled Paris for the Free Zone, only to be arrested as they crossed the border. On August 4 the Vichy authorities agreed to arrest Jews in both zones and launched new roundups in the South to sweep foreign-born Jews into camps. Lederman was concerned about camp conditions, particularly in Vénissieux, a military camp that had previously housed Vietnamese workers.

Lederman asked Abbé Glasberg for help entering the Vénissieux camp, and the abbé provided him with the cover of a Catholic working for his charity, L'Amitié Chrétienne. Lederman brought along a dozen Jewish Scouts from the Éclaireurs Israélites Françaises.* Their goals were to help the detainees and to facilitate escapes where possible.

"Once we were there," Lederman wrote, "the facts were clear."

We knew the internees were doomed to deportation. It was August 1942; the first trains had left in March, and we hadn't had any direct news of the "travellers." They had all left behind a horrible silence, a silence of death. If it was impossible to save the adults, we had to try to save the children.[15]

---

* The French branch of the international Scouting movement. Other groups involved in the effort included the Jewish OSE (Oeuvre de secours aux enfants) and the Protestant Cimade.

Suzanne's Children

On August 27, the team began to spirit Jewish children out of the camp.* Lederman's team had the heartbreaking task of persuading parents to hand over their children as they prepared for their own doom. Abbé Glasberg falsified documents concerning their legal status. For the next two days, streetcar workers conveyed the children to the local Red Cross office, and a friend of Lederman's found them temporary hiding places. Finally the police panicked and alerted their forces, to no avail—the children were gone. But Lederman's cover was now blown, and he was obliged to go underground.

He lived with the sorrow that hundreds of others in the camp could not be saved. Nonetheless, *les nuits de Vénissieux* represented a coup, thwarting the mechanics of deportation and introducing a new model of "kidnapping." The Nazis had resolved to exterminate the Jews of Europe. The MNCR responded that countless Jews might be murdered, but if children from the next generation could be saved, the Nazis would fail.

The rescuers in the South had important advantages. The transit camps in the Free Zone were overseen by French officials and guards, some of whom assisted with the escapes. The Vichy government refused to require Jews in the South to wear the yellow star, and there was far less surveillance there than in the German-occupied North. Hiding places in the countryside were more accessible, and the borders of neutral Switzerland and Spain were preferable to those of Belgium and Germany.

But in Paris, three hundred miles to the north, 4,115 children

---

* Accounts differ as to the number of children who were rescued from Vénissieux that August. The estimates range from 80 to Lederman's report of "about 150." Lederman adds that some adult detainees escaped and were recaptured. The accounts are in agreement that the children survived the war in hiding.

languished in detention. They missed their homes and puzzled over their circumstances. The grown-ups were always boarding trains; what lay at the end of the ride? In Drancy they conjured a magical destination called "Pitchipoi," but no one knew what it was. Could it be a shtetl, as in the stories from the old country? A beautiful city where they would find their families? Or nowhere?

The SS and the French police wrestled with the problem of the children for several weeks. They needed to decide whether the children would be deported now or later, with their parents or separately. Someone had to determine which approach would place less pressure on state resources and less emotional strain on the French police.

The plans for deporting children advanced. Adolf Eichmann had strictly forbidden convoys containing only children. His August 7 memo stated, "Children of stateless Jews can be deported in adequate proportions"—without specifying what those proportions might be. Vichy officials and the Gestapo decided that children could be added at a ratio of at most one child per adult. According to Serge Klarsfeld, "The reason is doubtless simple—the SS wants French and German railway workers and any others who may see the trains to believe that the children are being deported with their parents."[16]

The wheels began to turn. On August 15, a thousand children were transferred from Pithiviers to Drancy in sealed boxcars. They arrived in a piteous state, filthy, half-naked, and sick. On the morning of August 17, 323 girls and 207 boys in Drancy were transported to Auschwitz. Two days later, the unthinkable occurred. They were led into the gas chambers and their bodies incinerated.[17]

By the end of August, the prefect overseeing the camps at Pithiviers and Beaune-la-Rolande reported that there were only "a few sick or untransportable children" left.[18] The convoys would depart for Auschwitz on the average of every two days until the end of September. In later years, wrenching accounts would come to light of social workers arguing with jaded prefects and stealing children out of the camps one by one.

Over 1942 the Nazis' news blackout held fast. Only scattered flyers from the MNCR and a few other resistance groups announced the deportations, and even these fell far short of the reality. The Communist resistance still placed the July arrests in the context of forced labor, not murder. The August edition of the Communist paper *Le Franc-Tireur* was headlined "Against the Shameful Persecution," but it suggested that the Jewish deportees were merely the first in line for the same treatment awaiting every Frenchman:

> The monster Hitler needs slaves. He has our prisoners [of war]; he can't have our workers. The "hiring" isn't working, despite the bluffing and the unemployment. So Hitler demands that we send him 30,000 foreign Jews from the Occupied Zone, and 10,000 from the Free Zone. . . .
>
> Frenchman! Watch out. Don't ever imagine that Hitler's brutes will treat you any better than the poor foreign Jews, than the Polish and Czech martyrs![19]

In contrast, the Paris flyers from the MNCR emphasized the special plight of the Jews, including an apparent reference to the rescue at Vénissieux.

> The Catholic organizations of Lyon, in a magnificent gesture of Christian solidarity, have succeeded in saving 100 children whose parents were deported to the Occupied Zone to be placed in the hands of the Nazis. . . . A ferocious repression immediately came down on certain Catholics who opposed this act of vandalism and refused to hand over the children. . . .
>
> French fathers and mothers! Are you going to allow this odious crime to be committed? . . .
>
> Defend the persecuted Jews! In defending them, we defend our own freedom! Down with the anti-Jewish persecutions![20]

Another MNCR publication took the form of a brief letter, apparently mailed secretly to individuals, describing the group's mission to "defend France from the odious grip of racism." It politely asked the recipients to send anonymous letters to local police and civic officials to show their agreement with "this vast movement that we're organizing."[21] The authors chose not to mention that their "vast movement" consisted of at most a few dozen members.

Other resistance publications, including the Gaullist *Défense de la France*, condemned the Vel d'Hiv arrests, but they could not imagine the extent of the disaster. "We hesitate to use the term bestiality, because a beast does not separate a female from its babies."[22] The authors could not imagine that the children torn from their mother's arms were the lucky ones, with a far better chance of survival.

Hundreds of stranded children were now candidates for the next round of arrests and deportations. The Vichy authorities divided them into two categories: the "free" children were those who had escaped the original arrests, which gave them a relatively protected status. *Bloqué*, or "blocked," children were those who had been arrested and released for administrative reasons but whose names were recorded on a special list, making them subject to rearrest at any time.[23]

Both the blocked and the free children were assigned to the seven Paris orphanages and shelters run by the UGIF. Many of these had been Rothschild charities before the war, but they were now funded by forced contributions from the Jewish community to the UGIF. Conditions in the homes had sadly deteriorated, as the cheerful crèches gave way to bleak wards packed with anxious, hungry children tended by beleaguered staff members.

The four hundred beds in the UGIF children's homes were now constantly filled, and an additional 1,080 children had to be placed in non-Jewish homes and institutions.[24]

The children's fate rested with a complex web of organizations that often pursued conflicting goals. The official staff of the UGIF served the authorities' bidding, terrified of losing their own exemptions from arrest. Other UGIF staff members—including Dr. Fred Milhaud and his wife, Denise, and Hélène Berr and her relations—secretly undermined the UGIF's procedures, looking for ways to spirit the children out.

The rescue operations expanded, thread by thread. Entr'aide Temporaire increased its efforts to help the Jewish children. The Jewish Scouts, obliged to join the UGIF in 1941, founded a clandestine division called La Sixième for the purpose of rescuing Jewish children from deportation. The MNCR created a new ad hoc children's committee.

It was a ragged network, nearly impossible to coordinate and divided by status, religion, and geography. The triage was daunting. The starting point was the money and ration cards to keep Jewish families alive, whether they had gone underground or were living openly. The orphanages wanted for food, medicine, and clothing. Suzanne's associates scavenged for funds and moved children off the books and into temporary lodgings—anything to disrupt the system. They were inefficient but dogged.

Suzanne, a founding member of the children's committee, did what she could from Choisel. Claude was still in the South with Ruth, and Suzanne's children still needed her attention. Pilette, fifteen, had entered adolescence, and Bazou was a needy eleven-year-old.

But Suzanne felt guilty about their privileged life, constantly comparing it with the sufferings of Jewish children. Her MNCR colleague Jeanne List-Pakin wrote:

> We often heard her say, "My children are safe while others are threatened." After the July 1942 arrests in Paris, Suzanne was obsessed with the Jewish children who were herded into the Vélodrome d'Hiver, and taken from there to Drancy. She looked for a way to rescue as many as possible.[25]

8

suzanne and sophie

| JULY–OCTOBER 1942 |

The principals of the MNCR met furtively. One of them, Sophie Schwartz, first encountered Suzanne Spaak one summer day in 1942 when she had received instructions to seek an "elegant lady" on the Ligne de Sceaux, the railway line that ran through the southern suburbs of Paris.*

Sophie boarded a train at Denfert-Rochereau station in the fourteenth arrondissement and headed south. Suzanne walked or bicycled three miles from her house in Choisel to the station at Saint-Rémy-lès-Chevreuse. The exchange may have taken place there, or Suzanne may have ridden north through the lush Chevreuse Valley to a station farther up the line. At any rate, the Belgian heiress and the Polish organizer joined forces.

Sophie, a little overwhelmed, described her new contact as "indeed elegant, wearing a black tailored suit and blonde hair, really

---

* In 1977, the Ligne de Sceaux was incorporated into the RER B Line.

quite elegant."* If Suzanne recorded her impressions of Sophie they have been lost, but she might have described her as a hearty woman with unruly dark curls, dressed in her usual sober suit and white blouse; sturdy, spirited, and strong.

They met at the behest of Charles Lederman, who worked closely with Suzanne in the children's rescue efforts. Suzanne had opened an office in a pretty villa in Saint-Rémy-lès-Chevreuse using the government-sponsored relief fund Secours national as its front operation. She maintained the house as a communications hub for Lederman. A well in its herb garden served as a repository. Lederman and his associates rigged up a watertight container on a near-invisible wire that allowed them to lower documents into the water, where they could be stored until needed.[1] It was highly unlikely that the police would come knocking at a remote outpost of Marshal Pétain's favorite charity.

The women's encounter on the Ligne de Sceaux was the first of many. Their meetings were cautious and brief. Sophie recalled, "She gave me the money and she gave me addresses—the 'good addresses,' as we called them, for hiding the children. I don't know how many times I saw her, but each time we met, it was a Tuesday." Personal information was exchanged only on a need-to-know basis: "We didn't talk very much, she was very discreet, a *grande dame*."[2]

For Suzanne, the idea of deporting Jewish children was an abomination, but the children themselves were still something of an abstraction. Sophie's crèches had brought her into daily contact with the children and their mothers. Now that their parents had been arrested, the children were left to the whims of politics and circumstance. For Sophie, they were not just names on a list—they were flesh and blood.

---

* Pilette says her mother's good suit was burgundy and her hair was light brown. Sophie's recollections were recorded four decades after the fact.

Sophie had been born in 1905 (the same year as Suzanne) in Lodz, an industrial city southwest of Warsaw. Another outpost of the troubled Russian Empire, Lodz was occupied by the Germans during the First World War, an experience Sophie found redolent of "misery, typhus, and death. . . . They snatched the boys from the street and sent them to Germany to work, and they died of hunger there." The fifteen-year-old girl saw soldiers stumbling back from the front: "the ones that had been gassed, the ones with damaged lungs, people who were starving, broken, physically and morally."[3]

After the war, Lodz fell within the boundaries of the newly reconstituted Poland. Its 230,000 Jews represented a third of the city's population, making it the second-largest concentration in Poland after Warsaw. But the war's legacy was ongoing disruption. The region had passed from the rule of a distant czar to an arrogant kaiser to autocrats in Warsaw. The schools' language of instruction changed from Russian to Polish. As Sophie and her schoolmates gathered to learn the puzzling new alphabet, they began to question everything: government institutions, patriarchal family structures, and social inequalities.

Sophie was a gifted student, but her family couldn't afford school fees and sent her to work in a curtain factory. There she joined a Socialist youth movement and gravitated toward the new, illegal Communist movement. Around this time she witnessed her first pogrom, carried out by Polish soldiers who held Jewish men at bayonet point and cut off their beards.

The Polish police came for her one morning in 1924 at one o'clock. They threw her into a cell full of prostitutes, interrogated her, then released her. Her father gave her an ultimatum: abandon politics or leave home. She left for Belgium, where she married another Jewish émigré, Lazar Micnik, who had also been expelled from his home for political organizing. In 1929, the couple moved to Paris illegally and found work off the books, thrilling to the rise of Léon Blum's Popular Front government in 1936.

Suzanne's Children

Sophie joined a committee to support the Republicans in the Spanish Civil War and was disappointed that her husband refused to go and fight. "I've never held a pistol, I don't know Spanish, and I don't know what I'd do there," he told her. The couple settled into a secretive life of undocumented immigrants in an apartment off Place de la République.

Sophie turned her energies to a new women's organization created to help the Jewish refugees flooding into France. The working mothers were impoverished and isolated. Her group set up a center in Belleville to provide childcare and friendship. The women met regularly to discuss cultural topics, including the work of their favorite Yiddish author, Sholem Aleichem.

Aleichem's tales from the shtetls reflected both the women's Polish past and their French reality. They identified with his character Tevye the dairyman and with his musings on the Rothschilds, the leading patrons of Jewish charities in Paris.* When a pogrom arrives on his doorstep, Tevye looks to heaven and demands:

> There's no knowing what goes on in the mind of a rich Jew, of a Brodsky in Yehupetz, for example, or of a Rothschild in Paris—the Messiah may be the furthest thing from it. . . . Dear Lord God, I thought, wouldn't You like to play one of Your jokes on a Brodsky or a Rothschild for a change?[4]

Sophie made friends with a seamstress named Hannah Wozek. Hannah's husband had answered the call to fight in Spain with the Yiddish-speaking Botwin Company in late 1937. With the defeat of the Republicans, he was interned with other volunteers in a French camp, leaving his wife to care for their two-year-old

---

* The musical *Fiddler on the Roof* alters Tevye's "*Ven ikh bin Roytchild*" to "If I were a rich man."

daughter, Larissa. Hannah earned a meager living working twelve-hour days as a maid for a wealthy Russian family and entrusted her toddler to Sophie's nursery.

When war was declared in 1939, the nursery was closed and Sophie turned to Solidarité, work that led her to Suzanne Spaak. As the arrests began, the relatively mild conditions of the French detention camps misled the Jewish community. Families sent parcels, wives could visit, and inmates attended seminars and concerts. Everything, Sophie recalled, suggested that the prisoners would join the same labor details as the French POWs. "There were no instructions from the [Communist] Party that they should escape," she lamented. "That's the tragedy."

Sophie could do little when her own husband was arrested in 1941, but she could help others under threat. She led the 1941 women's march on the camp at Pithiviers, and took on the task of finding sympathetic French people to take in Jewish children. The more grueling assignment was persuading their families to let them go. One of the mothers was Hannah Wozek, who held fast to her Larissa.

On the day of the *Grande Rafle*, everything changed. Sophie had heard rumors the previous day that the authorities were going to put women and children in the camps, but no one wanted to believe it. At 6:00 a.m. the French police came for Hannah Wozek. She dressed quietly and hugged her daughter tight for the last time, leaving her with a friend. Then she was conveyed to the Vel d'Hiv and disappeared into the Nazi inferno. When Sophie heard the terrible news, all she could think was, "We've got to save Larissa."

Larissa, just short of her seventh birthday, was transferred to the Lamarck orphanage in Montmartre, repurposed as a warehouse for stranded children.[5] Annette Muller, a little girl who arrived around the same time as Larissa, wrote a vivid account of life in the orphanage:

> Bedlam ruled. We slept in large dormitories, beds jammed together and mattresses on the floor, with hardly any way to pass.

There was an epidemic of scarlet fever. Every day we had to lift our shirts to show our stomachs, where the spots appeared as the first symptom. They let us go out into a courtyard, and they installed a long table near the door. Sometimes visitors watched us from behind it, but we weren't allowed to approach them. They threw food to us, fruit, bread that we buried in the dirt to eat later in secret.

The lice swarmed, and hunting them became a game. Sitting on the ground in the middle of the courtyard, [my brother] Michel put his head on my lap. I looked for lice, which I crushed between my fingernails. Then it was my turn and I offered my head to Michel. All the children did the same, crouching or sitting in the yard like the monkeys in the Vincennes zoo.

Sometimes they took us to a steamy room in the basement where, to a deafening din, a barber with a little moustache officiated. The struggling children were hauled before him to the boos of the older ones who were already shorn. We sang at the top of our voices, "Go to hell, barber, God created you to make us miserable, you shave our heads all night. When will we hear the funeral bells for the barber?" He was our enemy. We all hated him.

Every day brought more batches of children, filthy, skeletal, and spotted, who were immediately put in quarantine in a crowded dormitory before they joined the others. They came from Drancy. Lamarck was a hub for deporting children.[6]

Sophie watched Larissa join the unhappy throng. Her dark curls were shaved off and a card was hung around her neck identifying her by number. She learned to go hungry. "We ate slowly because there was not enough food," Larissa recalled. "There was no organization among the monitors. Nobody looked after us or played with us, and there were lots of children." Within weeks,

Larissa had been transformed from her mother's darling into a juvenile inmate.

The occupation authorities used the UGIF's administration of the Lamarck orphanage and various Rothschild institutions to extend their control over the Jewish population and collect fees for their maintenance from Jewish households. Most of the money was stolen, and the UGIF institutions and Jewish indigents received the leavings as "charity." The UGIF children's homes registered the whereabouts of the small prisoners and controlled their movements.

Sophie found Lamarck to be "a fortress: very old, sad, damp, forsaken buildings." She asked for permission to take Larissa for an outing and briefly considered stealing her away. But she was haunted by the thought of the other children who would be deprived of outings if she failed to bring the girl back.

Riding the Métro, Sophie regarded the fragile child with her pale cheeks and dark, thoughtful eyes. Sophie noticed that Larissa had hidden the yellow star that her mother had fastened onto her brown coat. The child looked up and asked nervously, "Sophie, can you tell that I'm . . . you know what?"—not daring to say the word "Jewish" in public. Sophie reassured her, "No, not at all." Larissa smiled.

Soon Sophie learned that Larissa had been moved to another UGIF-run home at 9 Rue Guy Patin in the tenth arrondissement. She decided to try the official approach. She went to the UGIF office and announced, "I know that the children might be sent off somewhere and I want the child."

The female clerk responded, "If I give you that child, I'll be the one they take away."

Sophie bristled. "Listen, I don't know how old you are, but you've lived your life, and Larissa has her whole life in front of her."

The clerk told Sophie she had to seek an official letter at another office. There she was told, "Look, Madame, you can't have this child. We can only entrust her to a French family that will pledge to provide for the child's needs and guarantee that she can be located at any time"—to facilitate her arrest. That was when Sophie realized Larissa's safety depended on the assistance of non-Jews.[7] She was willing to risk her life on behalf of all of the Jewish children, but there were a few, including Larissa, who were family.

Sophie kept a low profile, moving around Paris with forged papers that might be detected at any checkpoint. Her husband was lost to her. Lazar had developed tuberculosis in Drancy and was transferred to the Rothschild Hospital, another UGIF institution. Sophie saw him for one last time in the waiting room under the stern gaze of the police. He was deported to Auschwitz on July 22 along with women and children arrested in the *Grande Rafle*. Sophie was told he died of typhoid, but camp records later showed he was sent to the gas chambers three days after his arrival.[8]

In the fall of 1942 Sophie wrote a report in Yiddish summarizing the MNCR's approach, developed in partnership with Suzanne Spaak:

> After the tragic days of July 16 and 17, hundreds of Jewish families went into hiding from the police. With their children, they stayed shut up in cellars and attics, with eight or ten people in the same place. Our organization immediately got involved in the fate of these unfortunates and sent a number of children into the countryside to stay with farmers. Between July 16 and October 1, nearly a hundred children in groups of three, four and five, were placed in the villages in the departments of the Seine, Seine-et-Oise, Marne, Aisne, Sarthe, Loiret.

It was not enough to find homes for the children; they required money as well. Many of the host families fostered city children for the income, and even those who acted out of charity usually needed funds and ration cards to provide for the children in a time of scarcity. Sophie wrote:

We created groups of "godmothers" and about twenty of them agreed to subsidize the upkeep of these children. Fifty-five percent of the children had one deported parent; ten percent had both parents deported. Twenty-five percent had parents in hiding; ten percent belonged to families that were untouched by the raids (e.g., French Jews and/or a father who was a prisoner of war). We paid 600–700 francs per month for each child. Our monthly expenses amounted to 50,000 francs.[9]

Suzanne Spaak's contacts were essential to the plan. So was the money she managed to squeeze out of her allowance. These funds were drawn from her inheritance but still dispensed by her husband—even though her generosity led to bitter fights.

It was still hard for Sophie persuade the parents to relinquish their children.

They often replied, "Sure, you Communists are always sowing panic and we're not budging. We don't have anywhere to go, and we're not rich enough to go far." That was also true, because the rich [Jews] had left for the Free Zone.[10]

Some Jewish leaders were opposed to placing children in Christian homes, fearing the action would result in their conversion. The arguments of the MNCR grew fiercer as the convoys continued to roll, with increasing numbers of children aboard.

Many families who yielded their children contributed to their upkeep when they could, but the collection process was painful. After the *Grande Rafle* it was nearly impossible to collect these funds from Jewish neighborhoods. One exception, for a time, was the Jewish furriers, who had been exempted from arrest on the grounds that their products were essential to the German war effort. Fur was a luxury in France but indispensable on the eastern front; German troops had already experienced one brutal Russian winter, and another was on its way.

The furriers became an important source of funds for the MNCR. One day Sophie sent a list of people in need to a furriers' meeting, with unexpected consequences. The host, Aron Walach, found his son Elie's name on the list. Elie had joined the FTP-MOI militants (he had helped the daring "Fifi" Feferman steal dynamite) and was under arrest. Walach was distraught. His commotion attracted the police, who arrested all of the furriers present and carted them off to the Cherche-Midi prison. There Walach saw his son, who had clearly been tortured.

Sophie was so distressed by the arrests that she cried out, "I want to die!" Two days later a German officer ordered the furriers' release, but twenty-one-year-old Elie Walach was executed by firing squad at Mont-Valérien.[11] The exemption would not last; the following year, the furriers, too, were rounded up.[12] Aron Walach was deported and murdered in May 1944.

The Jewish immigrant community was shrinking as its members were arrested, went into hiding, or fled. The October 1940 census had registered 25,646 immigrant Jewish families in Paris. Two years later, two-thirds had vanished, and the number of households dropped to a 7,926.[13]

July's *Grande Rafle* had targeted certain Jewish neighborhoods and nationalities, principally Poles and Russians. September brought another round of raids in the form of door-to-door arrests for petty infractions. The new targets were Romanians, then Belgians, then Greeks.[14]

A few French Jews, such as Raymond Berr, had been arrested, but in general they remained a category apart. The difference was explained by Maurice Rajsfus, a French-born child of immigrant parents who had registered him for citizenship. After his parents were arrested, he and his sister continued to live openly in Paris, wearing their yellow stars until near the end of the occupation. Rajsfus later wrote:

> There was never a massive roundup of French Jews in Paris, except the one [of Notables] in December 1941. It was not worth the trouble to go door to door. The susceptible Jews were those in groups, in orphanages, nursing homes, or hospitals, who could be picked up easily when [the SS] had room at Drancy or needed to fill a train. No one should ever have remained in a group. All should have been dispersed.[15]

This point was critical for the MNCR on two counts. It was essential to persuade both immigrant families and the Jewish leadership of the UGIF that housing the children in their orphanages was an invitation to disaster.

Following the *Grande Rafle*, the UGIF sent out a mailing urging Jewish families to entrust their children to them as "the only Jewish organization that is recognized and protected by the occupation authorities." Sophie Schwartz considered this a travesty. On September 25 she led another women's march on the UGIF offices and forced the door, demanding a meeting. The UGIF staff threatened to call the police, but the women cut the telephone wires. UGIF's vice president, André Baur, finally agreed to speak with them.

The women wanted to know the UGIF's plans for the children consigned to its orphanages, but Baur and his colleagues could only stammer a response. The women shouted, "Traitors of the UGIF, resign, resign! We're going to destroy you, we're going to blow you up!"[16] They demanded the UGIF officials' help in freeing the interned children but left without an answer.[17]

Paris was still home to thousands of Jews subject to arrest. It was impossible to know whom to trust. For decades, the Rothschild Hospital in southern Paris's twelfth arrondissement had served immigrant families. Now it had been absorbed into the UGIF, under the administration of Armand Kohn, a banker and distant relation of the Rothschilds. Kohn's family had lived in France for seven generations. He attended synagogue but otherwise lived the secular life of a wealthy French businessman, and regarded his family's exemption cards as a perquisite of its social position.

Kohn brought a methodical approach to his management of the Hôpital Rothschild, which became one more smoke screen for the Nazis. Its wards offered beds to ailing inmates from Drancy, such as Sophie's husband, Lazar, and women who were about to give birth. But there was every chance they could be returned to the camps or arrested in their beds.

Armand Kohn found himself in an impossible position. His job consisted of running the hospital according to regulations, and his family's exemption cards depended on him doing it well. But his efficiency aroused anger among the patients seeking means to escape. After several sneaked out the front door, Kohn ordered his staff to confiscate luggage and street clothes on arrival. Others fled through the basement, and he closed it off. He created a "reeducation system" with solitary confinement for the "delinquent" children of deported parents. The Jewish community began to refer to the hospital as one more *souricière*, or "mousetrap," in the service of the Gestapo.

Suzanne Spaak regularly visited ailing immigrants on behalf of the MNCR, helping where she could. One day she met a young member of the Jewish resistance with the nom de guerre of David Diamant. Summoned by a *billet vert* in May 1941, he chose to go underground, but he fell seriously ill and was obliged to seek treatment at the Hôpital Rothschild. Unlike most patients, he managed to escape.

Diamant recalled:

I had had major surgery and left the Rothschild Hospital by miracle, because this place had become a prison. I went back to my hideout [near Belleville], but it was damp and rank, with nauseating mold. That's when Suzanne Spaak came, on behalf of the MNCR, to place me in a clinic where I wouldn't have to breathe the foul air.

Suzanne found Diamant a bed in a non-Jewish clinic where he registered under a false name. She may have located it through Robert Debré and Léon Chertok's medical network. She kept in touch with Diamant. When she couldn't visit him she sent him encouraging letters by pneumatic tube, the express postal system that connected the post offices of central Paris.*

Like Sophie Schwartz and Charles Lederman, Diamant was dazzled by Suzanne. "She was slender, dynamic and full of energy, and she cared for me like a sister."[18]

Drancy's procession of convoys came to a temporary halt, but significant harm had been done. In the sixteen weeks between June 5 and September 30, thirty-eight convoys had carried some forty thousand Jews—overwhelmingly immigrants—to their fate.†
Twenty-six convoys had been concentrated over August and September, departing every two or three days, most of them bearing women and children arrested in July. These four months accounted for over half of the seventy-six thousand Jews who would be deported from France over the five years of occupation.

---

* Diamant's real name was David Ehrlich. He would survive the war to become one of the leading archivists and historians of the Jewish resistance in Paris.

† The second convoy, departing on June 5, marked the start of the most intensive four-month period of the deportations.

9

the unimaginable

I n October 1942 Adam Rayski discovered that Jews deported from France "to labor in the East" had been gassed in the Polish camps. "I recoiled, I rejected it," he wrote later.

It seemed to be accurate, coming from a reliable source: an old comrade from Spain, who left the camp at Gurs engaged as a driver for the Todt Organization, a construction firm working for the German Army.*

He returned to Paris on leave, after driving a transport through Poland to the front in the Ukraine. Along the way, he heard German officers talking about the tests for killing Jews with gas. In Krakow, not far from Auschwitz, he was able to confirm the murder of the deportees from France.

---

* Todt was a massive engineering conglomerate that executed many of the Third Reich's construction projects, both before and during the war.

Suzanne's Children

Hearing the news was one thing; knowing what to do with it was another.

Publish? Don't publish? If we circulated this information, didn't we risk provoking a reaction of fear and panic, and plunging people into despair and resignation? But what a responsibility it was not to divulge it! And what if it wasn't true, which is what we hoped in our hearts? Our leadership was distraught and torn before these questions, which couldn't be dealt with coolly from a distance any more, since it directly concerned people like us.[1]

Rayski decided to publish. The October 10 issue of *J'Accuse* had been relatively restrained. Quoting Cardinal Saliège's pastoral letter, it described the suffering of small children in the camps and urged, "Let every French family take in a persecuted child."[2] There was nothing restrained about the October 20 edition:

Deportations of French following those of Jews.
   Thousands of interned French are in danger of being deported and exterminated in the Nazi prison camps.
   The Boche torturers burn and asphyxiate thousands of Jewish men, women and children deported from France. . . .
   The news that is reaching us, despite the silence of the official press, announces that tens of thousands of Jewish men, women and children deported from France have been either burned alive in sealed rail cars or asphyxiated to experiment with a new poison gas. The death trains have delivered 11,000 corpses to Poland.[3]

These notices reveal the limitations and the achievement of the Jewish underground press. The staff of *J'Accuse* was working from anecdotal reports from Poland. Their article underestimated the number of victims at this point, reporting eleven thousand when the figure was closer to forty thousand. Nevertheless, these flawed reports were more accurate than anything published elsewhere in the French news media through the end of the occupation.

The French public's lack of knowledge could be blamed on the blanket of censorship. This was not the case in Britain and the United States, where officials lingered in a state of willful denial. They received early reports of the mass killings of Jews in the East in the "Holocaust by bullets," but these were difficult to verify and could be ascribed to battlefield casualties.

Over the summer and fall of 1942, accounts trickled out from concentration camps, some from escapees, others from German dissidents. In July 1942, the anti-Nazi German industrialist Eduard Schulte informed the Jewish World Congress in Switzerland about the plans for the Final Solution. The following month, the German diplomat Rudolf von Scheliha secretly confirmed this information to the International Committee of the Red Cross. He was arrested by the Gestapo in October and executed in December.[4]

British and American officials were disbelieving. In the summer of 1942, a US diplomat in Switzerland wrote, "There is what is apparently a wild rumor inspired by Jewish fears that the Nazis will exterminate all at once (possibly with prussic acid) in the autumn about 4 m. Jews whom they have been assembling in Eastern Europe." In late 1942 (after Schulte's and Scheliha's reports), an official from the British foreign ministry called the idea of the Final Solution "a rather wild story."[5]

But the evidence continued to mount, and in November the US State Department confirmed the reports. The following month, the Allies issued a denunciation of the planned extermination of the Jews of Europe—two months after *J'Accuse* published its report in Paris.

On the night of November 7, the Allies attacked strategic Vichy French ports and airports in Morocco, Algeria, and Tunisia. Their victory gave them a foothold in North Africa, exposing the southern coast of Europe to an Allied attack.

Hitler responded by sending troops to occupy the French Free Zone. This had enormous consequences for Jews and their supporters. Vichy France may have been a puppet government, but it had been able to extend some protection in small ways, such as refusing to require Jews in the South to wear the yellow star and relaxing controls at the borders. Lyon, the home of France's second-largest Jewish population, served as the base for the MNCR's southern branch.

With the events of November, threats to Jews mounted, and an important escape route was cut off. That month a twenty-nine-year-old SS officer named Klaus Barbie arrived in Lyon to head the Gestapo office, keen to pursue fugitive Jews and members of the French Resistance. He installed a suite in the Hôtel Terminus where he oversaw the torture and murder of men, women, and children by the hundreds. To the extent that the Southern Zone had been a haven for Jews, it was no more.

The MNCR responded by stepping up its criminal pursuits, and at the top of the list was forgery. The French government revered complex administrative processes, and the French public respected them—in the case of immigrant Jews, to their detriment. Everyone needed a panoply of official papers, or, in the case of *résistants* and fugitive Jews, skillfully forged facsimiles. Travel, work, and school depended on identity cards. The purchase of food, clothing, and fuel depended on ration cards. Manufacturing these became a central occupation of the underground. A few individuals, such as Léon Chertok, acquired the legitimate documents of a deceased non-Jew, but most turned to art and artifice.

The MNCR assembled its own forgery shops. Rayski favored a mobile operation, spiriting equipment from attic to cellar as required. Robert Debré had a more institutional approach, installing one in his medical laboratory at the children's hospital, which

Suzanne Spaak used to forge documents for the fugitives in her care.[6] Errors could be fatal. Creating documents from scratch required the skills of a professional forger; it was far easier to alter existing papers. There was a brisk market in virgin documents from government offices with blanks that could be filled in as needed.

The autumn of 1942 brought mixed signals. The convoys had abruptly halted at the end of September, but Adam Rayski received the horrific news of the gas chambers in October. The trains resumed with a vengeance in November, with four convoys departing between the fourth and the eleventh. Convoy 44 bore Greek Jews who had been arrested on November 5, along with their French-born children. Witnesses reported that the French police who escorted the internees onto the trains were friendly, offering words of encouragement.

The deportations were still largely invisible to the French public, and French newspapers were preoccupied with other problems. One was the national groundswell of support for de Gaulle: Allied and Free French forces had landed on France's doorstep, and much of the French navy had defected to their side. Pétain was losing his luster as the "protector of France." The German occupation of the Free Zone violated the terms of the armistice, and the marshal's countrymen increasingly regarded him as Hitler's dupe. British air raids were pounding German cities to dust, and the Soviet army was closing in on German forces in Stalingrad, cutting them off from the reinforcements and supplies they needed to survive the winter. The war hung in the balance, and with it the French Resistance.

On November 20, 1942, *Le Matin*, the leading collaborationist newspaper, published a speech by Marshal Pétain preaching his gospel of sacrifice and denial more urgently than ever: the French people should disregard the events around them and cling to the established order. He aimed his chastisement squarely at the new enthusiasts for the Resistance:

You have only one duty: to obey. You have only one government: that which I have been granted the power to govern. You have only one fatherland, which I embody: France.

That week the MNCR published a new tract of *J'accuse*, delivering a dramatically different message:

Two thousand Jewish children, aged 2 to 12 years, have just been sent to the East, to an unknown destination. Endless trains with sealed cars have delivered them to torture and to death. The heart-rending cries of innocent victims, drowning out the sound of the wheels, sowed terror and horror all along the road. . . .

French Mothers!

When you kiss your child in bed at night and see your child's first happy smile upon waking, think about those hellish trains. . . .

Is there anything in the world, is there anything in modern history more atrocious, more inhuman, more barbaric, than the torture of innocent children? . . . These children are just like yours, and their parents were ready to defend them. But they were ripped away from them mercilessly with an animal savagery. . . .

These horrors happened here, in our sweet land of France, with the complicity of the French government collaborating with those who starve us, plunder our wealth, hold our people captive, and murder the patriots fighting for a free and happy France. . . . Do not, by your silence, become accomplices of these murderers.[7]

The appeal rang in a new voice. The author was anonymous, but the language was fluent, vivid and poetic, reflecting the emotions of someone who had cared for small children. Reading it years later, Pilette found the language familiar. "It's just what mother would say." Suzanne Spaak was one of the few native French speakers in the group, and she was probably involved with the tract in some way, whether writing, editing, or typing it.

The MNCR was doing everything in its power to warn the Jews and alert the French to the deportations. Then, in mid-November, the convoys stopped again, this time from a shortage of rolling stock. With the Battle of Stalingrad in its final throes, the German army needed every available train to supply the eastern front. The SS had to wait.

The MNCR needed new strategies and alliances. Tens of thousands of Jews had been deported to their deaths, but tens of thousands remained at large in Paris, Lyon, Marseille, and other pockets of the country. What could be done to help them survive?

The MNCR found itself in a lonely position. The Allied governments in London and Washington had denounced the Nazi genocide, but time and again Jewish leaders were told that the best way to help the Jews was to win the war as quickly as possible. The Soviets were in no position to help, locked in their own life-and-death struggle. Charles de Gaulle was mired in political infighting in London, struggling to lead his movement in the face of Churchill's and Roosevelt's intense dislike.

In France the will to resist the Germans was growing, but the Resistance was split into a dozen factions, few of which considered the Jewish cause a priority. De Gaulle instructed his followers to lie low until the Allied invasion. But the members of the Yiddish-MOI had watched their friends and relatives disappear into the camps by the tens of thousands; why should they tell their youth to wait when they might find themselves on the next convoy? Better to let the youngsters build their bombs and shoot their antique weapons. The French Communists continued to let them down. The Jewish leaders of the MNCR, Adam Rayski wrote, were "sure they could count on the help of the Party, which could assign a number of non-Jewish members to make up the nucleus."

> But this didn't happen. The Communist Party in Paris had its own problems, and suffered from a shortage of manpower aggravated by frequent arrests. To fill the holes in their various divisions, the PC [Communist Party] kept coming to us to find men.

In other words, at the height of the Jewish deportations, the French Communist Party asked its Jewish members to redeploy their militants from Jewish rescue operations to general party functions.

In the meantime, the occupation authorities used petty anti-Semitic ordinances to regulate the flow of arrests. Fred Milhaud, the doctor from the UGIF underground, had observed the arithmetic:

> The rhythm of the arrests were governed by those of the deportations, which were governed by the crematoria. The Nazis didn't want all the Jews of Paris to be arrested in one week, as would have been the case if the infractions had been better monitored. It was enough to use them as harassment to maintain a certain anxiety among the Jews and to arrest some every day based on their infractions. When these arrests weren't enough, they carried out random *rafles*.[8]

The MNCR reviewed the overall situation and resolved to put the children first, in part because they represented the art of the possible. Children were simpler to hide and easier to explain, and more likely to speak fluent French than their elders.

Furthermore, the Jewish children could blend into the ranks of other children farmed out to the countryside. Many of these were the offspring of Parisian factory workers and prostitutes, and others were war orphans designated as *les pupilles de la Nation*. Infants and tiny children were lodged with *nourrices*, or nursemaids, while older children were placed on farms where they were expected to do their share of the chores. Others found refuge in Catholic convents and boarding schools. To hide a single child was fairly simple, but hiding masses of them under an urgent timetable was fiendishly difficult.

Suzanne Spaak devoted her days to the children's cause. Now she routinely left the house at 6:00 a.m. and returned around midnight. The curfew was a bother, but she could talk her way out of any problems with the French police.

There had been no further word from Harry and Mira Sokol; once they disappeared into the grip of the Gestapo they would not emerge. But dangerously, invisibly, the Spaaks' connection to their network remained alive in the form of Leopold Trepper. Living with his mistress in a pleasant apartment in Paris, he continued to run his intelligence network across Nazi-occupied Europe.

His operations grew increasingly precarious. Trepper had been trained by Moscow's top professionals, but many had perished in Stalin's purges. Now he answered to the same nervous amateurs who had kept Harry Sokol on the air for the lengthy transmissions that led to his arrest. Trepper added his own risky behavior to the mix. As the Gestapo swept across Europe in search of his agents, Trepper recruited phalanxes of clumsy replacements, some of them zealots from the international Communist movement, others naive chance acquaintances.

Whether it was fact or bluster, Trepper counted the Spaaks among his assets. He later informed his superiors that after their initial meeting, Claude helped him transfer money between Brussels and Paris. "I didn't recruit Claude Spaak as an agent," he reported, "but he worked openly with me, that is to say, he knew that his activities benefited the Soviet intelligence service."[9]

In the same report, Trepper stated that "I proposed to Madame Spaak that she help us in our work, which she accepted. Until my arrest, fully aware that she was working for the Soviet intelligence services, she passed information to me openly and periodically."[10] Trepper didn't specify what kind of intelligence Suzanne possessed. It's difficult to imagine any, beyond information shared among various resistance groups. If Trepper's statement was true, she would have been aligned with Allied policy. The previous August, Winston Churchill and W. Averill Harriman, a US envoy, flew to Moscow to advance the Anglo-Soviet alliance, and de Gaulle's Free French were engaged in a full-scale collaboration with the French Communists.[11]

The Spaaks may have seen helping Trepper as a practical contribution to the Allied cause. If this was the case, it was fraught with risk. The Soviets' sloppy operations had already reaped disastrous consequences across the continent, including the arrest of the anti-Nazi Germans in Berlin.

The Gestapo's success in Berlin energized its search for Trepper. The Rote Kapelle task force worked its way through its lists of suspects in Brussels and Amsterdam and made a new round of arrests in Lyon and Marseille, following the trail of evidence.

On November 24, 1942, they came for Trepper himself as the master spy sat in Dr. Albert Malaplate's chair, preparing to undergo some overdue dental work. The Gestapo officers, thrilled with their prize, decided to give Trepper favored treatment in the hopes that he would turn double agent and dupe his handlers in Moscow. He received comfortable accommodations, good food, and friendly conversations. Trepper considered his options, and talked.

The Gestapo officers were pleased. After the war, their chief told Allied intelligence officers, "From the moment Trepper was in our hands, the roll-up of the remaining Rote Kapelle was assured."

Trepper was much too clever to wish to die for a "lost cause." It was made clear to him that even during a war, men of his stature and importance did not need to be tried and die although law throughout the world condemned such men to death. Trepper did not need time to think over the proposition. He knew immediately what he wanted to do and, perhaps, what he had to do. Without hesitation he betrayed one colleague after the other. He made meeting arrangements so that we could pick them up while he was meeting them. . . .

Trepper told us much more than we ever hoped and much more than was necessary under the circumstances.[12]

The Gestapo cells in Berlin had already filled with suspects from the Rote Kapelle. Now the doors of the prison in Fresnes swung open to consume the fruits of the investigation in France.

In January 1943, at the same time Harry Sokol was meeting his death in Belgium, a German officer issued orders governing Trepper's associates in Fresnes. Several of them had tried to kill themselves. His memorandum, found in a prison garbage can after the war, stated:

To avoid every possibility of meetings or contact with accomplices, the prisoners of the Rote Kapelle conspiracy will henceforth be detained without names or personal details.

The prisoners will be kept in strict isolation. They must not have any possibility of being seen or getting in touch with each other. Therefore they will not go to the baths, or be allowed to walk. They will not leave their cells except under special orders. They will not leave for interrogation at any given moment, only on the orders of [SS] Captain Reiser and Secretary Berg.

The guards will only enter the cells in pairs.

The lights will stay on all night in these cells.

In the case of a male, and if there is no written counter-order, the prisoner will always be bound and on his back.

Be especially careful regarding escape and suicide.

[Signed] Major Gieseler[13]

10

la clairière

In December 1942 the Germans told André Baur to hand over the addresses of the UGIF's children's homes.[1] The UGIF tried to filter children out to rural areas of the Southern Zone, but its leaders were constrained by fears for their safety. By 1943 most Jewish institutions reached the conclusion that they needed Christian allies.[2]

The rescue committees turned their attention to locating the children scattered across Paris. In this regard, the Nazis had an advantage. Immediately following the Vel d'Hiv arrests, the SS instructed the UGIF to notify Jewish households that it was establishing "a central file of all Jewish children whose parents were arrested over the past few days. If these children were collected by a private organization or individual families, please report them immediately." A few days later, Vichy president Pierre Laval made his formal request to the SS to include the children in the upcoming deportations.

The convoys had paused at the end of November, but the wheels of bureaucracy continued to turn. On January 5, 1943, the

UGIF's André Baur told the authorities that 386 of the 414 beds in the organization's children's centers were filled. "We are obliged to keep a certain number of beds free to be able to receive children who are continually being sent to us, either by prefectures outside Paris or by internment camps. . . . As a result we are setting up family placements."[3] Baur neglected to say that many children sent to the UGIF had been whisked away into hiding before they were even registered.

The hiatus would not last. The Germans were set on resuming the deportations. On January 21, 1943, the SS officer Helmut Knochen wired Adolf Eichmann's office from Paris. When would freight cars be available? Knochen had some logistics to sort out concerning the transport of 3,811 Jews detained in Drancy, 2,159 of whom were French citizens.

A few days later Eichmann's office replied that the freight cars were ready. After the three-month pause, a convoy left Drancy on February 9 bearing 1,000 Jews to Auschwitz. Of them, 920 were immigrants, and 126 were children.[4] The reserves of immigrants in Drancy were depleted.

The SS informed the French police that one thousand victims were required for the next convoy. There were enough French Jews on hand, but Vichy officials still opposed their deportation and declared that French police would not participate in the action. They pointed out that there was still time to arrest enough Jewish immigrants to fill the quota.

The abrupt nature of the demand required the French police to alter their approach. They would drop the pretense of rounding up factory and farm workers and set their sights on easier marks. These were the sick, the elderly, and the children.

Over the following days, the French authorities dispatched 1,400 police, who made 1,518 arrests.[5] Of these arrestees, 1,191 were between the ages of sixty and ninety. The authorities had arrested and deported elderly subjects before, but never in such a concentration. Many spoke little French and had remained in their homes because they had previously been exempt from arrest.[6]

Children in orphanages were even easier prey. On February 9, French police arrived at the UGIF orphanages at 9 Rue Guy Patin and 16 Rue Lamarck. Most of the children there had been arrested with their parents, rendering them *enfants bloqués*, or "blocked." After an initial stay in Drancy, they had been released to UGIF orphanages until further notice. At each venue, the police asked the staff for a list of the foreign children who had been placed there by the UGIF. The police returned on February 10 and arrested ten children from Guy Patin and twenty-two from Lamarck. Over the next two days, the French police arrested a total of forty-two children from various UGIF institutions, and eight from outside the centers.

Fifteen-year-old Simone Boruchowicz, consigned to the orphanage at Guy Patin with her eleven-year-old brother, Armand, recorded the experience:

> The terrible *rafle* of February 1943 [was] the one where we saw some of the smallest and some of the biggest children crossing the street to get into the bus, each bearing a little bundle. Not one of them cried. The police, after accepting a hearty complimentary breakfast, held the door coldly.

Armand added:

> Once we were downstairs, a big *rafle* was announced, and the inspectors took the names of the children telling them they were going to the countryside. Two older boys hid in the basement, which couldn't have been guessed. But an unfortunate little boy of 5 gave them away, naturally without intending to.[7]

The sight of French policemen arresting small children was devastating. Hélène Berr described one officer in her diary:

On the night of February 10 he turned up to arrest the children at the orphanage—the oldest was thirteen and the youngest five. These were children whose parents had been deported or who had disappeared, but they needed "some more" to make up the next day's trainload of a thousand Jews. [The policeman said] "Sorry 'bout this, lady, I'm just doing my duty."

The arrests created a crisis among the UGIF staff. Thérèse Cahen was serving as the night supervisor at Guy Patin when the police arrived at dawn. Like Hélène Berr, she was a cultured French Jew from an affluent family. She wrote an agonized letter to her sister asking which was more ethical: to accompany the children in their fates, or to walk out in protest?

> I am paid and doubly protected by virtue of being French and having my [UGIF] card, so I can properly lock up at 6:00 p.m. and prevent the children from saving themselves. (The management thinks only about this.) This pleases me even less, given that nothing suggests that another *rafle* won't occur, and plenty of them. . . . Everything appears to happen in the following manner: an order to provide so many Jews; an order from the Commissariat for Jewish Affairs not to take the French; and then they take the [foreign Jews] between the ages of 2 and 100.
>
> Am I right to want to dissociate from it all by leaving the children who will miss me and whom I was helping? I don't know. . . . In the meantime, I don't tell the older ones to save themselves instead of returning every afternoon from school. But that would be the only decent thing to do, since these girls of 15 are too young to understand that their existence is not over, and that they're worth saving.[8]

Cahen chose to cast her lot with her girls, and would eventually die at their side.[9]

The chief rabbi of France, Isaïe Schwartz, deplored the arrests. That February, he met with a high-ranking French police official, who tried to placate him by explaining that "the increase in arrests affects only foreign Jews and has been necessary in order to protect French Jews." Schwartz protested that the French Jews "had never been consulted on the matter of whether they hoped for that kind of protection."[10]

The events of February 1943 stripped away another layer of fiction from the deportations. This time the trains were packed with immigrant Jews, dispatched whether or not they were suitable for labor. It marked the first time French police had arrested toddlers in orphanages.

Three convoys left Drancy for Auschwitz on February 9, 11, and 13, carrying a total of 460 children. The quotas were completed by children taken from UGIF centers. Some were individual children of parents who had already been deported; many were siblings, such as the three Sternschuss sisters: Mina, nine; Lola, seven; and Simone, six, from the orphanage on Rue Guy Patin.

Most of the passengers, including the children, were gassed upon arrival.

It had taken place over five days. The Jewish activists were stunned, as were the non-Jewish women, a passionate handful, who made it their business to know.

"*Il faut faire quelque chose.*" ("Something must be done.")

The following week Suzanne Spaak mobilized the most audacious rescue of the occupation. She and her coconspirators planned the operation a short stroll away from the German headquarters on the Rue de Rivoli and carried it out at institutions under police surveillance and SS control. Their mission did not end with a single operation; it created an expanding safety net for Jewish children that would continue to care for them for years to come.

The details can be found in the postwar testimony of five direct participants. (If Suzanne Spaak left an account, it did not survive.)

Suzanne's Children

The five recorded their versions in different eras, from different perspectives, based on different affiliations, and each includes some minor discrepancies. They agree on the fundamental facts, and all credit Suzanne Spaak with initiating and leading the operation.[11]

Despite Vichy's secrecy, Suzanne learned that the arrests in the orphanages had occurred and that more were imminent. Her most likely source was Sophie Schwartz.[12] Suzanne received confirmation from a member of the Resistance who worked for the Prefecture of Police.*

For Pilette, the story began when her mother told her that she had gone to see a relative of Julien Weill, the chief rabbi of Paris, on the elegant Avenue Victor Hugo.† She knocked on the door, introduced herself as Madame Spaak, sister-in-law of Paul-Henri Spaak, and said, "I want to help the children."

"He said 'All right, there are about fifty.' That's how she got in."

Pilette was unsure exactly who this man was. One possibility is André Baur, the UGIF official and Rabbi Weill's nephew.‡ The former banker oversaw the UGIF aid to thousands of indigent Jewish families, but also assisted in the mechanics of the arrests.

The outrage of the detainees at the Vel d'Hiv wasn't entirely justified: Baur was far from a Nazi stooge. In May 1942 he sent a strong but futile letter to the French Red Cross demanding to know the fate of Jewish deportees. He wrote many protests to

---

* Jacques Adler, a historian of the Jewish Communist movement, wrote that the warning was sent by the French Communist Party to the MNCR.

† Pilette did not recall the man's name. She thought he was the son of the chief rabbi of Paris, but it appears that Julien Weill was childless, making his nephew a reasonable guess. French researcher Gisèle Pierronet believed Suzanne learned of the impending event at a private dinner with Armand Kohn of the Rothschild Hospital.

‡ Another uncle was Dr. Benjamin Weill-Hallé, a leading physician who supported the UGIF underground, along with his colleague Robert Debré.

Vichy and SS officials over the course of 1942 and 1943, often provoking their ire.

What Suzanne needed from this man, whether he was André Baur or someone else, were details. The authorities would have given him, as a UGIF official, the dates and locations of the next arrests in order to expedite them. After the war, one of Suzanne's partners from the MNCR described her attitude.

> When she learned that the children were in danger, she—the "Aryan," who wasn't even allowed to cross the threshold of the UGIF—presented herself to the directors and demanded that the children be removed from the UGIF centers and put into safe hands.
>
> They hesitated, they stammered, they meant well, but they were afraid. "So shut down your shameful *Bastille*," Suzette Spaak told them. The UGIF people handed over most of the remaining children to her. She took care of them with all of her energy.[13]

The next round of arrests was planned for February 19. Armed with this information and the tacit support of the UGIF, Suzanne set to work.

The usual procedure of filtering children into the countryside singly or in pairs would not do. Dozens of children at Lamarck and Guy Patin required immediate evacuation. This called for a mass operation on a larger scale than any single group could manage; none of them had the personnel, the network, or the money to do it alone.

The maneuver would require trusted contacts within Jewish institutions, as well as non-Jewish families who would temporarily shelter the children in Paris. Then they would need multiple safe havens in the countryside.

This meant leaping over vast social gulfs. There were relatively few Jews who moved between the non-Jewish French and Jewish immigrant communities, such as Robert Debré and Léon Chertok, and they were under surveillance or in hiding. Non-Jewish resistance circles were distrustful of outsiders. Too many, like the Musée de l'Homme group, had been infiltrated and betrayed.

But over time Suzanne had forged diverse ties. Jewish Communist groups accepted her as a friend of Mira Sokol's. The Protestants knew her as the mother of a student at a prestigious Protestant school. Soon she would join forces with the wealthy matrons of Entr'aide Temporaire, who regarded her as a member of their class. As the *plaque tournant*, or "turntable," she could rally all of them for the emergency at hand.

Working closely with Sophie Schwartz, she devised a plan. The UGIF orphanages allowed visitors to take the children out for a walk one day a week. The children were starved for fresh air and exercise, but it was dangerous for their relatives to come out of hiding and make themselves known. Suzanne and her partners decided to remove the children from the orphanages. Now they needed a destination.

For this, Suzanne turned to the Oratoire du Louvre, a Protestant church on the Rue Saint-Honoré a few blocks away from her apartment. That fall she had met a friend of Pilette's who asked her to meet his pastor there.

French Protestants, a small minority in France, had experienced persecution in the past, and their theology expressed a strong affinity for Judaism. The Oratoire du Louvre had opposed the Nazis from the start. When the occupation authorities dissolved Jewish Scouting organizations, the Oratoire's troops absorbed local members into their ranks. When the yellow star was imposed in May 1942, the church's pastor denounced it from the pulpit. After the service a parishioner named Odette Béchard approached the pastor and asked how she could help. He referred her to Entr'aide Temporaire, where Hélène Berr and her relations volunteered. Béchard's husband, Fernand, like various other congregants, worked for the Kuhlmann chemical conglomerate, where Hélène Berr's father was the managing director. The Berr connection led directly to the UGIF underground. The network was perfect for Suzanne's purpose.

The Oratoire's efforts were led by Pastor Paul Vergara. A slight man approaching sixty with an exuberant mustache, Vergara lived with his wife and children in a church apartment. The family shared the spirit of resistance. One parishioner recalled that within days of the *Grande Rafle*, "Vergara was sending Jewish children [into hiding] all over the place." Vergara's son-in-law, Jacques Bruston, another Kuhlmann engineer, had joined the Gaullist resistance and took on increasingly dangerous assignments. Vergara's teenage daughter Sylvie secretly snipped fabric from German soldiers' pants and pinned the scraps to her lapel as trophies. One day the French girl-friend of a soldier spotted her and she was arrested. Her twin brother, Sylvain, raced home to hide the family's compromising papers.

Suzanne arranged to meet Vergara at the church, along with Marcelle Guillemot, the social worker who ran La Clairière, the church's soup kitchen.* Guillemot was a tall, brisk woman with neatly coifed blond hair and an elegant profile. The children at the Oratoire considered her "energetic, strong and a little forbidding."[14] (Pilette called her "a dry, humorless drill sergeant, but she got the job done.")

Marcelle Guillemot recalled the first meeting:

Madame Spaak had had a young catechist of Pastor Vergara's to lunch. He spoke to her about the magnificent sermon Vergara had just given with such a spirit of resistance. Madame

---

* The exact timetable and the number of children rescued vary among the different accounts. However, sixty-three is the most widely accepted number of children involved.

Spaak quickly judged that the pastor could be a great help to her in connection with her activity helping the Jews. She went to see him and disclose her goal, to save at least the Jewish children from the deportation that was awaiting them.

Vergara and Guillemot immediately agreed to help, and offered the facilities of La Clairière as a meeting point.

Suzanne visited La Clairière on Thursday, February 11. On Saturday, February 13, a group of Jewish women, Sophie Schwartz's lieutenants from the MNCR underground, began collecting addresses of individuals and institutions that would accept the fugitives. Suzanne returned to see Marcelle Guillemot and advance the plans.[15] The social worker typed up a brief appeal to the Oratoire's congregants and made multiple copies.

On Sunday, February 14, Pastor Vergara preached a sermon based on the text "God created man in his own image." The best way to serve God, he argued, was to help one's fellow man, starting with persecuted Jews.[16]

After the service Marcelle Guillemot positioned herself at the side door, surveying the women as they prepared to depart. She slipped copies of her appeal into the hands of those women she judged trustworthy.

The appeal asked the women to appear the next day at the UGIF office at 23 Rue de la Bienfaisance. There they were asked to visit a UGIF institution the next day, either the orphanage on Rue Lamarck or the one on Rue Guy Patin, and introduce themselves as "relatives" who had come to take the children "out for a walk." Once they had one or two children in hand, they would deliver them to La Clairière, where Suzanne Spaak and Marcelle Guillemot would take over. Sophie Schwartz organized a second group from her Jewish women's circle to carry out the same task. The participants would total about forty women, twenty-five Protestant and fifteen Jewish.

Suzanne Lorge was the oldest daughter of a wealthy Belgian financier from a Catholic family. The romantic fourteen-year-old fell in love with fifteen-year-old Claude Spaak, and the two secretly became engaged.

Claude Spaak, shown here with Suzanne and Pilette in 1928, was a member of Belgium's leading political family. A talented writer and connoisseur of the arts, Claude proved to be a moody, difficult husband.

3

The third party in the Spaak marriage was Suzanne's school friend Ruth Peters. The tall, ungainly Canadian became Claude's mistress while remaining Suzanne's close friend and becoming an "aunt" to the children.

4

Bazou, born in 1931, was a sunny, affectionate child who adored his parents and sister.

When surrealist René Magritte went broke, Claude and Suzanne provided him with a monthly stipend from her inheritance, and Claude shared a steady stream of ideas for his paintings.

Magritte worked from this photograph for his portrait of Suzanne. She looks puzzled and sad.

In 1937–38, Suzanne led relief efforts for victims of the Spanish Civil War, taking the children to French villages to collect contributions. She stands to the left; Pilette sits at her feet, and Bazou stands to the right, both wearing their dance costumes.

8

Claude's brother Paul-Henri Spaak became Belgium's prime minister in May 1938 at the age of thirty-nine. The following month he accompanied King Leopold III to a screening at the Palais des Beaux-Arts (shown here). Two years later, Spaak begged the king not to submit to the Nazi invaders.

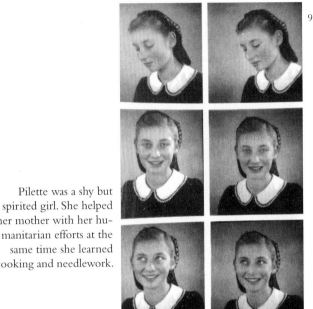

Pilette was a shy but spirited girl. She helped her mother with her humanitarian efforts at the same time she learned cooking and needlework.

In 1938, Mira and Hersch Sokol, penniless Jewish refugees, arrived on Suzanne's doorstep in France. Mira, a gentle intellectual, became her best friend.

The Sokols were recruited by Soviet intelligence. In early 1942 they began operating a radio transmitter for Leopold Trepper, but they were arrested by the Gestapo four months later. These photos were taken in Gestapo custody.

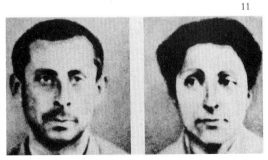

12

The Sokols' torture sessions in Fort Breendonk were overseen by SS officer Philipp Schmitt, assisted by his dog, Lump.

13

One of Suzanne's counterparts at the MNCR was Adam Rayski, a fiery young journalist. He helped to organize the Jewish Communist armed resistance during the occupation, but he reproached the party for its passive response to the Jewish crisis.

14

Léon Chertok, a handsome Jewish physician from Vilnius, acquired false identity papers through his female admirers. He worked closely with Suzanne in the children's rescue efforts. He is shown here with a rescued child in the village of Noirvault.

15

Sophie Schwartz supported Jewish families through her efforts in the MNCR. Childless herself, she devoted her life to promoting the welfare of Jewish immigrant children.

16

Charles Lederman was a Warsaw-born Jewish lawyer and a founder of the MNCR. His blond hair and flawless French accent helped him avoid detection by the authorities.

Suzanne's work with the Jewish underground bolstered her confidence and prompted a makeover that included a stylish hat, burgundy suit, and ochre blouse.

17

18

In July 1942, René Bousquet, the head of the French police, organized the Vel d'Hiv roundup in concert with the German SS. He personally extended the arrests to include children. This January 1943 photo shows him (in fur collar) in Marseilles with German officers preparing another roundup of Jews.

19

The arrest and deportation of immigrant Jews mounted over 1942, leaving their families stranded. These children were consigned to the Lamarck orphanage in Montmartre, shown here in early 1943.

20

Brussels-born siblings Sara and Simon Kejzman tried to escape to Switzerland but were turned back by the Swiss. The UGIF placed Simon in the Lamarck center and Sara in Guy Patin. They were among the children arrested at the centers on February 10 and deported (under the names of Marguerite and Simon Bogaert) on Convoy 47 on February 11. The February arrests inspired the rescue at La Clairière a few days later.

Suzanne turned to Paul Vergara, the Protestant pastor of the Oratoire du Louvre. A longtime opponent of the Nazis, he quickly agreed to help with the children's rescue operation.

Vergara's right-hand woman was the formidable Marcelle Guillemot, who ran the church soup kitchen at La Clairière. The pastor and the social worker offered it as a staging ground for *le kidnapping*. Guillemot would later make her own daring escape from the Gestapo.

La Clairière had served the immigrant community in the Marais for decades. Marcelle Guillemot turned the church facility into a clandestine base for Jean Moulin's Gaullist resistance.

Larissa Gruszow was left at the Lamarck orphanage after her mother was deported to Auschwitz. Sophie Schwartz was desperate to help her friend's forlorn daughter.

With Suzanne's and Vergara's help, Larissa was placed with the Cardons, a prosperous Catholic family in Normandy. In this photo, she dances in a meadow on their estate with Vergara's son, Sylvain. Vergara's daughter, Éliane, dances with another child.

Vergara's son-in-law, Jacques Bruston, was an active member of the Gaullist resistance. Bruston and the pastor's family paid a high price for their ideals.

Suzanne's famous neighbor Colette went down in history as an accommodationist, if not a collaborator. She was actually protecting her Jewish husband, Maurice Goudeket, shown here with her at their apartment in the Palais Royal. She also gave valuable support to Suzanne Spaak's rescue network.

28

Suzanne's rescue network expanded to include Hélène Berr, a member of a prominent French Jewish family. She is shown here with Jewish children from the UGIF institutions.

29

Dr. Robert Debré, an eminent Jewish pediatrician, shown here in 1935, used his privileged status to aid Suzanne's rescue network. Along with the Countess de la Bourdonnaye, he supported the publication of the classic resistance novella *Silence de la Mer* and directed some of its profits to the children's benefit.

30

Debré's partner was the dashing Countess de la Bourdonnaye, Elisabeth de la Panouse, known as "Dexia." She left the count, a Vichy supporter, for her children's pediatrician. Imprisoned as a member of the Musée de l'Homme group, she resumed her resistance work upon her release. She and Debré participated in a wide range of resistance activities throughout the occupation.

31

MINISTÈRE DE L'INTÉRIEUR
DIRECTION GÉNÉRALE
DE LA POLICE NATIONALE

RÉFÉRENCES À RAPPELER
EN TOUTES CIRCONSTANCES

Pol.Sûr.e N° 1075

ÉTAT FRANÇAIS

Vichy, le 18 Septembre 1943

CIRCULAIRE DE RECHERCHES 28/43

Chef d'un groupe de terroristes dangereux

In September 1943, Soviet agent Leopold Trepper escaped from German custody. The Vichy police put out a wanted poster describing him as "a foreigner who directs a group of foreign terrorists." The Gestapo followed his trail to the Spaak residence.

The head of the Rote Kapelle task force was Gestapo officer Heinz Pann-witz. He conducted the interrogations of Pilette, Bazou, and their relations.

32

33

After Suzanne's arrest, her funds were no longer available to support the hidden children. British SOE agent Dennis Barrett, a gentlemen's tailor in peacetime, learned of the crisis and came to the rescue.

Jacques Grou-Radenez, master printer of the resistance. He and his wife hid Jewish children for Suzanne, and his fate was her only regret.

35

Abbé Franz Stock, the German chaplain, secretly aided members of the French Resistance imprisoned at Fresnes. He had helped the Countess de la Bourdonnaye in 1942, and consoled Suzanne two years later. He was post-humously honored by both the French government and Pope John XXIII.

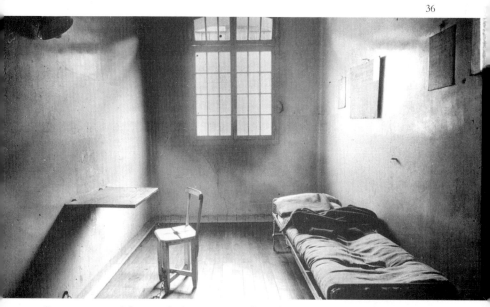

36

Suzanne spent eight months in a spartan cell in the women's wing of the Fresnes prison, a "factory of despair" outside Paris.

37

After the Liberation, the French government gave the MNCR a villa—previously a German military facility—to serve as a home for the hidden children who were left unclaimed. The children called it Renouveau ("Renewal") and named a room after Suzanne Spaak.

38

Pilette and Bazou Spaak in Paris in 2015.

Le kidnapping was scheduled for Monday, February 15. If the plan went well, scores of children would arrive at La Clairière over the course of a day, and they would need to be fed and occupied. More critically, they would need to be registered and dispersed as quickly as possible.

Suzanne enlisted every pair of hands she could find, including her fifteen-year-old daughter. Pilette would have to miss school on Tuesday; instead, she would accompany her mother to La Clairière to help out wherever she was needed.

The morning of February 15 dawned unseasonably mild. The curfew had ended at 6:00 a.m., but the streets were still dark and empty when Suzanne and Pilette left the apartment at seven. They walked past the Place des Victoires and the grand equestrian statue of Louis XIV and on through the shadowy streets to the Rue Greneta in the Marais.

A few miles away, in the northern eighteenth arrondissement, clusters of Protestant and Jewish women began to appear at the UGIF orphanages. One group made its way to the four-story building at 16 Rue Lamarck signposted ASILE DE NUIT, ASILE DE JOUR, ET CRÈCHE ISRAÉLITE ("Night Shelter, Day Shelter, and Jewish Nursery"). Others arrived at the smaller, equally bleak building at 9 Rue Guy Patin in the tenth arrondissement.

They told the staff they had come to take the children for their weekly walk and presented their identity cards for inspection. Then each departed with one or more children.

Once they were outside, the older children could make their own way to the Marais, but the smaller children had to be guided through the city. The women held their hands and spoke soothingly as they passed shops and produce stands stirring to life. When they reached Rue Greneta they entered La Clairière's dingy entryway, which led to a large room with a vaulted ceiling where lunch was served to the poor. Marcelle Guillemot had put up a notice that there would be no lunch that day.

Pilette watched them arrive. They were different from the children she knew. Their heads had been shaved for lice and many wore a Star of David on their clothing, required for all Jews over the age of six. She thought they looked like refugees in their ragged clothes and battered shoes with no laces. One stubbly-haired girl of seven gripped a newspaper over her star with one hand and clutched her little brother's hand with the other. Another arrived with a baby in her arms.

A pair of twin boys arrived wearing matching Dutch boy caps. Pilette was enchanted.

"Mother," she whispered, "can we take them home?"

"No," Suzanne answered firmly. "It would be too dangerous."

By nine o'clock many of the children had arrived—more than expected. There were some happy accidents. Two sisters were reunited with their two brothers who had been separated from them after their parents were deported. Suzanne worked alongside an MNCR activist named Marguerite "Peggy" Camplan, who would become her closest ally. An attractive dark-haired woman in her forties, Camplan was a Protestant by birth and a Communist by conviction. It was whispered that her husband was Jewish and had changed his name from Kaplan.[17] Of the five known accounts of the rescue, Peggy Camplan's was the most detailed. "The crowd of children arrived carrying their meager bundles, and some without anything at all," she wrote.

> They were either trusting or frightened, depending on how much they knew. By that evening there were 60 of them in the Great Hall of Patronage where their destiny would be decided. Madame Spaak was there to receive them, reassure them, amuse them.[18]

The children were hungry. The soup Pilette ladled out had been furnished by Marshal Pétain's relief fund, his propaganda showpiece. ("*O ironie!*" Peggy Camplan exclaimed.)

The children's next stop was a desk occupied by Suzanne and an assistant. Camplan reported:

The afternoon of the first day of the *Coup de l'UGIF* was devoted to carefully noting the children's names, birthdates, family addresses, and addresses of UGIF facilities. Their ages ranged from 3 to 18. We had to think of the possible return of parents who had escaped deportation and searched for their children, which had already happened.[19]

Once their data was recorded, the children were shuttled to temporary havens. "Everyone helped, the women from the [MNCR], the women from the Oratoire," wrote Peggy Camplan.

Madame Spaak appeared pleased from the beginning with this success, but she didn't lose sight of the rapid action required by this business, because it was impossible to keep all of these children in this spot for long without attracting attention.

Their deadline was the midnight curfew; the younger children needed to be safe in bed before then. At ten o'clock, Suzanne took stock. Her goal of placing all of the young children in homes was almost realized.

She had mobilized an extraordinary team effort. "Pastor Vergara telephoned in all directions to find temporary beds," Camplan wrote.

Madame Spaak provided the example; she took many children herself and placed others with her friends. . . . The women of the [MNCR] also took them and placed them, even with Jews who were already in hiding, and who thus showed proof of their great support.

Pastor Vergara and several of his [grown] children took some in, as well as Pastor Vidal and a large number of parishioners from l'Oratoire. Even people in humble lodgings in the neighborhood, and concierges. . . . It was *magnifique!* Of course, this temporary distribution was carefully recorded.

A handful of Jewish teenagers remained, but they could spend the night at La Clairière on benches. However, there were still five small children who needed beds. Suzanne located a spot for them with a concièrge on the Boulevard de Sébastopol, but it was a mile away and the escorts were already heading out, anxious to reach home before the Métro shut down for the night. Whoever took the children would have to travel on foot and still make it home before curfew. Suzanne turned to Pilette. She set out into the night with the five children in tow.

The streetlights were extinguished as a precaution against air raids. It was slow going in the dark, and the children were hard to shepherd. They had been starved and shut in for weeks, and now they limped along the blacked-out streets. Pilette prodded them, anxious about the time. Finally she arrived at the address and rang the bell.

The concièrge opened the door and peered out. "Bring them upstairs," she said. Pilette and the children trudged up seven floors to a small chamber. The woman's own five children were piled on the bed, sleeping soundly, and she shook them awake. "*Allez!*" They tumbled out of the bed and the new arrivals took their place. The concièrge's children stumbled down the stairs to sleep with their mother.

Pilette left for the Palais Royal, skirting police patrols and peering into the shadows. The darkness made it difficult. Some women installed small bulbs in the toes of their shoes to light their way, powered by batteries in the soles, but Pilette had no such device.

When she finally arrived at the apartment, all was silent. She tiptoed into Bazou's room. Her brother was sound asleep in his bed, Claude was off with Ruth, and Suzanne was, yet again, absent. Pilette had just completed the most terrifying mission of her life— but there was no one to tell.

Suzanne and her colleagues spent the night at La Clairière working on the formidable record-keeping challenge. They had assembled a list of people in the countryside who had agreed to accept a child, recording their preferences for a boy or a girl. This was compared with a roster prepared the previous day, listing the children and their attributes.[20]

"The next day, Tuesday, February 16, ten new children arrived," Camplan wrote.

> Like those who came earlier, they were fed and sheltered at La Clairière until we could find them a temporary spot. But the big job of the second day was to work out, in writing, the permanent distribution of this continually growing flock.
>
> Suzette—Madame Spaak's codename—had gathered an entire staff around her at La Clairière. The children were distributed among the placements on offer, taking into account as much as possible the requests regarding age and sex.

The next group to join the effort was the Oratoire's Girl Scout troop. Its twenty-three-year-old leader, Simone Chefneux, sent the girls to La Clairière to receive their assignments as *convoyeuses*, or children's escorts. Madame Camplan reported:

> On the third day, Wednesday, February 17 (which saw fifteen new children arrive), we executed the plans of the previous day. Each *convoyeuse* was given her assignment to take the children to either a temporary hiding place or to the countryside,

where they would be introduced to the neighbors as a little refugee. The child was saved!

The departures followed rapidly, but children from the Jewish quarter continued to arrive. By the end of the week, Marcelle Guillemot found the number of young guests had risen to ninety.[21]

She had reason to be anxious. The sudden influx of children had naturally aroused curiosity on the street. Nosy shopkeepers were told that the children had been bombed out of their homes in the suburbs by British air raids. Still, there were informers everywhere, and the unusual events at the soup kitchen could turn curiosity into suspicion. Once the children were safe, the women set to work erasing all traces of their operation. Camplan wrote:

On the fourth day, Thursday the 18th, we burned all of the papers and labels bearing the compromising names. We took the boxes of the remaining clothes to a neighboring seamstress and gave a brave grocer the lists from the children's files. She hid them for months in a bottle rack in the back of the store, and we opened a private door when we wanted to consult them.[22]

The seamstress removed the yellow stars from the children's clothes and burned them, then dismantled the garments and stored them with her rags.

On Thursday police appeared on the Rue Greneta asking questions. Shortly afterward, officers from the Vichy Commission for Jewish Affairs descended on the Oratoire, but by then all evidence of the operation had vanished. Peggy Camplan wrote:

From that point on, we adopted more discreet tactics. The children didn't come from the UGIF any more, because the

Coup had been so successful that it couldn't be repeated without danger.

The operation's success caused more complications. News of the rescue at La Clairière had flown through the Jewish community. Relatives, friends, and neighbors appeared on its doorstep, pleading on behalf of their children. The women at La Clairière gave them temporary addresses from their list of reliable hosts, and Suzanne or a colleague from the MNCR came by every day to drop off the name of the contact who would oversee the permanent placement. Remarkably, La Clairière continued to function as a soup kitchen and community center with only a brief pause.

After the war Claude Spaak reported that a dozen Jewish children were taken to the Spaaks' country house in Choisel—a fact that Suzanne successfully hid from her own children.[23] The other host families ran the gamut of French society. Many of Pastor Vergara's parishioners were families of professional men who collected the children from La Clairière the same day they were called.[24] The Meunier family had been hiding Jewish children since the Vel d'Hiv. Now the pastor turned to them again, asking them to take a group of children between the ages of four and seven. Michèle, sixteen, worried about her family's "mean concièrge."

"We were afraid she would turn us in, so the children came and went quickly so as not to attract attention," she recalled. "The children weren't traumatized. They didn't realize what had happened to their parents, and we didn't either. But one little boy, 5 or 6 years old, would pray, '*Mon Dieu*, please bring my parents back.'"[25] Over the coming months, Vergara continued to send children to the Meuniers until they could find places in the countryside. Michèle estimated that her family sheltered some fifteen children over the year.

Many more havens were needed, and Suzanne sought out every

node of her network, including the Countess de la Bourdonnaye. Dexia had been assisting Robert Debré and was known as his nurse (though some called her his "secretary"). She supported the operation at La Clairière and offered her luxurious apartment on 55 Rue de Varenne as a hiding place. She took in over a dozen children, including Armand Boruchowicz, the boy from Guy Patin whose friends had been caught hiding in the basement.[26]

For Dexia and Debré, resistance was a family affair. Their older children by their first marriages were fighting with de Gaulle's forces, but Dexia's youngest daughter, Oriane, was still living at home. She had sung the "Marseillaise" in the famous student demonstration against the Nazis on the Champs-Élysées in 1940; now she had to be more discreet. Nevertheless, she maintained her feisty spirit: "We used to cut Métro tickets in a V and the Cross of Lorraine and leave them on the floor of the subway."*

Oriane's new task was to hide the children. The countess's apartment had six bedrooms, a garden, and a grand salon, but there were logistical challenges. Her elegant street served as a thoroughfare for the occupation hierarchy. The Wehrmacht's military tribunal was located a few doors down, and Pierre Laval had lived next door at the Hôtel Matignon until the previous November. Only a year earlier, the countess had gone to prison and risked deportation for hiding her fellow Musée de l'Homme resisters in her apartment.

Dexia and Oriane sneaked the Jewish children, aged seven to ten, past the neighbors and the concierge and installed them in Oriane's room. "We played little games. They were *adorable*, hiding in the banquettes." Oriane also witnessed their pathos. "One of

---

* The French Resistance had adopted the "V for Victory" slogan, and the Cross of Lorraine was the symbol of de Gaulle's Free French.

them said, 'Madame, can you tell me, did they arrest *Maman* because I didn't know my catechism?'"[27]

Before they could be moved to the countryside, the children needed a new identity and ration cards. The rescuers started out by obtaining blanks or "scrubbing" old cards. Suzanne took on the task of scrubbing them using Dr. Debré's hospital laboratory. "Madame Spaak was in charge of the first ones," Camplan noted, "but her methods took a long time because she had to go through a group that worked outside Paris. She often traveled with the fake cards in her bodice or sent them through the mail, one by one, under the cover of a new hardback book marked 'printed matter.'"[28]

More shelters were needed, and Suzanne continued to reach out. One contact was Jacques Grou-Radenez. The master printer, known as a "friend of the poets," dined with the Spaak family on occasion. His most recent project was training members of the Gaullist student movement Défense de la France, offering them a printing press and lightning apprenticeships for their underground newspaper of the same name.

Grou-Radenez and his wife had five children of their own, but at Suzanne's request they took in five Jewish children and welcomed more over the coming months.[29] It was a courageous decision; Grou-Radenez was already placing his family at risk through his work printing *Défense de la France*. But he and his wife, deeply principled Catholics, would not turn the children away.

Next, Suzanne contacted the ladies of Entr'aide Temporaire, perhaps through the Oratoire's Odette Béchard. Suzanne began by meeting with the group's president, Denise Milhaud of the UGIF underground, and Hélène Berr's cousin Nicole Schneiderman.

"We didn't know about the action of La Clairière when Madame Spaak proposed to me that we take in children," recalled Milhaud. "I hesitated, because I wasn't even sure it was Madame Spaak."[30] But

Milhaud decided to trust her, and Entr'aide joined Suzanne's rapidly expanding network.*

The children were safe from immediate danger, but now the next stage began. More ration and identification cards were needed. Sophie Schwartz and Solidarité contributed counterfeits from the Jewish Communists and the FTP-MOI underground. Pastor Vergara and Marcelle Guillemot set up forgery workshops and collection points for Red Cross supplies in church facilities.

The Oratoire's Girl Scouts rode the rails accompanying the children to the countryside, and a young congregant named Maurice Nosley took children to four host families in Saône-et-Loire, working with Entr'aide Temporaire and Hélène and Denise Berr.[31]

Finally, the children were all registered, documented, and placed. After a cooling-off period, the rosters were placed in hermetically sealed jars and buried in a garden in the suburb of Goussainville, where Sophie Schwartz had her lodgings.

Sophie Schwartz's lieutenants served as a vital link between the rescuers and Jewish families in hiding: if relatives could be convinced to bring their children directly to the network, they would lessen their risk of arrest in the UGIF facilities. Sick children were sent to Léon Chertok and his MNCR medical committee, with the support of Robert Debré. Debré and his colleagues were often able to place them in non-Jewish clinics.

But the network required money, in large quantities. The MNCR paid an average of 1,000 francs a month per child to cover room and board in the metropolitan area. Areas outside Paris were less expensive but still cost around 750 francs a month. In one day,

---

* Unfortunately, Hélène Berr's journal falls silent over the period in 1943 when the operation took place. But other entries mention her collaboration with Denise Milhaud, Lucie Chevalley, and Odette Béchard, all members of Entr'aide who took part in the operation.

the operation at La Clairière added sixty-three children to the account, which meant an additional 60,000 francs a month. This was a daunting figure, even for a Belgian heiress.

Suzanne embarked on a massive fund-raising campaign. She had formerly shunned Parisian high society, but now her pedigree was useful. Pilette was delighted to see her dowdy mother decked out as a woman of fashion. The burgundy suit and hats were called into action, and she kept her hair trimmed and coiffed in the updated style that flattered her new nose. Claude had given her a gold bracelet the previous year. By the time she added her new fur coat, Pilette thought "she looked like a star!"

Suzanne continued to expand her network. Robert Debré connected her to the leading physicians of Paris, while Entr'aide Temporaire introduced her to banking and business circles. Scores of participants from half a dozen groups had taken part in the rescue; now they would cover the expenses of hundreds of Jewish children at a cost of some 300,000 francs a month.[32] The Oratoire took up regular collections, and Pastor Vergara commissioned a church deacon named Maurice-William Girardot to deliver the funds to Suzanne at the Palais Royal.

Suzanne gave her donors a choice of payment plans. Some of them opted for a onetime contribution; others chose a subscription plan. Suzanne's artist friend Valentine Hugo made a single contribution, while her screenwriter brother-in-law Charles Spaak signed up for a 5,000-franc monthly subscription, enough to support five children. (This would have surprised his critics, who took a dim view of the screenplays he wrote for the German-owned Continental Films.) Suzanne gave what she could from her own allowance and asked her relatives for more. Every possible source of funding was explored, from far-flung Rothschilds to destitute Jewish families in Belleville.

But Suzanne scored her biggest coup closer to home. She knew that Colette was sympathetic to the cause, but her neighbor had become more reclusive, tormented by her arthritis and her fears for the safety of her Jewish husband.

A few weeks after *le kidnapping* at La Clairière, Suzanne knocked at her door and explained the situation. The next day Colette's housekeeper, Pauline, appeared at the Spaaks' bearing a large donation, along with a long typewritten list of names and addresses: two single-spaced pages, front and back.

Suzanne showed the list to Pilette. Colette had scoured her address book for friends who were good for a contribution or a place to stay, and above all who were absolutely trustworthy. With one gesture, Colette added scores of aristocrats, artists, and perceived collaborators (like herself) to a mission that had been launched by Polish Communist Jews and Protestant reformers.

This convergence suited Suzanne—it was, at heart, the quality that defined her. One of her Communist Jewish partners, Jeanne List-Pakin, saw Suzanne's political independence as both her strength and her liability.

> Not being a member of a political party, she didn't believe that she was obliged to submit to strict discipline regarding clandestinity. In her impulsive heart, she wanted to offer her help to all of the resistance networks at the same time.[33]

Once the situation at La Clairière was under control, Suzanne returned to the house on Avenue Victor Hugo that had been the source of the original warning. She volunteered to take more children. "But please," she asked, "from now on, not so many at once."

11

le grand livre

T he rescue operation needed a business plan. In the months following the rescue at La Clairière, Suzanne Spaak helped build a major financial enterprise with a national reach. Its success was measured in the survival of Jewish children under threat of deportation, and every step had to be conducted secretly. Detection could result in deportation for broker, host, and child.

The groups were mindful of the need for records to reunite hidden children with surviving family members after the war. Toddlers with pseudonyms were likely to forget their actual identities, but that was preferable to their information falling into the wrong hands.

The rescuers devised an elaborate bookkeeping system. The impulse came naturally to the ladies of Entr'aide Temporaire, who, like Suzanne, were the wives and daughters of businessmen. They coded the entries, making them clear enough to read but cryptic enough to confound interlopers.

The Oratoire's Odette Béchard furnished Entr'aide with a ledger, a large, leather-bound volume with "1921" stamped on the spine. The group dubbed it "*Le Grand Livre*." One of the rescued children, Sami Dassa, later wrote a history of the rescue stating that the register commenced with *le kidnapping* at La Clairière and was maintained by Denise Milhaud.[1]

The original copy, which rests in the archives of Paris's Mémorial de la Shoah, offers a glimpse of the process. The entries mixed the actual names of rescued children with information that was backdated twenty years, to correspond to the stamp on the spine; thus a child born in 1939 would be registered as 1919, and so forth. Based on appearances, the *Grand Livre* was an obsolete registry of a charity for children long grown.

The handwriting and formats vary from page to page, suggesting that different women made the entries. Columns under the headings "*Soldes*," "*Entrées*," and "*Sorties*" listed figures for the balances, donations, and expenditures, which were principally payments to the women who hosted the children.

The names of the children's parents were also recorded. Most of them were assigned one of two designations: "Biarritz" meant a parent was a detainee in Drancy, and "Bayonne" indicated the parents had been deported to Auschwitz.

The information was often inconsistent, surely due to the haste and secrecy with which it was recorded. Birth dates were sometimes omitted. Chronologies were erratic, and there were wild variations in spelling, as French bookkeepers puzzled over Slavic names and immigrants struggled with the French alphabet. These elements render the *Grand Livre* a difficult document to parse, but it offers many clues.

One entry recorded a contribution from "Madame Lorge" (Suzanne Spaak's maiden name) for 25,000 francs, the equivalent of over $100,000 in 2017. Pilette believes that this was a contribution that Suzanne coaxed from her mother. Suzanne made donations from her household allowance when she could, but she risked rousing her husband's ire. Claude saw his wife's fortune as a path to the good life, and he frequently upbraided her for being too "proletarian." Suzanne, on the other hand, was almost superstitious about her fortune. She often told Pilette, "To have money is good if you share it with others. If you keep it, it makes you unhappy."[2]

Suzanne appeared again in the *Grand Livre* ledger later as a "*sortie.*" This could have been a term for removing children from a home or an institution to take them into hiding. One "*sortie*" was initially assigned to "Madame Lorge," but the name "Lorge" was crossed out and replaced by "Beaux Arts"—the name of the Brussels cultural center and museum where Claude Spaak had worked.*

The benefactors in the *Grand Livre* included many names associated with Entr'aide: in code, abbreviated, and in full. Odette Béchard made frequent *sorties*, as did Denise Milhaud, Lucie Chevalley, and Hélène's mother, Madame Berr.

There is an entry for "Madame la Baronne de Forest"; Peggy Camplan recorded that the Countess de la Bourdonnaye participated through her assistant, "Madame Laforest."[3] Several Rothschilds were named as donors, including the "Baronne de Königswartes," Pannonica Rothschild, who worked for the Free French and would later become the fabulous "jazz baroness."

Then there were the children. They were often listed in groups of siblings, with their birth dates and orthographically challenging surnames: the Boczmaks, the Nepomiatzis, and the Szwarcbarts. Many entries tell a heartbreaking story in shorthand. René Beugelmans, the ledger reports, was entrusted to Entr'aide by his aunt after his Russian-born father and Scottish-born mother were deported to "Bayonne" in 1942. The rescuers were able to save Henri Lemel but not his older sisters, *enfants bloqués*. There's a painful entry in red

---

* It may also have referred to Marguerite Camplan, who lived at 10 Rue des Beaux-Arts in Paris.

pencil for twelve-year-old Eugene Sommer: "*pas parti, refus de sa mère*" ("Didn't leave, refusal by his mother").

The women kept a careful eye on the hosts. Some were altruists; others were motivated by money and eager to exploit the situation. One entry fumed, "Upkeep paid from 1 July to 31 December. We learn that the *nourrice* has a sum of 16,000 francs from the parents, and we demand that the upkeep be deducted from this sum."

Most of the stipends ran about 1,000 francs a month, the going rate outside Paris, though some were as little as 600. The hosts were paid on a monthly basis, which required extensive travel on the part of the women serving as messengers. Many of the hosts expected to be paid in advance, and some took it out on the children when a payment was delayed. But in general the children were well fed, housed, and protected.

Suzanne Spaak's and Léon Chertok's working relationship with Robert Debré and the countess led to other collaborations. In May 1943 the French Communist Party asked the MNCR's Charles Lederman to find a way to contact London, and he learned that Debré's Gaullist contacts had the means for transmissions. Once the two men reached an accord regarding the radio, Lederman turned to Debré's partner. The countess ran Debré's clinic at the Hospital for Sick Children, which maintained extensive files on the children under his care. This gave Lederman an idea. Could the MNCR, he asked, secrete dossiers on its Jewish children in hiding among the hospital's files for safekeeping? The countess agreed immediately. The hospital guarded the secret files until the end of the occupation.[4]

Suzanne traveled frequently by train to the outposts of other resistance groups. One of her missions was to transport identity cards, some of them forged blanks, others pilfered from government offices or recovered from bomb sites. She would return on the train with a dozen of them packed into her girdle, looking stouter than usual.

Sometimes Suzanne conducted the scrubbing at home. She and Pilette worked from a table placed in front of a window (where "anyone could see what we were doing!" Pilette marveled later). Suzanne carefully schooled her daughter in the technique: first, place the old identity card under a damp cloth, then apply a hot iron. The old ink would come up into the cloth, leaving a ghostly blank. This was where the Jewish child's new identity would be filled in.

Suzanne also located homes in the countryside. One day Pilette asked her how she did it. She explained that her method was to get on a train and choose a small village not too far from Paris. She would enter the local church and ask the priest to hear her confession; then, from the privacy of the confessional, she would confide that she needed to place some children from Paris. Could the Father suggest any suitable homes in the community? She never mentioned that the children were Jewish; her wards could have been the children of prostitutes, factory workers, or war orphans, or perhaps they had been bombed out of their neighborhoods. The priests could advise which local families would be inclined to help or needed the income.

Pilette asked, "Couldn't it be dangerous?"

"Yes," Suzanne admitted. "*Mais il faut le faire.* It's got to be done, and it never fails."

Pilette took pride in serving as her mother's assistant and some-time confidante. Bazou was a different story. The boy loved his mother intensely and missed her terribly. He became a latchkey child of the Resistance, coming home more and more often to an empty house. Sometimes, when pressed, Suzanne asked him to carry out small errands—harmless, she thought. The blond school-boy never attracted suspicion, and the task was simply dropping off an envelope here and there, perhaps at the printer's shop of their friend Jacques Grou-Radenez at 11 Rue de Sèvres. The message might concern a resistance meeting, an exchange of information, or perhaps a Jewish child to hide. Bazou, always eager to please, never asked and never found out what the envelopes contained. Suzanne was constantly in motion, riding the rails to villages to seek host families, setting out for Lyon to pick up forged documents, or traveling south on the Ligne de Sceaux to hand off money and "good addresses" to Sophie Schwartz.

Most of the Jewish children were processed and placed without their guides ever knowing their real names, but sometimes there was a personal connection. This was the case for Sophie Schwartz and Larissa Wozek. Sophie visited her at the orphanage when she could, distressed by the child's mournful expression and keenly aware that, as the child of a deportee, she was in constant peril of deportation. There were frequent reminders; Larissa recalled that one Sunday in the orphanage "there was a *rafle* of the parents who came to visit. It was terrifying, because the adults were hiding everywhere."[5]

Sophie wanted to remove Larissa from the orphanage as soon as possible, but there were complications. First she needed a place to take her. She found a couple, both hairdressers, who agreed to take the girl and signed a paper to that effect. But when Sophie went to fetch Larissa from Guy Patin, she was sick with a high fever. She needed a safe haven. Sophie dropped her off at a friend's and turned to Suzanne Spaak for help.

Suzanne reached out to Paul Vergara, who knew the perfect spot. The pastor's family had a small country house in Normandy in the colorfully named region of Faute d'Argent ("lack of money").[6] Vergara had many friends among the local inhabitants; he had already placed two Jewish children, Denise and Monique Jackiel, with a retired schoolmistress. He knew another family that would be perfect for Larissa.

In April, Larissa, now six, was taken to the Cardons, a prosperous Catholic family with a lovely eighteenth-century château in Bézancourt. Its grounds teemed with their cheerful offspring, and they immediately took to Larissa. Her new name was "Madeleine Petit," but the Cardons called her "Mado."

It would be one of the sunniest periods of her life. The child thrived on a diet of affection, hearty food, and fresh air. The Cardons took a picture of Larissa sitting proudly astride a horse led by their son Pierre. Another photo shows her in a meadow wearing an airy summer dress and white sandals, dancing dreamily to a gramophone with Paul Vergara's handsome son Sylvain, jaunty in his plus fours. Vergara's daughter Éliane Bruston danced with another Jewish child while other hidden children and Cardons watched, seated in the grass.

Despite the wholesome surroundings, Larissa experienced moments of alienation. She recalled later:

> [The Cardons] explained to me that if anyone asked who I am, I would say that I'm a niece from Paris who came to restore her health, that I'm from the same family. Also, they told me that there was a good God, and that I had to pray every night to God and the Virgin Mary for my mother to return. Of course, I prayed. And I went every Sunday to Mass. They weren't bigots, but, well . . .[7]

The Oratoire's Girl Scouts continued to serve as escorts for the children, as did churchwomen, social workers, and members of the Jewish women's group. Their destinations included many Protestant enclaves, including the village of le Chambon-sur-Lignon. Before the war the village pastor André Trocmé had served as a presbyter at the Oratoire alongside Michèle Meunier's father. Now he shared the Oratoire's mission. According to Michèle, "Many of the children rescued by the Oratoire went to Chambon-sur-Lignon." In all, the village was credited with saving the lives of at least eight hundred Jews.[8]

The Countess de la Bourdonnaye had offered her vast apartment on the Rue de Varenne as a way station for some time. Robert Debré wrote admiringly that she hosted

> successive groups of children torn from the *rafles*. It was necessary to accept them when they were ill. She washed them in soapy water, got rid of their parasites, clipped their long hair, broke them of the habit of covering their heads with grimy caps and dressed them properly. They were transformed, really unrecognizable, and after some nourishing meals, recovered their natural high spirits. Then they were ready to be dispersed into the provinces.[9]

Other members of the network used their own contacts to find havens. Léon Chertok went back to the remote hamlet of Noirvault, the home of his friend Eva Fradin. In 1941 Chertok had begun visiting Fradin's mother as a respite from the "hell of Paris." The Fradins had taken in Adam Rayski's son, Benoît, after the Vel d'Hiv arrests; now they took in three more.[10]

When children contracted minor illnesses, their hosts were obliged to take them to local doctors. If they needed hospital care, they were tended by the Countess de la Bourdonnaye and Denise Milhaud, who brought them to Debré's clinic. Debré's network extended beyond his medical staff.

> We weren't only helped by the complicity of our fellow radiologists and laboratory technicians, but also by certain officials, including some in the police. My laboratory at Enfants-Malades was far from being the only one that distinguished itself as forgery dispensary.[11]

Debré also offered his services to a broad array of resistance organizations.

In the hospitals, who were we not able to hide, to "camouflage," you might say, among those the police were pursuing!

Many victims of racial persecution, communist militants, resistants threatened by the different police forces, [were] treated for imaginary diseases in the hospitals, where some nocturnal admissions and narrow escapes were quite dramatic.[12]

One member of Debré's underground medical committee was Robert Merle d'Aubigné, a pioneering orthopedic surgeon and the bearer of an old Huguenot name. His wife recruited leading specialists to care for the hidden children's ailments.[13] Another member was Louis Justin-Besançon, a professor whose wife, Madeleine, worked with Entr'aide. As the French Resistance gained momentum, the doctors were pulled in different directions, hiding fugitives and documents, treating wounded militants, and secreting medical supplies. Everyone was constantly asked to do more.

Suzanne had already hosted clandestine meetings for the Jewish underground in her apartment, but now "her apartment became the headquarters where representatives of different resistance movements met," one of her associates wrote later. "Over twenty-four hours, university professors, workers, priests, Jewish social workers, Communists and Gaullists would pass through."[14]

Suzanne drew her famous neighbor further into the intrigue. Adam Rayski wrote, "The leadership of the [MNCR] met over a certain time at Colette's apartment on the Rue de Beaujolais, where the windows opened on the gardens of the Palais Royal. The relations were established thanks to her neighbor, Suzette Spaak."[15]

But then, to his alarm, Rayski learned that Colette's husband was Jewish and under threat of rearrest, even though he slept in the attic and never left the building. "We gave the leaders of the MNCR—for reasons of security—the order not to meet there any more," he wrote.[16]

Suzanne's Children

Few people outside Rayski's circle were aware of Colette's involvement, even though she was one of the best-known writers of her time. Her masterly biographer, Judith Thurman, wrote:

> Colette's reluctance to take any sort of stand, even privately, or to voice any sentiment of outrage at the persecutions, even in her letters, is a symptom of that moral lethargy she admits so candidly in "Bella-Vista," where the narrator bears witness to crimes she does nothing to stop. "I was born under the sign of passivity," she writes then. And she writes, now [to a friend in 1942], "Save your aggression for your work. For the rest of your day-to-day life, passivity suffices."[17]

Years later, Jean-Louis Debré (the grandson of Robert), echoed this judgment:

> The attitude of Colette during the Second World War is disappointing and disconcerting. . . . Of course, Colette needed money, but her attitude is ambiguous, as though, outside reality, she was turning her back on events.[18]

If it weren't for Pilette's recollections and Rayski's memoirs, Colette's role may never have come to light. She never publicized her support for Suzanne's rescue efforts or the Jewish militants. Her attitude was, "Let them think what they will."

By 1943 the French were exhausted by the hardships of the occupation and shocked by its mounting abuses. Germany no longer appeared invincible; the epic Battle of Stalingrad ended on February 2, 1943, with a massive German defeat. Collaborationists were dismayed and resistance sympathizers were energized. In London, de Gaulle tackled the challenge of uniting France's fractious resistance movements under a single command.

The Oratoire du Louvre found itself in the middle of the action.

The church's connection to the Gaullist resistance had begun at the outset of the war with a glamorous young congregant named Jacques-Henri Schloesing, the son of a neighboring pastor and the cousin of Vergara's son-in-law, Jacques Bruston.

After France's surrender, Schloesing joined de Gaulle's forces in London and was assigned to a French fighter squadron to hunt German planes and escort American bombers over France.* On February 13, 1943—the day before the rescue at La Clairière— Schloesing's plane was shot down by four Focke-Wulf 190s. Badly burned, he managed to parachute out over the Somme. The following week, Bruston spirited him into hiding. Schloesing made it back to England and insisted on going back into service despite his injuries.[19]

Other Frenchmen were harder to convince. Early resistance initiatives were easily crushed before they could achieve traction. De Gaulle's base in London was another issue. The French public nursed a lingering resentment of Great Britain, stoked by the British bombardment. Nonetheless, Britain's Special Operations Executive, or SOE, became one of the engines of the French Resistance. The Oratoire du Louvre played a role in advancing these interests, and they would intersect with the children's rescue efforts and Suzanne Spaak.

De Gaulle chose a charismatic, coolheaded official named Jean Moulin to unite the resistance forces within France.[20] In March 1943, Moulin, who was based in the Southern Zone, sent his secretary Daniel Cordier to Paris to launch a new operation. Remarkably, it would be based at the Oratoire with La Clairière as its hub. The connection came about through Moulin's trusted courier, Hugues Limonti. The twenty-one-year-old mechanic was appointed chief liaison in Paris, a terrifying position involving the

---

* Schloesing was shot down and killed in August 1944 over Normandy.

oversight of a dozen agents and some thirty contacts a day, as well as communications with the Southern Zone. Limonti was also expected to recover parachute drops, distribute their contents, and make arrangements for clandestine visitors to and from Britain. Finally, he was charged with guiding downed Allied flyers to escape networks.[21]

Hugues Limonti needed help.

He turned to a close friend of his sister's, Marcelle Guillemot. The Oratoire's social worker had already begun her life of virtuous crime, supporting rescue operations for Jewish children from La Clairière. The rescue work provided Marcelle Guillemot with many of the resources Limonti sought: a quiet street with a busy storefront, a trusted staff, and office supplies. Guillemot could do nothing without Paul Vergara's consent. Daniel Cordier went to visit the pastor on Moulin's behalf, and Vergara agreed to place La Clairière at Moulin's disposal. The operations would function under the supervision of Limonti, code-named "Germain."

The modest soup kitchen became a frequent stop for the various groups united under Moulin's resistance council.* Couriers appeared at the door with the passwords: "I come on behalf of Germain, to carry out a commission for Claude" or vice versa, and Limonti arrived every day to collect the messages. Sometimes Guillemot had to vacate her office to allow him to use it as a dressing room.

La Clairière continued to feed the hungry and care for children as its underground operations grew rapidly. Soon it was being used as a warehouse for weapons, radio transmitters, and underground

---

* These groups included the Organisation civile et militaire (OCM), a Paris-based group of conservatives and Socialists; the Communists' Front national (FN); the conservative Ceux de la Libération; and Ceux de la Résistance, a centrist group that included Robert Debré's son Michel.

publications. Limonti gave Marcelle Guillemot the daily task of buying all the Vichy newspapers. Their contents were dissected and communicated to London, where the BBC's Radio Londres crafted broadcasts to counter their arguments.

Moulin's affiliates met at La Clairière twice that spring. One meeting lasted until lunchtime and the soup kitchen clientele had begun to gather downstairs. Mademoiselle Guillemot introduced the visitors as church elders who had come to make an inspection. In return for her support, Moulin's delegation furnished Guillemot with identity and ration cards that she shared with Suzanne Spaak and the MNCR to use for the Jewish children.

As the activity mounted, so did the risk. La Clairière was getting too busy for comfort, but it was too practical to give up. Marcelle Guillemot was always on hand, ever available and ever vulnerable.

The unified Resistance was buoyed by Moulin's stubborn diplomacy and the promise of an Allied invasion in the foreseeable future. Their progress culminated in the first historic meeting of the National Council of the Resistance in Paris on May 27, attended by Moulin and representatives of eight resistance movements, two trade unions, and six prewar political parties.

The Jewish Communists looked for ways to participate. On May 21, 1943, Sophie Schwartz, Adam Rayski, Charles Lederman, and several others met to discuss how to expand their initiatives, including Solidarité and the MNCR. They were stirred by the Soviet victory at Stalingrad and the ghetto uprising in Warsaw, where Polish Jews awaiting deportation armed themselves and attacked German forces over April and May. They were crushed, but word spread of the first urban uprising in Nazi-occupied Europe. Inspired, the Jewish underground in Paris founded a new umbrella organization, the Jewish Union for Resistance and Support (UJRE).[22]

Throughout the country, the balky gears of the Resistance were finally starting to mesh. A new leadership structure emerged and the ranks filled with eager volunteers, many of them young men drafted into Germany's new forced-labor force, the Service du travail obligatoire (STO). Begun in January 1943, the wildly unpopular program drafted hundreds of thousands of Frenchmen over the age of twenty to work in the Reich, beyond the hundreds of thousands already there. Thousands of youths known as *réfractaires* decamped to the countryside, where they joined resistance bands called *maquis*.*

They included young men from the Oratoire. Forging their documents became one more task for Marcelle Guillemot's workshop at La Clairière.

---

* Named after the scrub brush of their mountain enclaves.

12

the unraveling

| JUNE–SEPTEMBER 1943 |

The dark days descended in the early summer of 1943. The Gestapo and the French police had been hard at work trailing suspects, planting informers, and interrogating detainees. The French Special Brigades had mastered methods refined by the Gestapo, monitoring suspects for as long as nine months as they compiled names and addresses, then striking on multiple fronts.

On June 20, the police moved in on Défense de la France. Suzanne's friend Jacques Grou-Radenez, who had hidden Jewish children, was squarely in their sights. His office and printing shop were searched, but his resourceful wife, Madeleine, had been tipped off in advance and hid the incriminating materials. However, an informer's tip led the French Gestapo to arrest scores of members of the group. They included General de Gaulle's niece Geneviève and the blind student leader Jacques Lusseyran. Both were taken to Fresnes, then deported to concentration camps.*

---

* Remarkably, both de Gaulle and Lusseyran survived the war. Lusseyran

On June 21, Jean Moulin was arrested in a suburb of Lyon with eight members of his organization. Moulin was savagely tortured under the personal supervision of SS officer Klaus Barbie. He died without revealing names or intelligence.

Over the summer, the authorities concentrated on British agents and French contacts, and the SOE may have played a part in a debacle. One question reigned in the minds of the German military and the French resisters: When and where would the Allies invade? The London strategists set about misleading the Germans, and instructed the SOE to operate as though it were preparing for a 1943 invasion, specifically in the northern Pas-de-Calais region. They multiplied the numbers of agents and arms parachuted into France. The French Resistance took heart, believing the invasion was at hand, and relaxed security. (There have been allegations that the SOE misled its own agents to make the fiction more credible if they broke down under interrogation.)[1] In late June, five SOE agents were captured by the Germans and sent to Fresnes, and the toll continued to mount over the summer.[2]

In July, it was the Oratoire's turn. The disaster began with Pastor Vergara's son-in-law, Jacques Bruston. The thirty-four-year-old engineer had blood ties to the Gaullists through his cousin the fighter pilot, and Bruston was eager to support Moulin's resistance council and its London backers. On July 22 he left Paris by car en route to Tours to pick up some cases dropped by parachute. The Germans, perhaps through individuals who cracked under interrogation, had identified the field and the ground personnel. As he drove back to Paris, Bruston was halted at the Porte d'Orléans, and the Gestapo found the cases hidden in the trunk. The Oratoire operation was

---

was an inspiration for Anthony Doerr's novel *All the Light We Cannot See.* See the Goodreads interview with Doerr (https://www.goodreads.com /interviews/show/995.Anthony_Doerr) from December 2014.

compromised. Hugues Limonti and Bruston's wife, Éliane, learned of his arrest and warned Marcelle Guillemot. Limonti went into hiding at La Clairière.

One of the three occupants of Bruston's car may have broken down under questioning. The following day Guillemot received a suspicious phone call. "Do you want to carry out an assignment from Lise to Madame Bruston?" the voice asked. Guillemot played dumb, and the voice answered irritably, "So you don't understand! Fine, we'll come."

It was 1:00 p.m. The soup kitchen had just finished serving the noon meal. Hugues Limonti collected his messages and fled. Moments later he passed Gestapo vehicles turning onto Rue Greneta.

Marcelle Guillemot raced through La Clairière, destroying evidence. A postwar interviewer recorded her description of the next harrowing moments:

> She barricaded herself on the second floor, closing all the doors and securing all the locks. She threw into the toilet all the identity cards, photos, etc. of the young *réfractaires* of the Oratoire that she was just finishing. She lit the boiler and burned the boxes holding the radio messages, newspapers, lists of Jews, etc.
>
> Over this time that the Gestapo was ringing the bell, knocking, telephoning. The unsympathetic concièrge herself tried to open the door with some keys. Having finished everything, and even having eaten a bit, Mlle. G. prepared to escape, judging that all was now in order. She almost made it downstairs, but her clothing snagged on a key—one she walked past a hundred times a day without snagging.
>
> This made her stop and think. Perhaps she could use another exit without being seen. She made her way to the skylight. She saw that the cleaners in the next building, by sheer chance, had left a window open that she could reach through

the skylight. She climbed out and tranquilly departed from 58 Rue Greneta, under the gaze of the concièrge who knew her. Mlle. G. warned her with a look, and she kept her silence magnificently. The Gestapo waited patiently at the exit of number 60![3]

Then the Gestapo came for the Vergaras. The pastor was warned in time and escaped, but his family did not. His wife, Marcelle, was held and interrogated for three months in Fresnes. The Gestapo also arrested seventeen-year-old Sylvain—little Larissa's dancing partner and the twin brother of Sylvie, the snipper of German uniforms. Sylvain was deported to Buchenwald, a second blow after Vergara's son-in-law, Jacques Bruston, was sent to Mauthausen.

For the past six months, Marcelle Guillemot had been juggling her roles as church social worker, MNCR supporter, and secret agent for the Gaullist resistance. Now she fled to the countryside. The arrests took her out of action as far as Paris was concerned, but she remained in touch with Hugues Limonti and carried out various services on his behalf.[4]

The children's escorts from the MNCR suffered a loss that month. Régine Grumberg was on her way to pick up some children to take into hiding when she noticed some police inspectors following her. They grabbed her as she was entering the Métro. Fortunately, she had followed protocol and wasn't carrying any compromising addresses.[5] She was sent to Drancy, then to Auschwitz.*

The Jewish resistance was also battered. The young Jewish militants, suffering from their families' deportations, launched increasingly violent attacks, on the principle of "an eye for an eye." The French police's Special Brigades responded by escalating their surveillance and arrests. As the losses mounted, the Jewish

---

* Mercifully, she survived the war.

underground's leaders searched their ranks for possible informers, fixing their attention on a new recruit for Solidarité. Lucienne
Goldfarb was a striking red-haired teenager who fit the profile of
the ideal volunteer, as the daughter of Polish Jewish parents detained
at Drancy. Then her associates learned of her intimate friendship
with a French policeman, which had coincided with dozens of arrests. Lucienne—aka Katia la Rouquine, or "Katy the Redhead"—
would profit from her relationship with the French police through
the occupation and beyond.[6]

Adam Rayski reported, "By late July nearly the entire Jewish leadership had fallen"—at least sixty individuals in all.[7] Only
a handful escaped; Léon Chertok and Rayski fled to the South.[8]
Sophie Schwartz owed her escape to an attack of appendicitis. She
had been hospitalized in a clinic under a false name; otherwise she
would surely have been arrested with the others.[9]

Over the month of July, three groups of critical partners in
Suzanne Spaak's rescue network had been crippled. Pastor Vergara
and Marcelle Guillemot were in hiding in the countryside. Sophie
Schwartz, Léon Chertok, and Adam Rayski had gone underground.
Jacques Grou-Radenez's Défense de la France had been decimated,
even if the printer himself was still at liberty.

The legal Jewish charities were attacked. In June the Gestapo
arrested David Rapoport, the head of children's services for the
Amelot Committee, and in July they came for the UGIF. The SS
had gotten wind that children had been disappearing from the
UGIF's facilities, and on July 13 the UGIF headquarters informed
its children's homes in Paris that "the German authorities demand
with all urgency the complete list of children currently in our centers, 'blocked' or not."[10] Ten days later the Gestapo arrested UGIF
official André Baur, Suzanne's possible source, along with his wife
and their four children, aged three to ten. The Baur family was held
in Drancy until December 17, then deported to Auschwitz and
gassed upon arrival. The week after Baur's arrest, the Gestapo came

for more than twenty women on the UGIF's children's staff, and they, too, were deported.

The rules had changed. Throughout the summer of 1943, the SS took over the mechanics of the arrests and deportations from the French. French policemen had tried to spare French Jews, but the Germans made no such distinctions.

In September the Gestapo came looking for Robert Debré and two of his associates. The German police had made several visits to his colleagues, but they fended off their questions. Debré was visiting his house in Touraine to review arrangements for hiding Jewish children and to explore the potential use of a nearby field to receive parachute drops from London.

The phone rang; it was Dexia, calling from his Paris office. "They're here." Debré didn't know what to do, but the countess advised him to return to Paris. He was examining a child in his clinic when the Gestapo returned. The countess and his servant held the police at bay while the doctor fled through the kitchen and out the back on an escape route to a prearranged hiding place nearby. An associate, the Baroness de la Chevrelière, coolly informed the police, "He's out on an emergency call and will return any minute." Stymied, the police left, stating that they would return. They did, thirteen times. As their fury mounted, they tore the curtains, ripped out the telephone wire, and smashed his possessions.[11]

Debré and his colleagues went underground. A friend in the Gaullist resistance procured forged identity and ration cards, and Debré shaved off his beard and mustache. The couple found refuge outside Paris with friends.

On a visit back to the city, Dexia was arrested and delivered to Gestapo headquarters. Trembling but summoning every ounce of her sangfroid, the countess demanded a chair. Then she proceeded to lecture the Germans. Yes, she was Debré's secretary, but he had vanished, she informed them. He was probably under arrest somewhere in the South. She had already been tried with the Musée de l'Homme conspiracy and imprisoned in Fresnes; didn't they know? The agents didn't know, and they were astonished that she would volunteer the information. Did they think anyone in her right mind, she demanded, would care to repeat the experience?

The Germans, impressed by her performance, released her that night, and she and Debré went deep underground. Both of them had sons fighting with the Gaullist resistance. That would have to do for now; others would need to take their place in the Jewish rescue network.[12]

The resistance circles were wounded but not destroyed. Rayski's hotheads from the FTP-MOI hit back in September, relying on an unlikely source of support: a French Resistance cell within the German navy. The relationship had begun with a twenty-one-year-old German telegraph operator. Hans Heisel had made friends with a French barber and a tailor, who turned out to be recruiting members for the FTP-MOI. As a result of their conversations, Heisel reported, "I realized that I was an accomplice of a state-organized gang of murderers. I didn't want to be, so I decided to join the resistance." Heisel recruited two other German sailors and began to prospect in facilities frequented by German soldiers, slipping anti-Nazi leaflets into toilet paper rolls and lifting guns from uniforms from swimming pool locker rooms.[13]

In September, Heisel received a visit from a resistance contact code-named "Mado."

"We need a gun urgently," she told him.

Heisel answered, "I can get one tomorrow."

"No, that's too late," she replied, "I must have it today." Heisel reluctantly handed over his service revolver. "That was really idiotic," he reflected later. "If [the Germans] had noticed me running around with an empty holster, I would have been in for it." After the war Heisel learned that the FTP-MOI had used his weapon to assassinate SS colonel Julius Ritter, the director of the despised STO forced labor program. Heisel approved, taking special pride that Leo

Kneler, a Jewish fellow German, took part in the attack.[14] Besides Kneler, the hit squad consisted of a Polish Jew, an Italian Communist, and a Spanish Republican.[15]

The assassination raised the profile of Jewish militants. Himmler took a personal interest in the investigation. Following Ritter's elaborate funeral at the Madeleine, the Gestapo informed Vichy officials, "Of 102 persons recently arrested as guilty of terrorist attacks, 52 were foreign Jews."[16] The Special Brigades intensified their surveillance, and three of Ritter's four attackers (all but Kneler) were captured and executed. The Germans resumed their reprisals, which had been suspended over the previous year. In October, fifty Frenchmen were shot in revenge for Ritter's death.

The remaining members of Défense de la France also expressed defiance. The arrests had been a major blow, but on September 30 the group published its thirty-ninth edition, titled "The Fruits of Hatred." It included the first photographs from concentration camps to appear in the French press, showing starving Greek Jewish children and the emaciated bodies of Russian prisoners piled in a pit. The paper reported the mass murder of Jews in Poland and the torture methods the Gestapo used in France. Publishing photographs was a feat. It had required Grou-Radenez's support to acquire the equipment and the technical ability, which the Jewish publications lacked.

The photos of the Jewish children had arrived through the Gaullist network: flown in from London, parachuted into Lyon, then passed on to Paris.[17] The photos of the Russian POWs had arrived several months earlier, via a Sorbonne professor who was a POW who hid them in a package sent back to France.

Jacques Grou-Radenez was proud of his apprentices; his star student, Charlotte Nadel, was a cofounder of the movement and ran the newspaper. In only two years, it had evolved from 5,000 copies of a primitive flyer to a serious newspaper with a circulation of 150,000, as well as numerous subsidiary publications and forgery operations. Its stories jolted its readers and provided a striking contrast to official propaganda. The same week *Défense de la France* published photos of the concentration camps, Vichy's lackey newspaper *Le Petit Parisien* reported, "English, Americans and Russians Want to Dominate Europe and Make Its Inhabitants Slaves, says Monsieur von Ribbentrop."

The "Fruits of Hatred" was a gesture of defiance, but it was also a strategic act. The students had possessed the camp photos for months but had held them back out of consideration for the families of French prisoners. Now they decided to publish, Charlotte Nadel explained, "to show the Gestapo that they hadn't beheaded our movement—to demonstrate that they hadn't arrested our leadership, and thereby exonerate the ones they had arrested."[18]

But following their bold move in September, Nadel decided that greater caution was in order. "I refused to maintain contacts with other movements, especially with Suzanne Spaak, with whom I had regular meetings in the garden of the Palais Royal. Spaak and her husband were involved in a Belgian intelligence network, and they also hid Jewish children with Jacques Grou-Radenez." In Nadel's judgment, the contact with Suzanne Spaak wasn't worth the risk.

Her precautions were not sufficient. Nadel herself was arrested the following year. By the end of the occupation, some two hundred members of Défense de la France would be deported or killed.[19]

Suzanne Spaak's position grew lonelier. She may have wondered, given the relentless pursuit of her coconspirators, why the surveillance teams of the Special Brigades had not found their way to her door.

13

flight

The Spaak family arrangements continued in their peculiar fashion. Suzanne and the children occupied the apartment at the Palais Royal. Claude usually stayed with Ruth, who had returned to Paris in July and rented a pied-à-terre over a couturier's shop off the Champs-Élysées.

"Our parents were never home," Pilette recalled. Suzanne still slipped out the door before dawn, riding the train to who-knew-where and creeping back at midnight. The apartment was haunted by a procession of anxious strangers. One "maid" stayed for months; a bright Jewish student tutored Pilette in math in return for hot meals until Suzanne found him a refuge in a seminary in Normandy. (Pilette claimed the math lessons were an utter failure.)[1]

School vacation ran from July to October. Suzanne sent Pilette to Belgium for the summer, which suited her fine. Her aunt Bunny Happé owned a large country house in the town of Limal, south of Brussels. "I was happy in Limal and miserable in Paris," Pilette recalled. Bunny gave her new dresses, and her house had a cook, a live-in maid, and gardeners who put fresh food on the table. The visit also gave Pilette a chance to spend time with her beloved grandmother Lorge, who had moved in with the Happés when the Germans took over her Brussels mansion. Bazou stayed in Paris with Ruth.

In Paris, the atmosphere was tense. French police officers spent the summer of 1943 rolling up resistance groups and helping the Gestapo's task force hunt down Allied intelligence agents. Leopold Trepper's network was high on their list. The Allied intelligence services had, in many respects, converged. The British and the Soviets had agreed to offer "every possible assistance in making contact with their respective agents" since 1941, and in late 1943 the new US intelligence service, the OSS, would initiate collaboration with the Soviets.[2] There was no doubt among the Allies and the French Resistance that if the Soviets crushed Germany on the eastern front, victory in the West would follow.

Leopold Trepper was in detention, but his network still operated, and the Rote Kapelle task force was dedicated to its destruction. Over the summer of 1943 it made rapid progress. Trepper's network had already lost a string of radio operators, including Harry and Mira Sokol. Fernand Pauriol had a better run of luck, building and operating clandestine transmitters. But in August 1943 the Gestapo lured him to Paris, arrested him, and sent him to Fresnes. Pauriol's interrogation was crueler than the "special treatment" Trepper received over his months in captivity.

Trepper's interrogators, like his other acquaintances, were impressed by his intelligence and sophistication. They dispatched three SS doctors to examine him, and an officer informed him that they "concluded, on the basis of anthropological criteria, that you aren't Jewish." Trepper maintained that he was. Finally a Gestapo search unearthed his authentic passport, listing his birthplace. The Gestapo sent investigators to the site, but the town's Jewish population had been wiped out the previous August.

Trepper's interrogator read the report aloud: "Neumart is *judenrein*. The records have all been burned. The cemetery has been destroyed and plowed up, so it is impossible to search the tombstones for the name of Trepper." This is how Leopold Trepper learned that his family had been exterminated: mother, siblings, aunts, uncles, cousins; forty-eight in all. He managed to conceal his emotions and received the news with a smile.[3]

That August a new Gestapo officer arrived from Berlin to oversee the Paris investigation. Heinz Pannwitz, thirty-two, was a baby-faced former Boy Scout who had worked directly under Reinhard Heydrich as a Gestapo and SS officer in Prague. Trepper ingratiated himself with Pannwitz and his men, tantalizing them by writing reports on his operations, naming members of his network, and setting up deceptive radio transmissions to Moscow. He later claimed that he wrote the messages in a code designed to alert the Soviet recipients, protecting Soviet intelligence interests rather than the hapless beings he sacrificed.

The Gestapo fanned out to arrest over a hundred of his agents and employees, many of whom were tortured and executed. Trepper avoided naming certain strategic contacts, above all those who might hold the keys to his future survival. These included Claude and Suzanne Spaak.

In mid-September Gestapo agents told Trepper they were on the verge of breaking the code, which would endanger both the operation and Trepper himself. He had to take action. He decided to exploit his friendly relationship with his Gestapo guard, a lumbering sad sack named Willy Berg, who suffered from chronic bellyaches. Trepper had told him he knew of a surefire remedy but withheld the details. Then, on September 13, he answered Berg's groans by volunteering to obtain the medication at the Pharmacie Bailly on the Rue de Rome. As the gullible Berg waited patiently in his car, Trepper entered the crowded drugstore and slipped out the back door.

Trepper thought the French Communist Party was his surest route to safety. His first step was to locate his young mistress, Georgie de Winter. She hadn't seen him for months, but immediately came to his aid. However, in order for her to help him, Trepper had to correct some falsehoods. Earlier he had told Georgie that he was working for British intelligence. Now he admitted that he was a Soviet intelligence officer and needed to establish contact with the French Communists.

Georgie followed his instructions. On September 17, Trepper succeeded in meeting with a Communist Party contact. They exchanged information, and the contact gave Trepper a cyanide pill in case things went wrong.

On September 18, the French police distributed wanted posters for Trepper illustrated with a Gestapo mug shot. The three-quarter view showed the suspect with a tense mouth and narrowed eyes.[4] The poster, placed in post offices across France, was captioned "Leader of a dangerous terrorist group."

> The person represented here is a foreigner who directs a group of foreign terrorists and who in recent months has continuously executed acts of sabotage against the installations of the French State. As a result, the provision of vital necessities to the French population has been compromised. It has been established that the group works in close collaboration with communist circles.

This was a fabrication. Trepper steered clear of military operations. His front companies were major suppliers to the German army. But the occupation authorities were continually trying to win public support by inflating the threat of terrorism.

Otherwise the text offered an accurate description, indicating that its authors had studied him closely:

Height 1m70. Stature: short and stocky. Broad back. Stiff pos-
ture. Rounded chest and head held back. Left eyebrow raised.
Eyes blue-gray. Birthmark on left side at cheekbone height.
Short, thick neck. Sometimes wears glasses. Slow pace with
small steps. Slightly overweight.

When walking, he points feet out [walks flat-footed].
Recently he was dressed in a blue suit without stripes, single
breasted with a single row of buttons. He wore a light gray
shirt with narrow dark stripes, a burgundy tie and low shoes.
Without hat or coat.

Trepper's walk was an interesting detail. The German and French
police knew that their quarries were adept at changing clothing, fa-
cial hair, and other aspects of their appearance, so they were trained
to recognize a subject's stride. (Some British agents put cardboard
in their heels to alter their gait.)[5]

Trepper and Georgie de Winter spent a week moving among
her friends' apartments, aware that the Gestapo was close behind.
On Saturday, September 25, Trepper sent his mistress to the Spaaks'
apartment to ask for help.

Claude recalled:

A very pretty woman called at my home in Paris and said she
had been sent by Trepper. She said to me, "He would like your
wife to go and see him at once."

Trepper was hiding out in an apartment in western Paris, she added.
"He can't leave because the Gestapo is looking for him." Claude
gave her the money he had been keeping for Trepper and set off to
see him.[6]

There was obviously some danger, so I preferred to go myself.
This was in Suresnes, in a big building. He opened the door

and threw himself into my arms. Then he said, "The Gestapo is on my heels. Can you help me?"[7]

Trepper told Claude he needed to get back in touch with the French Communist Party, this time at a higher level, but his channels of communication were cut off. He needed an intermediary. The Soviets told their spies to keep their distance from local Communist parties, and Trepper was forbidden to meet with French party representatives more than once a year. Furthermore, the Communist leadership had gone deep underground following the attrition of the previous summer. Trepper believed that Suzanne's contacts at Solidarité could help. The Jewish members of the party leadership maintained an intense interest in the children's rescue operations.

Suzanne's role took on new implications. The same web of contacts that had saved the lives of Jewish children represented Trepper's best hope for escape. Her network connected to the London-based Gaullist intelligence bureau (BCRA)* and wove through British intelligence, the MNCR, and various Communist organizations. Suzanne agreed to contact Léon Chertok and Charles Lederman.

Although she didn't yet admit it, Suzanne was highly exposed. According to Claude, "She received several warnings that she ignored. Once, for example, a priest came to tell her that she should be careful, she had been reported to the local police station."[8]

The Spaak children were unaware of these developments. At the end of the vacation, Pilette wrote to her father from Limal, asking if she could stay. Claude replied, "If you want to stay you can, but we'd be very sad, especially now that Ruth is in Paris. We want to make a fresh start being a family." She reluctantly boarded the train for Paris.

---

* Bureau Central de Reseignements et d'Action (Central Bureau of Intelligence and Action).

Trepper was nervous about prolonging his stay in Suresnes. On September 26 he showed up at the Spaaks' apartment, and Pilette answered the door. He tried to remain calm. "Would you tell your father Monsieur Henri is here?" he asked. The girl conveyed his message to Claude. To her amazement, her father leaped out of bed "like a jack-in-the-box" and, still in his dressing gown, pulled Trepper into the library.[9] For the next three nights he slept in Pilette's bed while she camped out in her mother's sitting room.[10]

Trepper asked the couple to help send word to Moscow via London that the Germans were about to break their radio code. Suzanne's friends in the Gaullist resistance had radio contact with London. With La Clairière's activities suspended and Robert Debré in hiding, the most direct route to the Gaullists was through Jacques Grou-Radenez. She dispatched the faithful Bazou with a message to the printer's home.

The Spaaks had moved mountains to help Trepper, but he wasn't sure they suited his purpose. He found Suzanne's rescue operations especially inconvenient:

> In spite of the great confidence I had in the Spaaks, the fact was that this was the least safe of all the places I had hidden since my escape. I knew that both the Spaaks belonged to the resistance, but at that time I did not suspect the degree to which Suzanne, in particular, was involved in a variety of underground activities.
>
> In 1942, she had devoted herself to rescuing Jewish children, and had been a militant in the National Movement Against Racism. But I did not realize that by September 1943, at the time she took me in, she was also working with several Gaullist and communist organizations. She took part in the most perilous actions, without regard for danger. Consequently she was very much exposed. We decided it was wiser to part company.[11]

For Trepper, "parting company" meant taking advantage of other members of her rescue network. First Suzanne took Trepper to the Oratoire du Louvre. She had remained in touch with church elders after Pastor Vergara's and Marcelle Guillemot's flight. Despite the increased risk, parish families continued to hide Jewish children, and deacon Maurice-William Girardot continued to deliver funds to Suzanne at the Palais Royal.[12]

Now Suzanne asked the Oratoire to harbor another Jewish fugitive, this one a full-grown Soviet agent, and his young mistress. The pastor agreed, though with reservations. Trepper and Georgie de Winter spent the night of September 28 as guests of the Oratoire, but they were sternly required to sleep in separate rooms and depart at dawn.[13] They were back at the Spaaks' the following night. Trepper gave them a colorful account of his adventures, emphasizing the importance of the intelligence he'd gathered. Next, Suzanne found a place for him at La Maison Blanche in Bourg-la-Reine, a suburb south of Paris where she had found two boarding houses to use as stops on her underground railroad.

Again, Trepper considered Suzanne's rescue operations a personal inconvenience. "I noticed that several of the boarders seemed to be having as much trouble as I did in playing the role of peaceful old men," he reported. He feared that that the Jews in hiding would endanger him, but events would prove just the opposite.[14]

As Trepper bided his time, the Gestapo task force worked its way through Georgie de Winter's circle of friends. Each arrest and interrogation prompted another round of arrests, leading the Gestapo closer to its quarry.

Trepper decided it was safer to separate from Georgie de Winter. He knew that as long as she relied on her own circle, she was leaving a trail that the Gestapo would find easy to follow. Nonetheless, Georgie continued to tap her friends for places to stay; more surprisingly, Trepper also asked them for help. One of them was an elderly widow who went by the name of Madame May.

She agreed to move into the retirement home in Bourg-la-Reine as Trepper's "nurse" and carry messages to the Spaaks at the Palais Royal.[15]

Trepper was desperate to reach the French Communists, especially Édouard "Arek" Kowalski, the leader of the FTP-MOI's immigrant fighting units.[16] He had met Kowalski before the war, and Léon Chertok knew how to reach him.

Chertok wasn't easy to find. Over the previous six months, scores of his friends and fellow activists had fallen. He wrote, "One knew that Paris was the most dangerous place because of the French police in the Special Brigade, the 'scientific' police from the Préfecture. The Gestapo could never have done the job themselves."[17] By this time, over a hundred members of the Special Brigades had been assigned to Paris, charged with the pursuit of only sixty partisans from the FTP-MOI. Chertok's security restrictions were more severe than ever.

Now the Spaaks gave Chertok what he called "the biggest scare of my life." One day in October, Claude asked the doctor to meet him at La Trinité, an ornate church in western Paris. Chertok was thunderstruck by what Claude had to say:

> There he told me an *abracadabrante* ["preposterous"] story: a Russian spy, head of an international network, captured by the Gestapo but who succeeded in escaping from the Pharmacie Bailly's back door, who's hiding out in a boarding house in Bourg-la-Reine, and wants to meet with the Central Committee of the Party![18]

Chertok had long trusted Suzanne, but this was his first encounter with Claude. He knew only that he was a writer and the brother of the Belgian minister-in-exile, Paul-Henri Spaak. Chertok tried to put him off, but Claude insisted that Suzanne knew that Chertok could reach the committee. Chertok was aghast. "I was sure that they had been taken for a ride by a pathological liar," he wrote. "But they were old enough to know where it could lead."[19]

Chertok reported to Charles Lederman several times a week. The lawyer listened to what Chertok had to say and passed it on. It turned out that the tale was true. A few days later, Lederman told Chertok that a meeting between Trepper and Kowalski had been arranged for October 22.

Unknown to them, Trepper's plans had been derailed. The previous Sunday morning, the Gestapo had arrested the elderly Madame May. She had fallen into a trap laid by the infamous "French Gestapo," known as the "Bonny-Lafont Gang," which ran a torture shop at 93 Rue Lauriston in western Paris.

Madame May found the Gestapo agents waiting in her apartment. Heinz Pannwitz, the officer in charge, found her to be a "very resolute and energetic woman": "She screamed at us, kicked me quite vigorously in the leg and hit me over the head with the handle of her umbrella."[20] She was carted away for interrogation and held out as long as she could, but when the Germans threatened to murder her son, a prisoner of war, she surrendered Trepper's hiding place and Spaaks' address.

Trepper had been scheduled to meet with her, and when she didn't appear he guessed what had happened. On Sunday, October 17, he set off by taxi from Bourg-la-Reine to warn the Spaaks. As he climbed the stairs to their apartment he clutched his cyanide capsule tightly in his hand in case the Gestapo was waiting.

Claude, who was on his own, answered the door. Trepper regarded him anxiously.

"Are you alone?" he asked. "Or are they here?"

Trepper realized from Claude's calm demeanor that the Gestapo had not yet arrived. For the moment, the cyanide was unnecessary. He felt, he recalled later, as though the blood had begun to flow through his veins once more.

"Your family must disappear," Trepper told him. "The Gestapo could be here any minute."

"What about Suzette?" Claude responded. Suzanne had gone to Orléans for the day to pick up some blank forged documents. She was due to return with several dozen ration cards hidden in her girdle, the possession of which was punishable by death. There were other people to consider, such as the woman who had hidden Trepper along with her Jewish charges in Bourg-la-Reine. Trepper had placed them all in danger.

Claude walked Trepper to the door. "Where will you go?"

"I don't know," he replied, and left. He spent the night shivering on a park bench.

That evening, in a house in a northern suburb, the Gestapo arrived to arrest Georgie de Winter.

At the Palais Royal, Claude prepared the family's evacuation. Claude gave Pilette the bundle of gold coins and told her to take them to Ruth's flat off the Champs-Élysées. She left them with Ruth, saying, "Father wanted me to tell you that mother's going to come stay with you."

Pilette returned home and found the large leather suitcase Mira Sokol had left with Suzanne. She packed it with items she thought her mother would want—some clothes and a few pieces of jewelry—then added some clothes for herself and Bazou.

Suzanne arrived at the Gare de Lyon around 6:00 p.m. Claude was waiting to intercept her. She tried to make light of the matter, but Claude cut her off. "We have no right to risk the lives of our children." She finally agreed to go into hiding, but first she had to warn her contacts and make arrangements for her absence. She told Claude she would meet him and the children at Ruth's.

After she left, Claude enlisted Pilette to help him go through the apartment, starting with Suzanne's desk in the vestibule. They ransacked it for incriminating evidence, incinerating it as they went along. Well after midnight, Claude stopped short in front of the huge bookcase at the entry. He looked at Pilette. "Do you think?"

He picked a book off the shelf, opened it, and gasped. "*Nom de Dieu.*" To his horror, a flurry of paper fell out containing names, addresses, and forged documents from various resistance movements. He picked up another volume, and underground tracts spilled to the floor. They went through each book, page by page, working until four in the morning. Claude piled the evidence in the stove to burn and sent Pilette to bed.

The next day, Pilette and Bazou were told to attend school as though nothing had happened. Claude stopped by the Belgian consulate to request authorization for his wife and children to visit their family in Belgium, and Suzanne arranged a hurried meeting with Peggy Camplan from the MNCR.[21]

Suzanne was directly responsible for forty-five children; now she entrusted Camplan with the records of their identities and their whereabouts.[22] But this was only part of the challenge, as Suzanne was an essential thread in a network that served hundreds more. She had been responsible for delivering some 50,000 to 60,000 francs a month for the children's upkeep, and Camplan and her associates would be hard-pressed to replace the funds. But Suzanne was confident that this was a temporary arrangement; she told her friend that she expected to be back to work as soon as the threat blew over.

Trepper continued to press Suzanne to help him contact London, and Jacques Grou-Radenez agreed to send a Gaullist representative to meet Trepper at a church in Auteuil. But as Trepper approached the church he spotted a black Citroën, the Gestapo's vehicle of choice. He fled and telephoned the boardinghouse in Bourg-la-Reine. A stranger answered. Now Trepper knew that the Gestapo was only a step away.

On October 19, Claude accompanied Suzanne and the children to the Gare du Nord, and stood with them on the platform waiting for the train to Brussels. Pilette regarded the other passengers.

"You could feel the fear in the air," she recalled. Nonetheless, Pilette thought her parents looked relaxed. "I remember the two of them talking before the train started to move."

Pilette recalled:

He said that should there ever be the necessity to correspond between the two of them, if he meant what he was asking, he would sign the letter "Toutou" (a nickname he had when he was very young—in common language it's the name of a nice little dog). And if he did not mean it he would sign it "Claude." And she would sign "Suzette," but if she did not mean it, it would be "Suzanne."

The atmosphere was not as tense as it could have been. I truly believed that I would be back before the end of the month. So did mother. Dad always seemed to be so prudent and certainly mother went through life light-hearted. The reason to go to Belgium was to cool off and be sure that everything was all right before continuing.[23]

Claude waved farewell to his family as the train pulled out of the station. The journey from Paris to Brussels was arduous in wartime, lasting from seven in the morning to six in the evening, but the Spaaks had made it before. The children knew there would be a long stop at the border, requiring everyone to leave the train for it to be searched. Passengers waited fretfully in line to show their papers. With a single nod from the police, an unfortunate soul would be hauled off to a room to be undressed, and some would not return.

Claude went back to the Palais Royal. He knew it was risky, but he had arranged for Léon Chertok to call at noon, and he had to be warned. At noon the phone rang. Claude picked up the receiver and blurted, "We've been burned. No one should budge." He hung up and returned to Ruth Peters's flat.

Chertok was flabbergasted. It meant that the Gestapo had laid a trap for Trepper, who was scheduled to meet with Kowalski, a key leader of the Jewish resistance. "No one should budge" was an impossible demand. Kowalski was on his way to the meeting, and his arrest would be catastrophic. Chertok and Lederman set out for Bourg-la-Reine, hoping to intercept Kowalski in time. Finally Chertok spied him on a street ahead. He quickened his pace to catch up with him and hissed, "*Fous le camp, Édouard, fous le camp!*" ("Get the fuck out of here!")[24]

Claude met Trepper on the evening of October 21 at La Trinité, both men visibly trembling with fear. Trepper was weak and exhausted from sleeping rough. After they parted, he hailed a bicycle taxi and convinced the elderly cyclist to give him shelter for the night. The next morning, he telephoned the Spaaks' apartment at the Palais Royal. A woman answered, claiming to be Claude's secretary. Trepper knew that Claude didn't have a secretary. The Gestapo had arrived, and Claude, who was staying at Ruth's, didn't know.

Claude's birthday fell on October 22, and he was feeling cheerful. He and Ruth were planning to dine with his brother Charles and his wife, and he was in the mood for a good bottle of wine. Claude told Ruth that he was going back to the Palais Royal to fetch one, but, concerned, she persuaded him to call ahead.

Claude had set up a code with the maid; if she addressed him as "*Cher Monsieur*," all was well, but if she called him just "*Monsieur*," there was trouble.

He telephoned. "All is well, *Monsieur*," she blurted. "*Certainement, Monsieur, oui, Monsieur.*" Then he heard her ask someone, "*C'est tout?*" followed by the sound of a blow. The line went dead.

Claude later learned that the maid had spoken from his living room surrounded by a squad of armed Gestapo agents.

14

all saints' day

Suzanne and her children arrived in Brussels on the evening of October 19 and went straight to her family. It no longer felt like her city. The Germans had taken over her mother's mansion for the use of their female military personnel (known as the "little gray mice"). Her sisters and their husbands were treading carefully, doing business with the Germans when necessary, helping the Belgian resistance when they could.

Suzanne decided it would be wise to split up; no one had room for all three of them. She stayed with Claude's mother, her beloved role model, and sent Bazou to Limal with Bunny and Pilette to the home of Claude's sister Pichenette. Suzanne took minimal precautions; she even attended a public concert at the Palais des Beaux-Arts with her sister-in-law Marguerite, Paul-Henri's wife. Suzanne told Pilette that they were being overly careful; the Gestapo would never look for her in Brussels. She seemed to have a magical belief in her own invulnerability.

On Sunday, October 24, Suzanne and Pilette went to lunch at the home of Suzanne's sister and brother-in-law, the Fontaines, on the outskirts of Brussels. Halfway through the meal, they heard a knock at the door and the conversation came to an abrupt halt. An elderly neighbor of Suzanne's mother-in-law arrived with chilling news: That afternoon, the Gestapo had arrived at Madame Spaak's house asking for Suzanne. She had played dumb, and they had left. She had dispatched her friend by streetcar to warn her daughter-in-law.

Suzanne and her relations went into intense deliberation. The security of the entire family was at stake, and Suzanne must disappear. The question was how.

One of the dinner guests, a blond young man in the Belgian resistance, offered to help. He had arrived on his motorcycle and had a studio apartment in central Brussels. He volunteered to hide Suzanne and Pilette until the family decided what to do.

It was nearing curfew, and the three rushed out of the house to the motorbike parked outside. The young man helped them climb astride, Suzanne in front and Pilette in back, then took off for his studio. A few days later Suzanne told Pilette, "You're a big girl, you can go on your own," and sent her to stay in Limal with Bazou.

Suzanne's quandary was more difficult, and it fell to her sister's husband, Maurice Fontaine, to address it. He owned a hunting estate in the depths of the Ardennes Forest that included a gamekeeper's cottage. Suzanne was conveyed to the remote outpost, where she waited nervously as the Gestapo investigation swept up her friends and relations.

Suzanne was wrong about the limits of the Gestapo's reach. Pannwitz had been busy in Paris, filling his detention centers with Leopold Trepper's acquaintances, whether or not they had any knowledge of his espionage. He had the full cooperation of the Brussels Gestapo.* The danger extended beyond the Spaaks. The

---

* The Gestapo's Brussels headquarters were located at 347 Avenue Louise, directly across the street from Suzanne's mother's mansion at 368A.

Gestapo had posted surveillance outside the Palais Royal, and the members of Suzanne's rescue network were in their sights. When Oratoire's deacon Maurice-William Girardot came by to drop off donations for the Jewish children, the police pounced. He would spend three months in prison.

The Gestapo also came for Odette and Fernand Béchard. Odette had been the first Oratoire parishioner to join Entr'aide. Now Suzanne's connection to Trepper set up a chain reaction that led to her door. "The Germans came to arrest us," Odette wrote later. "I had left the evening before, having been warned. My husband barely escaped and our children were dispersed. That that's how, with great regret, I had to discontinue my [rescue] activity."[1]

With Girardot's arrest, the Jewish children lost access to the Oratoire's financial support. With the flight of the Béchards, they lost both donors and an active escort. If Léon Chertok and Charles Lederman hadn't been so quick to act, Trepper would have compromised the entire Jewish resistance.

Claude Spaak took precautions on his own behalf. He and Ruth packed up her studio and found separate hiding places. Claude eventually got in touch with a playwright friend who contacted his surgeon brother, who lent the couple the maid's room in his house in Saint-Cloud—the same one Claude and Suzanne had shared when they first moved to Paris. Saint-Cloud was quiet and out of the way, and their friends there helped them keep out of sight.

Suzanne's family expected the Gestapo to interrogate her children. Bazou was only twelve. His uncle Milo Happé, never dreaming of Suzanne's practices in Paris, instructed him to simply answer their questions. This instruction, faithfully followed, would have fatal consequences.

Pilette presented more of a problem. She had disappeared with Suzanne and needed a cover story. Suzanne's sister and sister-in-law spent hours on the phone concocting a tale: "I was supposed to say that I had been given the maid's room in the attic. I had sneaked out and gone to the movies, and I was afraid of being punished so I stayed out all night." Pilette found her cover story absurd. "Remember, it was the cold, rainy, dark end of October! I remember the two of them talking at length about which film I could have seen and where." Her aunt Bunny coached her on the plot of the film until she had it memorized.

Pilette was unenthusiastic about the ruse—"I must have been playing a half wit!"—as well as alarmed. "I knew they would be coming to pick me up, but I couldn't run away without harming my brother and grandmother." Pilette wasn't afraid of just the Gestapo; she had heard horror stories about juvenile detention and was terrified by what could happen at the hands of the "*mauvais enfants.*"[2]

Pilette's aunts called the Gestapo and told them their wayward niece had returned from her unlikely adventure and was going to be punished. Before they arrived, Pilette put on her favorite blouse that her mother had sewn for her, decorated with white rickrack on the collar. Then Bunny took the girl to her dressing room and applied rouge around her eyes to make her look as though she'd been crying.

Suzanne's sisters had reasons to be fearful. One was the complication of a downed British flyer the Happés had been sheltering. Over the course of the Gestapo's first visit, he had hidden for eight hours in a large bread oven. Milo Happé's nerves were already raw. He was an anxious man who spent his evenings scanning the nighttime sky for bombers. He walked a delicate line; his cigarette sales to the Germans were rewarded with permission to keep a car and purchase the gasoline to run it, but he also donated money and cigarettes to a nearby monastery that helped resistance fighters.

The Gestapo made the rounds, arresting Claude's sister, Pichenette, her husband, Jean Masson, and their nineteen-year-old son, Paul, as well as Paul-Henri's wife, Marguerite.

Late in the morning of November 1, All Saints' Day, the Gestapo came to Limal. They surveyed the family and singled out Pilette. They asked her some initial questions, then told her to pack her bag. She used Mira Sokol's good leather suitcase she had brought from Paris. The agents promised the family they would take her to her grandmother Spaak's.

Pilette recalled:

> I came down with my suitcase packed. Everyone was waiting by the front door, even the maids. I said good-bye to all of them, but Bazou was nowhere. I looked for him and found him all alone and crying in the bathroom. At that very moment our fate was sealed; I really fell in love with my brother, and nothing will ever separate us.
>
> The fact that I had my suitcase with me with everything I owned made the departure very definite. I felt that I had "gone," with no one to know where I would be. No one talked. It was cold. I was seated in the back of a car between two men. I remember arriving in Brussels; the night was wet, and the leaves on the ground sparkled when the tram went over them. It was sinister.

Rudolf Rathke, the burly Gestapo agent who dropped her off at her grandmother's, told Pilette she had to report back the next morning. Her grandmother was surprised to see her but took her in and lovingly cooked her an egg—the best thing she had ever tasted.

The following day Pilette left, accompanied by her grandmother's elderly friend, and equipped with a bar of soap and a towel in case of an extended stay. The Gestapo agents questioned her for a few hours, then sent her back to her grandmother. That same day, they arrested Suzanne's sister Teddy Fontaine and her husband, Maurice.

Pilette's grandmother packed a box of food donated by friends for their relatives in custody. These were luxuries by occupation standards: wrinkled yellow apples, sardines, and other rarities. Pilette's eyes widened at the sight of Godiva chocolates, an unheard-of extravagance in wartime Brussels. Her grandmother shooed her away. "Those are for the people in prison."

The next day the Gestapo called and told her to come pick up some paperwork. Instead, SS officer Heinz Pannwitz detained her. "At first he tried to be nice and gentlemanly," Pilette recalled, "but then he started shouting. To his left a soldier on one knee was aiming a machine pistol at me. The officer screamed like a mad puppet. He slapped me and at one point he rushed at me and punched my shoulder."

"Do you know Trepper?" Pannwitz demanded. "Was he on the train with you?" Pilette was rattled, but she kept her head and gave nothing away.

Rudolf Rathke was gentler. As he waited with her between interrogations, he turned on the radio and adjusted the dial. When he reached the BBC, he paused for a moment, regarded her apologetically, and kept turning. At the end of the afternoon, Pilette sat alone watching the Gestapo office workers go home for the day. Rathke came in and told her they would take her to prison as soon as they had a car. He handed her a phone and told her to call her grandmother.

The Gestapo agents drove her to Saint-Gilles prison, constructed in the nineteenth century to resemble a massive medieval fortress. By the time Pilette arrived, everything had been locked up for the night. She passed through a huge rotunda that reverberated to the sound of metal doors, heavy boots, and barked commands. The guards took her up to a second-floor cell, flipped on a light switch, and opened the door. Her aunts Marguerite and Pichenette were in the cell, sitting on straw mattresses.

Her father's sister Pichenette said, "What are you doing here?" Laughing, Pilette answered, "I came to say hello." To her amazement, they believed her. Pichenette pointed a finger at the door and said, "*Pars—tout de suite!*" ("Out—now!"), thinking she had a choice. The guards brought in another straw mattress and a thread-bare blanket and told Pilette she had two minutes to undress and go to bed.

Pilette's mother was hiding in the Ardennes, and her father and his mistress had disappeared, but the family grapevine still functioned. Claude's mother was friendly with a woman named Ventia who had been Claude's lover when he worked at the Palais des Beaux-Arts in Brussels. She was in touch with a friend of his in Choisel named Monsieur Brousse—the only person who knew Claude's whereabouts—and he passed the word. This was how Claude Spaak learned that his daughter had been imprisoned by the Gestapo and was being interrogated about his activities.

The Nazis frequently practiced *Sippenhaft*: arresting family members of suspects as hostages and for blackmail. They rounded up more Spaak relations, over a dozen in all. The family was concerned for Suzanne's nephew, who was of an age to be shipped off to Germany for forced labor.

There were more secrets: the Spaaks maintained contact with Paul-Henri in London. His position linked him to both the Belgian resistance and the Allied command, and his son Fernand served in the British navy. Before his wife, Marguerite, went into German custody, she warned her teenage daughters, "Remember—you know nothing about anything!"

Pilette's interrogation ended, and she realized she was being held as a hostage. Unlike other prisoners, she wasn't allowed to receive visitors or walk around the prison courtyard. She was hungry: "The food was pretty bad, mostly soup with peels, ladled out by prostitutes." But the day after her incarceration, her grandmother's package arrived, and Pilette devoured the Godiva chocolates.

On November 9, Pilette's aunt Pichenette was taken away for questioning. Suzanne's brother-in-law Maurice Fontaine was already in the Gestapo vehicle. Upon their return, Pichenette noticed that his face was flushed, and he stayed behind in the car. She guessed that he had talked. The next day, Pichenette learned that "another Madame Spaak" had been arrested.

It is likely that the Gestapo threatened Maurice Fontaine that if the family didn't surrender Suzanne, all of them would face the consequences. His wife and son were in custody. Family members believe that he broke down under pressure and agreed to take his interrogators to Suzanne's hiding place in the Ardennes.

The Gestapo agents parked the car near a bridge behind some foliage. Fontaine walked down the steep hill approaching the cottage and Suzanne came out to meet him. Fontaine told her about the arrests, and she answered that she would turn herself in to free her family. He didn't tell her that the Germans were waiting for her just across the bridge.

Pilette had no idea that her mother had been brought to Saint-Gilles, but she noticed that her aunts were unusually tense. She would tap-dance in her cell to pass the time, and one day her aunt told her sharply to stop. Later she wondered if her aunt wanted to spare her mother the pain of hearing her familiar steps.

On November 10, Rudolf Rathke signed a memorandum stating that Suzanne Spaak had been taken into "preventive detention" at Saint-Gilles and would soon be transferred. He took her to the station to board the train under guard, bound for the Fresnes prison in Paris. As they waited on the platform, Suzanne slipped off her engagement ring, a platinum band with a small pearl, and asked Rathke to give it to her daughter. (Pilette would wear the ring for decades until the pearl wore away to a grain of sand.) Then Suzanne told Rathke, "I forgive the man who gave me up."

Shortly afterward, Maurice and Teddy Fontaine were released.

The Gestapo was not finished, however. Bazou had been brought in twice for interrogation, under his uncle's instructions to tell them about everything he knew except Leopold Trepper. The agent told Bazou that his mother had run away with a lover named Trepper, and his father had asked them to help find her, but Bazou didn't blink. Then the agent took another approach. As Bazou recalled:

> The Boche interrogator read me a list of names that included Trepper's. I pretended I didn't know it, and the others on it I actually didn't know—except for a certain Grou-Radenez, whom I had met many times because Maman entrusted me with messages that I took to him so he could transmit them to London by radio.
>
> At that time the Germans, aided by the French police, often rounded up people on the streets. Since children were spared, Maman gave me these messages to give to Grou-Radenez.[3]

On November 12, the Gestapo came for Jacques Grou-Radenez: father of five, protector of Jewish children, and master printer for the largest underground newspaper in France. Then they came for his wife, Madeleine Legrand. She wrote later:

> Seven men in raincoats. Seven goons with their hands in their pockets, and their pockets containing revolvers.
>
> "German police. Madame (they tried to be polite, forgetting their hats, of course), we've come to conduct a search because your husband is distributing Communist propaganda."
>
> But this astonishes me, because we're not Communists. So, why?
>
> Why? It doesn't matter. They have us now.[4]

Legrand was taken to the Gestapo headquarters on Rue des Saussaies. Her husband was tortured, and both of them were transferred to Fresnes and held for trial.

The Gestapo agents were pleased to have Suzanne Spaak in custody, but they were more interested in her husband, whom they regarded as the likelier conspirator and bait for their quarry, Leopold Trepper.

The arrests in Paris continued. Claude's brother Charles and his pregnant wife, Claudie, were next on the list. Charles, on contract for the Germans' Continental Films, was midway through a script of the Georges Simenon novel *Les Caves du Majestic* (*The Cellars of the Majestic*). The murder mystery took place in the opulent Paris hotel, which was currently requisitioned as the headquarters of the German high command.* Charles was struggling with the screenplay—the Germans had ordered him to change the main characters from Americans to neutral Swedes, which obliged him to alter other elements of the plot.

The Gestapo consigned Charles to Fresnes as well, more as a means to get to his brother than for any information he had. His German bosses from Continental were livid; their production was under way and they needed their script. A representative visited him in detention. "It's evident that the murderer isn't the same as the one in the novel, but it's no less evident that you're the only one who knows what it's about. So, Monsieur Spaak, would you please give us the key to the mystery and tell us who the killer is?"[5]

Spaak used his unfinished screenplay to win concessions: improved rations, writing materials, and cigarettes—but no matches. The tobacco addict sat stewing in his cell until he finally asked his guard, "*Feuer, bitte.*"

Continental sent assistants to Fresnes every day to pick up the new pages covered with Charles's tiny handwriting.† His wife was

---

* The Majestic, located on Avenue Kléber in the sixteenth arrondissement, is now the Hotel Peninsula.

† *Les Caves du Majestic* finally premiered in France in October 1945, six months after Germany's surrender. Charles had written the first screenplay Continental produced under the occupation as well as *Majestic*, the last.

imprisoned for three months; he was held for five. For the rest of his life, the only explanation he offered for his detention was that "his younger brother and his wife were involved in resistance activities and were threatened as a result," never hinting at his contributions to the upkeep of Suzanne's Jewish children.[6]

Suzanne entered the women's wing of the "factory of despair." If Saint-Gilles resembled a medieval castle keep, Fresnes was an industrial-age horror, constructed at the turn of the century on the so-called telephone-pole design, with cellblocks branching off from a main corridor. (New York's Rikers Island was another example.)

There were currently 1,200 cells for males and a separate section for 300 female prisoners. The usual population of thieves and pimps had swollen with the addition of hundreds of political prisoners: authors of tracts, scribblers of graffiti, and collectors of airdrops. Its female inmates had included members of the Musée de l'Homme group, including the Countess de la Bourdonnaye and the students from Défense de la France, including General de Gaulle's niece Geneviève, who had barely escaped imprisonment with the Musée de l'Homme. Suzanne and Geneviève de Gaulle would be neighbors in the women's block for several months before Geneviève was deported to Ravensbrück.*

Political prisoners in Fresnes could be held for days, weeks, or months. They were shuttled to the Gestapo headquarters on Rue des Saussaies at a moment's notice for interrogation—often, but not always, accompanied by torture. The Gestapo favored a form of water torture that involved holding the prisoner's head under freezing water to the point of drowning. Their chambers were full of bathtubs requisitioned from the homes of Jews and arrestees across Paris for this purpose.

---

* Geneviève de Gaulle survived to become a leading reformer in French politics.

Suzanne's Children

The common criminals in Fresnes usually stayed on-site to serve out their sentences, but for most politicals sentenced by German military courts, Fresnes was a way station to a darker destination. For many, including the gallant men of the Musée de l'Homme, the next stop was the firing squad at Mont-Valérien. (One Marxist philosopher shouted his last words to his German firing squad: "*Imbéciles, c'est pour vous que je meurs!*"—"Imbeciles, it's for you that I die!")

Other political prisoners were deported to German concentration camps—generally the men to Buchenwald and the women to Ravensbrück. There they frequently perished from starvation, exhaustion, and disease, the women at a far higher rate than the men.

Over the summer and fall of 1943, Fresnes also collected a number of SOE agents, many of them female radio operators and couriers. The men's blocks accumulated Allied crew members shot down over France. Airmen occupied a dangerous middle ground between POWs and political prisoners, especially bomber crews captured wearing civilian clothes. The Germans designated these men *Terrorflieger* and treated them similarly to SOE agents.

Suzanne underwent extensive questioning. The record of her interrogation has not been found. It was initiated by Heinz Pannwitz only days after he had questioned her two children in Brussels. Pannwitz was aware that Suzanne was the sister-in-law of the Belgian minister and held special value as a hostage.

The French author Gilles Perrault later recorded Pannwitz's claim that he had gone easy on her and had taken measures to prove it:

He asked two friends, both of them war correspondents from the German army, to attend all of Suzanne Spaak's

interrogations, so they could eventually testify that he had behaved correctly. This was a flagrant violation of the task force's
requirements for secrecy, but the chief considered it a reasonable precaution for the future.[7]

After the war, Pannwitz gave extensive interviews to the CIA in
which he described Suzanne's interrogation.

She talked openly and freely, withholding nothing in the belief that we already knew too much. He testimony agreed
with the facts as we knew them. What we did not know and
learned from her was that she had supported the SOKOLs,
she claimed, out of pity. She had sent a message through her
contacts to her brother-in-law (Paul Henri SPAAK) concerning TREPPER and had arranged with TREPPER to use this
channel of escape.

Suzanne knew that Trepper's operation had been rolled up, and
that she was giving nothing of value away. On that count she was
secure.

But the Gestapo officers had no idea that the gracious lady
sitting in their office held the key to numerous resistance groups,
as well as the directory to a network sheltering hundreds of Jewish
children.

Suzanne's genius lay in convincing the Gestapo that she was
utterly inconsequential. Pannwitz observed:

In spite of her involvement with TREPPER, Mme. SPAAK
was a very likeable woman who made an unforgettable impression. She was a serious, calm woman who looked at everyone with her large, protruding eyes in a composed fashion.
Obviously she had followed her parlor-pink sympathies.

Suzanne's Children

Pannwitz regarded Suzanne as a lady of leisure.

> She regarded all of her actions as an intellectual game and could never bring herself to sacrifice her comfortable living to become an effective and active worker for any cause. She was above all an artist with very modern taste in painting, which the pictures, painted by her and hung in her apartment, indicated.[8]

In other words, Suzanne convinced the Gestapo that, instead of devoting herself to rescue and resistance, she spent her time dabbing the paintings that hung in her home, among them the two dozen Magrittes.

Now her long months of waiting began. The cells at Fresnes were spartan and cramped. A postwar visitor described them as resembling

> a large, immobile ship. The 1500 cells are identical, naked. A mounted shelf, a chair on a chain, a comfort station in the corner (the word doesn't work, there is no comfort in Fresnes), a bare bulb, and four walls. Four white walls to write on, four cold walls to talk to, damp walls on which to complain.[9]

The registers of the prison were destroyed at the end of the war, but the walls bore witness to the life within. One stated, "Arrived July 7, 1943, condemned to death January 1944. . . . Juliette."[10] "Juliette" was the nom de guerre of Huguette Prunier, who cheered other inmates with stories of her husband and children. There were also messages of contempt: "*Les Boches sont foutus,*" wrote Monique. "The Germans are fucked." Allied airmen scribbled messages in the margins of a book called *Wild Justice*: "If you are a First Lieu. in the USAAF and the war lasts two years you will have saved approximately seven thousand five hundred dollars." Another complained, "If they took the bugs out of the soup, we would all starve to death, dry up and blow out the window."[11]

The prisoners found some relief by speaking through windows and into heating pipes, even if they had to "perform acrobatics" to get to them. Sometimes they managed to send messages through chains of prisoners to specific individuals.

One of Suzanne's fellow prisoners was Madeleine Legrand, the wife of Jacques Grou-Radenez. After the war, Legrand wrote a vivid account of her time in prison. "The soup has arrived. It's a tepid liquid the color of sand. Stirring it, I find five noodles and two pieces of unpeeled potatoes." She and her cellmates recited the rosary for *les garçons* in the adjoining block. They heard the airmen's shouts when Allied planes passed overhead, and the voices of those who would die at dawn singing their anthems: the "Marseillaise," the "Internationale," and "God Save the King."[12]

Anyone caught exchanging messages or gifts was subject to solitary confinement. One day Legrand heard someone calling out for "Suzanne" and began a conversation through a brave intermediary, a prisoner named Chantal. But then a German guard arrived with a gun, an attack dog, and a new batch of prisoners. Legrand tried to warn Suzanne, but she was identified. "Suzanne punished is Suzanne in solitary," Legrand wrote. (She didn't specify whether her "Suzanne" was Suzanne Spaak).[13]

The prisoners' only exercise was taking walks around a courtyard that contained a cabbage patch and the graves of inmates who had succumbed to injury, illness, or suicide.[14] Sometimes women were hauled off to trial and sentenced to deportation to Auschwitz; on those days the "Marseillaise" sounded in treble voices. One day Legrand was ordered to pack her things; the Gestapo was waiting. "You're going to be deported for two years," they told her. But then, to her surprise, she was released.

The Gestapo may have believed that holding Claude's wife and daughter hostage would bring him out of hiding; if so, they were wrong. Claude and Ruth remained ensconced in Saint-Cloud in silence.

Pilette was released on December 23, 1943, and returned to her mother's family. Other prisoners, including most of her relations and the Oratoire's hapless deacon, were freed around the same time, though Charles Spaak remained in his cell at Fresnes, chain-smoking and polishing his screenplay.

Pannwitz and his men had spent months staking out the Spaaks' apartment at the Palais Royal, gradually moving in and inhabiting it. Now they plundered it, removing furniture and silverware to their headquarters on the Rue de Courcelles, a mansion seized from a prominent Jewish family. The Gestapo left behind a houseful of Magrittes and Delvaux, which held no interest for them. They raided the house in Choisel as well, expropriating its square bathtub.

Suzanne Spaak's fellow prisoners described her as unfailingly kind and reassuring. She spent her solitary hours touring her memory palace, revisiting beloved quotations and recording them on her walls. Every evening, the other prisoners heard her singing the same melody from the serene final movement of the Pastoral symphony, the one that Beethoven called "Happy and Grateful Feelings After the Storm." But her hands needed to be busy. She unraveled thread from her blanket and went to work with two toothpicks knitting a tie for Bazou, and began to fashion a doll for Pilette from strands of her hair.

May crept into Paris, while across the Channel, the Allies secretly assembled ships, tanks, and troops for the invasion and dispatched squadrons of bombers to soften their targets.

That month, the guards came for Suzanne and a group of other prisoners arrested in the wake of Leopold Trepper. They were taken to a Paris building belonging to the Coty perfume company that the Germans had requisitioned for an "accelerated" court-martial for the Luftwaffe.[15] The prosecutor was a relentless officer named

Manfred Roeder, known as "Hitler's bloodhound" and famous for seeking the death penalty wherever possible.* The Gestapo's Heinz Pannwitz was also present.

As the French historian Guillaume Bourgeois wrote, "Trepper left a field of ruins in his wake. Among those who helped him, around twenty were arrested and deported to places where some would die."[16] Louise Parrend, who had sheltered Trepper and Jewish children in Bourg-la-Reine, was found guilty of "hiding resisters and Jews in her boarding house." She was deported to a prison in Germany. Madame May, Trepper's messenger, was condemned to death, but Hitler, who personally reviewed the death sentences for women, commuted her sentence.[17]

Suzanne Spaak was given a death sentence, but in her case, due to her tie to Paul-Henri Spaak, no pardon was mentioned. She was stunned to learn that another death sentence had been handed down to Jacques Grou-Radenez, arrested as a result of Bazou's testimony. Soon after the trial he was sent to the concentration camp at Flossenbürg, where he performed crippling slave labor alongside SOE agents, Soviet POWs, and members of the German resistance (among them the theologian Dietrich Bonhoeffer, who was hanged there in April 1945).[18] The camp was the site of daily mass executions. Suzanne Spaak never learned the printer's ultimate fate, but she felt horribly responsible.

---

* Suzanne and her counterparts were tried by a Luftwaffe court-martial because of events in Berlin. One of the German anti-Nazis in contact with Trepper's radio network was air force officer Harro Schulze-Boysen. Everyone connected to him was tried by court-martial; over fifty of them were executed. Some sources record Suzanne's trial as taking place in January, but the records have never been found.

15

the last train

I n her cramped cell, Suzanne Spaak agonized about those she had left behind, even though she had made every possible arrangement on their behalf before her flight. Her lieutenant Peggy Camplan struggled in her absence. The group had barely been able to make payments on the children's stipends for October. Once Suzanne and some members of her financial network disappeared in November, Camplan judged it prudent to cut off all contact with those who remained.

Camplan appealed to leaders of different resistance groups: Jacques Maillet from the trade unions and Émile Laffon from de Gaulle's Free French, besides the usual Jewish supporters. Between them, they came up with 50,000 francs a month. Next she turned to Entr'aide Temporaire. Denise Milhaud and her associates increased their contributions; so did Charles Spaak (presumably before his arrest).

Another source of funds was Éditions de Minuit, an underground publishing house launched with support from Robert Debré and Dexia.[1] Its maiden effort, Jean Bruller's novel *Silence de la Mer*, had sold briskly. Bruller and his partners devoted the profits from the novel and subsequent works to resistance causes, including the rescue of Jewish children. After Suzanne Spaak's arrest, Robert Debré arranged for it to step up its contributions to the children's network.

But the greatest windfall literally dropped from the sky, borne by an SOE agent named Dennis John Barrett. Johnny Barrett was a dapper Englishman who had grown up in France and followed in his father's footsteps as a gentleman's tailor. Barrett was slender, high-strung, and newly wed. The SOE's training reports on the twenty-seven-year-old were harsh: "Both mentally and physically frightened of being hurt, and would like a nice cushy job somewhere he felt perfectly safe," and "a very disappointing type."

Nonetheless, the SOE was desperate for Barrett's language skills. He parachuted into France on April 10, 1943, alongside his superior, Benjamin Cowburn, who had served as best man at his wedding. There, serving under the code name "Innkeeper," Barrett quickly proved his worth. His next evaluation found him "keen, intelligent and thoroughly reliable." Cowburn was delighted to learn that Barrett's keyboard skills extended to the piano.

Barrett's reports offered hair-raising accounts of his brushes with the Gestapo, along with the occasional haberdashery review:

> Source did not find that his clothes were in any way conspicuous, indeed, he looked more French than the French themselves, many of whom affected an English style of dress, tweed jacket and flannel trousers, which they managed to obtain on the Black Market.[2]

After Suzanne's arrest, Peggy Camplan told members of the SOE network about the urgent state of the children under her care. Somehow the news reached Barrett. He was flown back to London in November 1943, and returned four months later bearing the princely sum of 100,000 francs for the children. Later, Benjamin Cowburn delivered another large installment.

"Both of them were extremely interested in the question of the persecuted children," Camplan wrote, "and in the course of a leave in England, Barrett was able to obtain this money that he gave me 'for your little friends.' As one can imagine, it was very welcome here."[3] It is not clear where the money came from. The donations were recorded in the annals of the MNCR but not in Barrett's SOE files.

Barrett and Cowburn were in constant peril, especially after the D-Day landings on June 6. As the Allies fought their way across France, they relied on the support of SOE agents and their French colleagues.

On July 13, 1944, the Germans trapped some British Special Air Service (SAS) forces in the forest of Fontainebleau. Barrett and another SOE agent rushed to their aid. The two were captured and sent to Fresnes.[4] Benjamin Cowburn parachuted back into France two weeks later hoping to rescue them, but Barrett and his partner were already trapped behind prison walls. Now Johnny Barrett and Suzanne Spaak, who had unknowingly supported the same Jewish children's network, were imprisoned yards away from each other, with no knowledge of each other's existence.

With Germany's defeat in sight, Heinz Pannwitz turned his attention to Suzanne. There were loose ends to tie up. Pannwitz thought his "very likable" prisoner was unlikely to know much about Soviet espionage and claimed he had no desire to see her dead. Instead, he designed a plan to use her to entice her husband into captivity. After the war he described his strategy:

> I proposed to Berlin that Mme. Spaak be asked to assist the search for her husband with the promise that the death sentence never be carried out if her husband was found and both of them remained in prison for the remainder of the

war. Berlin agreed clearly and unequivocally to this proposal. Madame Spaak was in the military prison of Paris, Fresnes, in which the [Gestapo] security police kept all their prisoners, but which was administered by the military authorities.[5]

Pannwitz understood that Suzanne couldn't simply mail a letter to her husband, but he also presumed, correctly, that her family had a way to communicate with him. He proposed that Suzanne send her children the letter outlining his offer and ask the family to pass it along to Claude. He maintained that his pledge could be trusted.

> I asked the prison officials prior to writing the letter whether we were certain we could keep our word. The officials arranged for her to talk with me once more. I once more wrote Berlin asking for reassurance and emphasizing that in this case I had to keep my word. I received a firm, positive answer that the promise would be kept. After the second assurance, Mme. SPAAK wrote the letter as instructed and enclosed two small dolls which she had made out of her own hair for her children. Her children, who were with their grandmother in Brussels, received the letter.[6]

This was the first time they learned of their mother's arrest. Suzanne addressed the first page to Claude and the second page to Pilette, emphasizing that some things were not intended for her eyes. She also made it clear that her primary motivation for writing was her distress regarding Jacques Grou-Radenez.

"My dear little Pilette," Suzanne wrote:

> *I would very much like to stop my letter here. I hope that you will be spared this, and that Bonnette and Bonne Maman Spaak [her mother and mother-in-law] can do what I must ask of you. If, despite everything, you read this, my dear little Pilette, don't be frightened, you are a big girl and I know that you are a courageous little Belgian.*

On May 24, the military tribunal of the Luftwaffe condemned me to death for helping an enemy agent escape.

On June 8, a German police officer ordered me to write the following: "If you have the possibility of sending this letter on to your Papa, do it. If he doubts the promises that they've made to me, he can respond with a letter that his mother can give to the police."

I was asked to stress this, that this approach is not directed against Claude or anyone from the Spaak family, but only against the man [Trepper] who is responsible for my sentence. Claude has NOTHING to fear from him.

The officer, in the name of the GERMAN POLICE, made me two FORMAL PROMISES.

Claude will not be tried, but simply interned until the end of the war, perhaps even under house arrest, obliged to sign in on a daily basis at the mayor's office.

My death sentence will be dropped.

My dear, I would NEVER have agreed to write this letter if it was only a matter of myself. I place the life of Claude infinitely above mine, and I wouldn't risk his life to save mine for anything in the world. I also think of your and your brother's ages, and the presence of a good father is even more important. But a man [Grou-Radenez] was arrested because of me and condemned to death on the same day as me, and the second formal promise of the German police is exactly this: "The sentences against you both will be suspended, and we will just intern you until the end of the war."

I have asked for some days to think, and after carefully weighing the pros and cons I made up my mind today. I think it is my duty towards this man arrested because of me (there is no possible doubt, it's my fault), towards his wife, and towards his children (of whom the oldest is about Bazou's age). Everything that I have told you about my life is correct, but I can't hide from you that when I learned on May 24 that he had been condemned to death, I was profoundly unhappy. We returned from the court together and he had nothing but admirable words. He said to me, among other things, "Above all, [there's] no spirit of hate or revenge."

Regarding myself, a long time ago he told me that he had for-given me. I believe that it is my duty to do everything that I can to save this man who is so morally great. And now, I don't think I can do anything more than write this letter.

Since May 24, I have been profoundly unhappy, and this wasn't because of my sentence, but because I understood what it is not to have a tranquil conscience. As I have written in my appeal for a par-don: "I hold that human life is sacred and, for me, to live with the knowledge that I am responsible for the death of a man is a punish-ment worse than death." I believe this very intensely.

If I am mistaken, if I am wrong in writing this letter, I ask my dear Claude not to be sentimental. I have tried to act as intelligently as possible in carrying out what I believe to be my duty. And I finish with a verse by Peguy that I repeat every day: "Hope sees what does not yet exist, and what will be."

I embrace you all.
SUZANNE

Her signature—in capital letters—was emphatic.

Pannwitz was convinced that her message had reached Claude and that he met it with silence.[7] Claude later maintained he didn't receive it.[8] Pilette believes her father's statement—but also holds that he wouldn't have responded if he had received it. "Why should he? It was a set agreement that you don't fall into their traps."

There was no logic to Suzanne's death sentence. So far as the Germans knew, all she had done was to help hide Trepper's money and find him a few nights' lodging. Trepper's mistress Georgie de Winter, on the other hand, had played a supporting role in his es-capades, but she was spared a death sentence, and so were the two career Soviet agents sent to assist him.

As the Allies advanced on Paris, the Germans and their Vichy counterparts faced a difficult decision: How should they spend their final weeks in power? In futile combat, in rampant looting, or in the destruction of evidence of their crimes?

The debate was suspended by an unexpected event. On July 20 a large group of German officers, officials, and intellectuals, sickened by Nazi excesses and fearful of their postwar futures, launched a coup attempt against Hitler. An erroneous report reached Paris stating that Hitler had been assassinated and a new regime was taking over. For the next few hours, German dissidents within the military took over the Gestapo headquarters in Paris and prepared to parley with the Allies. But soon they stood corrected: Hitler was not dead, and the Nazis maintained control. The Gestapo swarmed the military installations in Paris, arresting the mutineers. Over the following weeks almost five thousand German military and civilian leaders were executed in Berlin for their involvement in the conspiracy, including Carl-Heinrich von Stülpnagel, the military governor of France.

It is not known whether Suzanne and her fellow inmates were aware of the German coup attempt that would have saved them, but they could hear the roar of Allied bombers and the rumble of artillery in the distance. The prisoners anticipated the advance with high excitement, and triumphant graffiti blossomed on the prison walls.

The Germans began to move their prisoners in preparation for flight. At the end of July, Georgie de Winter was transferred from private quarters to Fresnes, receiving special privileges as an American citizen. One of the female German guards offered her books and a sweater, adding, "When your countrymen arrive, I'm counting on you to tell them that I've treated you well." Georgie learned that Suzanne Spaak was also in Fresnes, and sent her a message via the prison grapevine. Suzanne sent her a gracious reply.

Later, on one of their walks around the prison cabbage patch,

Georgie and Suzanne fell into step. It was Georgie's indiscretions that had led the Gestapo to Madame May and Suzanne's address. Georgie looked at her regretfully and said, "I'm sorry, it's because of us you were arrested." Suzanne responded with a gentle smile. "Don't worry about it, it's of no importance."[9]

As the Allies fought their way to Paris, their commanders considered skirting the city, but de Gaulle loudly objected. The future of France, he argued, depended on a highly symbolic event: the liberation of Paris led by Free French troops loyal to him. The Communists, including their Jewish divisions, had carried out many of the earliest and most aggressive acts of resistance, but the general wanted to prevent them from getting the upper hand.* The Allies decided to let de Gaulle get his way.

Leopold Trepper had been lying low for months, waiting it out as his friends and recruits were imprisoned, deported to concentration camps, and executed. Now he sought his moment of glory. He approached Arek Kowalski, the leader of the Jewish resistance, and asked him for thirty men to attack the Rote Kapelle task force headquarters on the Rue de Courcelles. Kowalski was agreeable, but the decision had to be approved by Moscow.

Moscow was silent.[10] This did not bode well for Trepper. His operation was put on hold.[11]

The final days of the occupation brought chaos. Thousands of German troops looted whatever they could carry, while French Milice paramilitary units went on a rampage, murdering hundreds of enemies and witnesses to their crimes.

The SS was determined to use every remaining opportunity to deport a final round of victims. Several hundred Jewish children

---

* De Gaulle was only partially successful. The Communist Party benefited from its record in the Resistance, reflected by its large number of seats in the postwar French Parliament.

were stranded in the UGIF orphanages, where they made an easy target. Jewish organizations had begun to disperse the children from the UGIF homes in the Southern Zone the previous November, but they were slower to act in Paris.

The arrests had been going on for months, now carried out by the Germans. The convoys continued to roll, carrying increasing numbers of French Jews among the immigrants. Hélène Berr and her mother had continued their work with Entr'aide and the UGIF underground along with Fred and Denise Milhaud. There was a reasonable chance that the Berrs' citizenship and status would have protected them. (Over thirty thousand French-born Jews survived the war living openly in Paris at their registered addresses.) But the Berrs may have forfeited their privilege through their work with the immigrants. For a while Hélène and her parents had taken the precaution of spending the night in other locations, but one evening they decided to sleep at home. They were arrested and deported to Auschwitz. They would not return.

The threats to the Jewish children mounted. In March a member of the Communist Party brought fearsome news to Denise Milhaud's father, a partner in the rescue efforts: the Gestapo had planned another roundup of "all the Jews still free in Paris, and in particular the children who had been entrusted to the UGIF."

The Entr'aide network prepared to take action, aiming to "kidnap" as many children as possible. The organizers took their plan to the UGIF officials in charge—the group's new president, Georges Edinger, and Juliette Stern, a social worker—but the two rejected it, fearing they would personally suffer the consequences.

With the approach of the Allies, the choices became even more agonizing. On July 20, Alois Brunner, the SS officer in charge of Drancy, told a detainee there that the arrests were about to take place. On July 21—the day after the German coup attempt—Brunner dispatched police officers to nine UGIF centers to arrest the children.[12]

Once again, Denise Milhaud's father was the first to hear the news. He reported that the police had taken all the children except for the twenty-eight who remained in the UGIF orphanage at Neuilly, just west of Paris. The UGIF's Georges Edinger authorized his staff to release the children to the rescuers.

The twenty-eight children were spirited away from the orphanage, but Juliette Stern panicked and sent her staff members out to retrieve them before they could be hidden. The UGIF telephoned the orphanage every ten minutes to find out how many children had been rounded up. Stern's staff brought back twenty of the twenty-eight, who were promptly taken to Drancy with an escort of Jewish policemen. One of them, a boxer, flew into a rage of remorse when he arrived at the orphanage, shouting that he didn't think any children remained at Neuilly.

Between July 21 and 25, the Germans arrested more 250 children, aged three to thirteen, 80 of them from 16 Rue Lamarck. They arrived at Drancy in a state of pathetic confusion, wandering around the camp alone or in small groups. A few days later they were joined by orphanage attendants who had refused to abandon their charges.

SS officer Brunner told his subordinates that they faced a "painful task" in loading the children into boxcars, and he praised their "alacrity and skill" in carrying out the job.[13] Of the 250 children arrested in the *rafle*, 232 were deported to Auschwitz on July 31, and, of those, 199 perished.

Georges Edinger submitted a report on the incident to the General Commissariat on Jewish Affairs. He merely recorded the arrest of the children, but he condemned the arrest of his staff. "The children housed in the Neuilly home were the object of an administrative measure by the authorities of the camp at Drancy, on Tuesday the 25, numbering 16. We must deplore any measure taken against our personnel in this home."[14]

There is no doubt that Juliette Stern and others used their

positions in the UGIF to support large-scale rescue operations of the children in their care, but the survivors would never forgive the UGIF for the events of July 1944.* As historian Paula Hyman wrote, "Even in 1944, when the Nazis' genocidal intentions were obvious, the new head of UGIF North, Georges Edinger, refused to destroy its files and hide the children still under its supervision."[15] The debate would continue for decades.[16]

The railway was busy at Fresnes. On August 8, Johnny Barrett and twenty other SOE agents were loaded onto a train for Buchenwald. Barrett would be executed along with three other SOE agents on October 5.

On August 10, Georgie de Winter was escorted from her cell. Her guards returned her possessions, including her jewels, and showed her to a waiting car. "Where are we going?" she asked anxiously. "It's summer, my girl," the guard answered. "We're taking a spin." They reached the Gare de l'Est, where she found Pannwitz and his men waiting. The platform was wild with panic as invalid German soldiers and women clutching small children fought for places on the train.

Pannwitz tried to reassure Georgie, saying, "You're leaving for

---

* The historian Serge Klarsfeld criticized the UGIF's actions of 1944 but, pointing to its broader record, wrote, "This shameful task forever tainted the UGIF, leading people to neglect the contribution of this institution, originally designed by the Germans to facilitate the Final Solution, which, undeniably, statistically did far more to help the Jews than to do them a disservice." As previously noted, André Baur, the vice president of the UGIF, was deported with his family in 1943 and murdered. Juliette Stern would survive the war. In the final days of the Occupation, a Jewish resistance group seized the UGIF offices and arrested its president, Georges Edinger. He and other UGIF members were questioned by a Jewish honor court after the war for their failure to protect the children. See Simon Perego, "Jurys d' honneur," in *Jewish Honor Courts*, eds. Laura Jokusch and Gabriel N. Finder (Detroit: Wayne State University Press, 2015), 144.

Germany. It's impossible to guard you here, you'd be in danger. I'll join you before long, and we'll probably have news of Trepper." She asked about her small son, Patrick. Pannwitz gave a menacing reply. "If you escape, I'll send him to the Black Forest and you'll never see him again. If you don't try to flee, I promise that all will go well."[17] Pannwitz was only half-right. All did not go well; within weeks Georgie found herself in the first of a series of concentration camps. But in the end she was reunited with her son.

On August 12 the Germans loaded another convoy with 2,500 prisoners from Fresnes, most of them members of the French Resistance. They also included 168 fliers from Britain, the United States, Canada, Australia, and New Zealand. Other prisoners were added along the way. Suzanne Spaak would have recognized names from her past: one was Christian Dior's twenty-five-year-old sister Catherine, a courier for the Resistance, who was shipped to Ravensbrück and would barely survive the war.[18]

The final weeks of August brought strikes and street fighting across Paris, but SS officer Alois Brunner was ready to compromise military objectives to pursue his bloodlust. He prepared to fill another convoy, but the German army thwarted his plans by requisitioning the train to evacuate a thousand troops. Brunner bartered food and weapons with the Wehrmacht in exchange for three railroad cars. He filled them with Jewish members of the Resistance imprisoned at Fresnes and prominent Jews who had been held as hostages. They included Armand Kohn, the director of the Rothschild Hospital, along with his family. Brunner rode out of Paris on the same train on August 22.[19]

In Paris the hidden threads of the Resistance appeared and entwined. Hans Heisel, the boyish German sailor who had joined the French Resistance, could finally take off his loathed German uniform to fight alongside the French. His comrades renamed him "Albert Roche," and he fought the Nazis until liberation.

British and French SOE agents surfaced from the shadows and

leaped into the street fighting with gusto. Across from the Palais Royal, resistance fighters fired from the sandbags piled in front of the Comédie Française.

Robert Debré and his medical committee assumed an official military role. The doctor came out of hiding and took charge of the field medicine for the resistance forces across the Paris region. Jean Moulin would have been pleased to see the fruits of his labor: Debré's colleague Frédéric Joliot-Curie had supported Moulin from the start; now he alternated first aid with the expert production of Molotov cocktails. Another member, Louis Pasteur Vallery-Radot, had been working with the SOE for over a year. He used his position to place orders with London for drugs, antiseptics, and surgical instruments to care for wounded agents and *résistants*.[20] The doctors were supported by Léon Chertok, who added his contacts in the Jewish underground.[21]

Hitler ordered the commander of the German forces in Paris, Dietrich von Choltitz, to reduce Paris to a "field of rubble," but the general had no stomach for vindictive slaughter or a suicidal last stand. In the final days of the occupation, the Swedish consul, Raoul Nordling, pressed Choltitz to surrender after presenting a token resistance; Nordling made an additional plea for the lives of the political prisoners in Fresnes and elsewhere. The German general finally conceded and agreed to a fragile cease-fire. The fate of the prisoners was not a central concern; Choltitz's goal was to get his men out of Paris ahead of the Allied advance. Sporadic skirmishes held them up, but on August 25 Choltitz signed the surrender, disobeying Hitler's orders.

The streets of Paris erupted in celebration, and Free French forces poured into the city. It was a homecoming for many. The Countess de la Bourdonnaye's oldest son, Geoffroy, met his mother and sister Bertranne for the first time in four years. The young officer, lean and weathered, posed beside his battered tank, the *Wagram 30*, on the Boulevard Saint-Michel. He had joined de Gaulle's forces at the beginning of the occupation, and he would fight almost to the end. Bertranne had run a celebrated escape operation for downed Allied airmen. There was no news of the countess's younger boy, Guy, not yet twenty, who had been captured as he tried to slip across the Spanish border to join the Free French.

Robert Debré entered Paris with his Medical Committee of the Resistance. Once the wounded were treated, he turned his attention to public health issues. Debré's son Michel had also joined de Gaulle, but he was in London working directly under the general, planning the architecture of France's postwar government.

Parisians emerged into the bright light of August looking to pick up the pieces. On the twenty-fifth, de Gaulle stood before a cheering throng at the Hôtel de Ville looking out on Notre Dame. His speech set the tone for the mythology to come as he greeted

Paris liberated! Liberated by itself, liberated by its people with the help of the French armies, with the support and the help of all France, of the France that fights, the only France, of the real France, of the eternal France!

—ignoring the scores of British SOE agents, thousands of American infantrymen, and millions of Russians who lost their lives on the way to France's liberation.

De Gaulle's speech also advanced the myth that "all France" had fought for liberation under his banner. His version of history would overlook crimes of the Vichy bureaucracy, the French paramilitary Milice, and the nefarious General Commissariat on Jewish Affairs. It would shortchange the roles of immigrant Jewish resistance movements and, indeed, of foreigners in general, whether they were German sailors, Spanish veterans, or Belgian housewives.

The occupation of Paris was over, but secrets remained. Vichy officials buried their tracks and offered elaborate excuses for their actions over the previous four years. Records went missing. The Germans had destroyed vast numbers of documents concerning the occupation, and others vanished as Vichy officials fled their sinking ship.

But one record that remained was the manifest for the trains from Fresnes to Germany, and one name on the list was Suzanne Spaak.

16

liberation

On August 26—the day after the official liberation of Paris—Leopold Trepper finally seized his moment of glory. Moscow had given the green light for him and the Jewish street fighters to attack Heinz Pannwitz's headquarters on the Rue de Courcelles. They engaged in a brief skirmish with German stragglers near the Hotel Majestic along the way, but otherwise Trepper's expedition was mere drama. When they reached the headquarters they learned that Pannwitz and his men had fled two hours earlier.[1]

That afternoon, Claude Spaak and Ruth Peters returned to the Spaaks' apartment in the Palais Royal for the first time in ten months. The Gestapo had looted almost everything they could carry, leaving behind only the largest pieces of furniture, the books, and the scorned surrealist paintings—the most valuable items on the premises. The Gestapo agents had sat in the salon day after day, waiting for Claude to return. He marveled at his luck: beside the mantel was the large wicker trunk the family had used for its various moves. Had the Gestapo bothered to turn the trunk around, they would have found the address of Claude's hiding place in Saint-Cloud written on the side.[2]

Claude and Ruth had barely settled in when Colette's maid, Pauline, appeared at the door on behalf of her mistress, who wished to see him. "Do you need anything?" she asked him. He said he did not, but he did accept a bar of soap.[3]

There was no word of Suzanne. Claude traveled to Fresnes to look for her. There he found the printed roster of the prisoners who had been deported to Germany in the final days of the occupation, with Suzanne's name among them. So there was hope. In the months following her arrest, Claude's brother Paul-Henri used his position to make back-channel inquiries to the Germans. They sent back heartening responses, assuring him they had no wish to antagonize him.

On September 4, Brussels was liberated. The next day, Claude hitchhiked there to see his family and fetch the children. Pilette and Bazou moved back into the Palais Royal with Claude and Ruth ten days later, finding their old home oddly familiar yet also much changed. No one knew where their mother was. The Gestapo had stolen their silverware. In the formal gardens outside their windows they could see American GIs mysteriously hurling a large ball through a basket nailed to a post.

One day a man who worked for a moving company brought news. "Last March I came here with the Germans and hauled a big load from your apartment to a private mansion on the Rue de Courcelles," he reported. Claude set off to investigate, and took Pilette along.

The building in question was the elegant Hôtel Veil-Picard at 63 Rue de Courcelles. Formerly the home of an Alsatian Jewish banking family, it had been taken over by the Gestapo's Rote Kapelle task force.

When Claude and Pilette arrived at the gate, they were admitted by a female caretaker. As they stood waiting in the vestibule,

Pilette spotted some glowing blue opaline glass on a shelf inside the house. She recognized it instantly; it was part of a group of seventeen pieces that had once belonged to Victor Hugo. Claude had bought the pieces from their friend Valentine Hugo (the former wife of the writer's great-grandson). "That's when we knew we were in the right place," Pilette recalled.

Year later, the French author Gilles Perrault recorded Claude's recollection of the visit:

> They were taken to an immense room with sumptuous *boiseries*, but the only furniture was a table, two chairs and a stove. Prostrate beside the stove, wrapped in his overcoat and wearing a hat, a small elderly man shivered: Monsieur Veil-Picard. He summoned the caretaker, and she took Spaak to the second floor, which was piled high with furniture. She told him with a sweeping gesture, "Go ahead, help yourself, don't hesitate. The owners are dead." [Claude] . . . energetically refused, to the caretaker's surprise, to take a superb oriental carpet that didn't belong to him.
>
> The bathtub from Choisel was in the cellar.[4]

They departed through a gallery whose carpet was stained with blood. Claude and Pilette returned to the Palais Royal with only his opaline glass.

The months wore on. Over the fall of 1944, battles raged on both the western and the eastern fronts as Allied forces fought their way to the heart of the Reich. Hundreds of thousands of French POWs and political prisoners were still captive in Germany and Poland, but some began to trickle back from liberated zones.

Suzanne's friends from the MNCR started a weekly group for returned deportees and their families at the Pam Pam Café on Rue Marbeuf, near its offices. Pilette went a few times, but she found it difficult. "Mother was supposed to be in Germany, and people would spend all their time talking about atrocities in Germany. I stopped going—I couldn't bear hearing it."[5]

Then the MNCR pressed her into service to raise money for Jewish orphans. One day they sent her to a sumptuous apartment near the Opéra to ask for a donation. "It was a huge room with mirrors everywhere, and on the desk there was a scale for gems and precious metals," she recalled.

She was surprised to recognize the man sitting at the desk. Two years earlier her mother had sent her to a shabby apartment near the steps of Montmartre, where she made a seven-floor climb to a small attic. There she had found an elderly man in a shawl and a woman shuffling about in slippers. "They were going to give me a child, eight or nine years old, to hide." She took the child back to Suzanne, who guided him safely into her network.

Now she saw the same old man sitting before her. "I told him who I was and that mother was in Germany, she hadn't come back. We needed money for the rescued children. He sat down at the immense desk and said, 'Everyone's asking me for money, but in honor of your mother I'll contribute.'" He wrote out a check for 50 francs—the equivalent of a dollar. "I took it back to the group and said, 'I'm not doing this any more.'"[6]

With the liberation of Belgium, Paul-Henri Spaak was more prominent than ever. The Allies had groomed him to lead the reconstruction of Western Europe. Amid his official duties, he worked tirelessly on behalf of his family members. For several months after Suzanne's flight, he lived with the knowledge that his wife, daughter, sister, and other family members were held hostage in a Belgian prison under threat of deportation.

He also worried about his uncle, the elderly former prime minister Paul-Émile Janson, who had been arrested in 1943. After the other family members were released, he applied to the Belgian ambassador to Berlin to negotiate his uncle's and Suzanne's release. But it was already too late for Janson; he was deported to Buchenwald and died on March 3, 1944.[7] However, Spaak did receive a message from Heinz Pannwitz, now back in Germany. Don't worry, it promised, every possible measure was being taken to protect the life of his sister-in-law. She would wait out the hostilities in full security.[8]

There were more signs of hope. That fall a man from Luxembourg showed up at the door of Suzanne's mother saying that his sister was engaged to marry Suzanne's Gestapo interrogator. Rudolf Rathke had told him that Suzanne was on a farm in Prussia, he said, and for a certain sum of money he could bring her home. But Suzanne's sister called in the police to investigate his claims, and he was arrested. Such scams were becoming commonplace as hustlers preyed on the war's distressed survivors.

Paul-Henri Spaak returned to Brussels, where he resumed his post as foreign minister and eventually took a leading role in the creation of NATO. Then, in October, he received a brown envelope via the Belgian embassy in London containing two letters from his missing sister-in-law, dated August 12, 1944. When Paul-Henri turned over the envelope, a slip of paper fell out. It was the burial record for a grave in the Bagneux cemetery a few miles north of Fresnes.

Suzanne had entrusted the envelope to the German prison chaplain at Fresnes, Abbé Franz Stock. Stock had served in France before the war and sympathized with the Resistance. Three years earlier, Robert Debré had sought his help for Dexia and the Musée de l'Homme group when they were imprisoned in Fresnes. Over the occupation, the priest and his two aides ministered to some two thousand imprisoned *résistants* and other political prisoners, smuggling in books, food, and clothes to the captives and messages out to their families.[9] Stock couldn't stop the Nazis' slaughter, but he served their victims where he could, at great personal risk.*

Stock confided to a friend, "I witnessed so many deaths, and not just firing squads—humans can be so horrible." His aid to Suzanne was one of his last acts as chaplain at Fresnes.[10]

Suzanne's letters were penned in her large, round handwriting: one to Claude, one to her children. She wrote to Claude:

> Today I have a great hope because my appeal has been denied, and I really think that's because you are still free and that soon our dear children will be in your arms again. I write this to you, my dear, because it's difficult to write a "collective" letter, but I think with great and profound love of all those who love me.

But she was tormented by the thought of Grou-Radenez.

> I would truly GIVE MY LIFE TO SAVE HIM because I can't forgive myself for having given his name to the police. My dear, if this terrible misfortune didn't spare poor Madame Grou, I ask that you offer her all the moral and material aid you can. I would like her to know about my appeal and my letter in June to the children.

Suzanne berated herself for being "stupid" in giving the couple's address to Bazou "on that morning in September" without foreseeing the possible consequences.

---

* Stock's aides were transferred to the front lines as punishment, in one case for accompanying two Jewish youths to their executions at their request. Franz Stock, his health broken by the war, died suddenly at the age of forty-four in 1948. As of 2017, initial steps have been taken toward his canonization.

Then she recalled earlier times, when life and love were less complicated:

My dear, I would like to tell you all of the thoughts I've had for you since October 18, all of them, with such deep love, but I'm a little annoyed because I can't find the words to tell you, and I also know that you'll understand what I mean—yes? Do you remember that beautiful summer twenty-three years ago? I haven't changed.

To her children, she wrote:

I want to express all my love for you and I can't find the words. . . . My little Bazou, continue to imitate your dear papa. You can't find a better example, and when you are grown up, ask him to talk to you about my friends, and you'll see another example to follow.

My little Pilette, be GOOD, SIMPLE, GENEROUS, and do me a favor: read, and from time to time, reflect on some verses of the Gospel and try to follow these principles that I find so admirable.[11]

This religious note was unexpected for the self-described atheist, but perhaps she was reflecting the influence of Father Stock.

Another slip of paper bore the words, "I'm thinking of Mira."

Paul-Henri Spaak took charge of the situation and sent his wife and sister to Paris. They learned that two bodies had been hastily buried in Bagneux in August, identified only as "a Frenchman" and "a Belgian woman." The Frenchman's family had recently claimed one body as that of Fernand Pauriol, the radioman who had built and maintained Leopold Trepper's transmitters. Pauriol's family had reburied him in the South of France as a hero of the Resistance. The "Belgian woman" had not been identified, and her remains were about to be moved to a common grave.

Suzanne's Children

Paul-Henri told Claude what they had found: a gravesite, but with no means of identifying Suzanne's remains without a physician to conduct an exhumation.*

Once again, Claude hesitated. He didn't give his children the news until a few days before Christmas, and he was unwilling to go to the morgue himself. He turned to Léon Chertok for help, handing over Suzanne's dental records and authorizing him to identify the body. Heartsick, Chertok compared the dental chart with the remains and saw they matched. Suzanne was dressed in her burgundy suit and ochre blouse.

It has never been established who killed Suzanne Spaak, or why. Heinz Pannwitz maintained that Berlin had commuted her death sentence to a prison term with every intention of exploiting her as a hostage. Her execution took place amid pandemonium. American pilots in Fresnes described hearing sporadic volleys of gunfire and the bellowing of guards. "Prisoners were breaking their windows, trying to see what was going on in the courtyard below," fearing they would all be executed on the spot.[12]

In that last frantic week, Germans, Vichy French, and even Ukrainian fascists murdered and pillaged their way across Paris, driven by greed, vengeance, and the desire to obliterate incriminating evidence; there was a massacre of over a hundred prisoners from Montluc. But if a marauding band attacked Fresnes, no report of such an event has survived.

What is certain is that on August 12, 1944, Suzanne Spaak and Fernand Pauriol were taken from their cells to the prison courtyard.

---

* In his memoirs, Leopold Trepper claims credit for discovering the remains of Suzanne Spaak and Fernand Pauriol "after a thorough search of the cemeteries in the suburbs"(*Great Game*, 321). It appears that he was greatly exaggerating his role, given that his version directly contradicts the accounts of Chertok and the Spaak relations, including Claude.

There they were murdered with the infamous *Genickschuss*—a shot to the nape of the neck—that had stolen the lives of so many Nazi victims across Europe.

A decade later, a seemingly chastened Heinz Pannwitz told the CIA:

> The responsibility can only lie with the administrative offices of the prison where the commuted death sentence may have been overlooked in the files. It was neither possible for, nor the responsibility of my *Kommando* to supervise the prison transport from Paris during the final hectic days of the withdrawal.
>
> It is most regrettable that all our efforts to save this woman's life were in vain because of a stupid, horrible administrative mistake.[13]

Pannwitz implied that the Gestapo held the copy of Suzanne's stay of execution and that, in the last frantic days of the occupation, the prison guards accidently consulted the wrong file. This suggests that, in toying with her appeals for clemency, Pannwitz had cut the margins too close. His explanation is far from verified, but no more credible account has come to light.

The confirmation of Suzanne's death devastated her mother, Jeanne Lorge. When the news arrived, she disappeared for six months to be alone in her grief.

Claude shut himself away in his study at the Palais Royal. The end of the war restored the property of the Lorges and the influence of the Spaaks, but a deafening silence surrounded the subject of Suzanne. Pilette's Lorge cousin Tommy Happé recalled, "The family had a great esteem for Suzette, but my parents were eager to protect us from the dramatic aspects of the war, the sad things." Paul-Henri's daughter Antoinette added, "The Spaaks remembered Suzette as a beloved family member. But I'm always surprised how little they talked about Suzette and women in the resistance."

Suzanne's Children

Pilette and Bazou were left alone in their pain and confusion. According to Pilette, "Marguerite [Paul-Henri's wife] was the only one who talked to us about mother's death. She was affectionate and kind. No one else—not Ruth, not Claude—talked about it. We were just pawns."

Suzanne was reburied at Bagneux under a simple cross in the military section of the cemetery, amid rows of soldiers from every corner of the French empire, their graves marked with the cross, the Star of David, and the Muslim star and crescent.

The Oratoire's Paul Vergara spoke movingly at her funeral:

> She believed with all her heart in that which is stronger than might, she wagered against might and she won. Nietzsche sneers: "Mercy, and respect for what is right and for the weak are virtues of slaves, good for cows, women, the English, Christians, and other democrats." Despite these boasts she believed in the "virtues of slaves" that are revealed to be sovereign, and without which men are no more than educated animals.[14]

Suzanne's plot faced another section containing the empty graves of Jews who had died in concentration camps. Photographs mounted in the stones depicted entire families who had been wiped out within a few months.

Pilette and Bazou weren't invited to their mother's funeral; they weren't even told it was taking place. Pilette finally learned where her mother was buried around 1952, when Bazou showed her a picture of the grave. "That was the first time I really believed she was dead," Pilette said.

Claude told Gilles Perrault that it was only with great difficulty that he brought himself to visit the cemetery. He found "a vast necropolis where three thousand soldiers were buried," he said.

"There were flowers everywhere . . . and in the middle of these men, Suzanne and another one, the only women."[15]

Claude wrestled with Suzanne's legacy. Shortly after the liberation of Paris, one of Suzanne's fellow inmates visited him to express her admiration for his wife, who had been a great help to the other prisoners. "She especially asked me to tell you to visit her cell," she added. Claude wrote to the prison to ask permission, but the director brushed him off. The prison was full of collaborators now, he said. (One was Vichy prime minister Pierre Laval, who would be shot in the Fresnes courtyard after arguing that he had sacrificed immigrant Jews to save French citizens.)

No one had seen anything special in Suzanne's cell. Claude persisted, and the director finally acquiesced. It turned out that the cell had been converted into a storage room, and no one had seen anything because it was stacked high with objects blocking the walls.

Now Claude regarded the narrow surfaces, covered from floor to ceiling with three hundred inscriptions in her hand. Suzanne had always been an avid reader, and she had battled despair by mining quotations from the recesses of her memory, each imbued with a profound meaning.

"To understand all is to forgive all."

"Oh! Let my keel split, let me fall into the sea!" (from Rimbaud's *Le Bateau ivre*).

"You might have found a better wife than me, but I have given you our son."

"Ah, I am sitting in the shadow of the forests . . ." (from Racine's *Phèdre*).

"My enemies can kill me. But they cannot harm me" (Socrates).

"Alone with my thoughts, I am still free."

"Greetings and courage, comrades."

"Where the children are, the mothers should be, so they can
   watch over them" (Kipling, drawn from *The Jungle Book*).
"Melodious nightingale, sing a song to close my eyes" (from
   Shakespeare, *A Midsummer Night's Dream*).
"I regret nothing."[16]

Claude later told Gilles Perrault:

I don't remember how long I stayed. Sobbing, I went from
one wall to the next, copying all of the inscriptions on a piece
of paper the prison director had given me. There were say-
ings, poems, and also kind of a journal she kept over her final
days. She noted with hope that American tanks had reached
Chartres. She was also surprised that she was still in Fresnes,
since most of her companions had been evacuated.

"There's something else I can't forget," Claude added. "That
large brown stain that I saw on the floor of her cell."[17] It may have
reminded him of the other brown stain at the Gestapo quarters on
the Rue de Courcelles. Was Suzanne tortured? Her family would
never know.

Suzanne had left a sizable estate, and a family council gathered
to discuss its disposition and her children's future. Pilette and Bazou
had been left at loose ends. Claude married Ruth in 1946, a year
after Suzanne's death was confirmed—the minimum period for re-
spectability. The couple didn't inform the children that the wedding
was going to take place, nor did they invite them to the ceremony.

"You will call Ruth 'Mother' from now on," Claude told Bazou.
Pilette rebelled at the idea and clashed with her father. She watched
resentfully as Ruth took her mother's place in the home and even
started wearing Suzanne's gold necklace. As Pilette matured, she
increasingly resembled Suzanne. One day she was experimenting in
front of a mirror and pinned her hair up in her mother's style. When

she emerged from the room, Ruth flinched as though she'd seen a ghost, and harshly told her she must never do it again.

Soon after Claude's death, Pilette and Bazou learned that he had burned their mother's letters and photographs, as well as their own. Only a handful of papers remained. Claude never offered an explanation for his action, but his favorite great-nephew, Anthony Palliser, had an idea. "Claude spoke about Suzanne with respect, but he didn't speak about her much. He felt a little guilty. He hadn't behaved like a perfect gentleman."[18]

Claude had a hard time living with Suzanne's letter containing the Gestapo's offer to spare her if he turned himself in. Yes, it was ambiguous, and she did employ their private code indicating that he shouldn't take her words at face value. But the fact remained that while she was preparing to die a hero's death, he was holed up with his mistress, ignoring their children and her distress.

But Claude also struggled with the contrast between his wife's actions and his own. After the war, some of the rescued Jewish children wrote letters expressing their gratitude to Suzanne and trying to contact her children. Claude destroyed those letters, too—Pilette and Bazou never knew they existed. For years they wondered why the beneficiaries of their mother's efforts remained silent. Finally, after Claude's death, some now-grown children reached them. One of them was Larissa Gruszow, the child who was hidden in Normandy, who became a close friend.

Money was another factor. Claude and Ruth liked the good life. Suzanne's estate gave Claude the use of her property, but it was ultimately tied up in a trust for the children. He was required to show proof for anything he purchased himself for reimbursement. Pilette recalled him rifling through files, looking for receipts for petty household items such as towels and napkins. Ruth was in line to inherit a handsome fortune, but it had to wait for her mother's death a decade later.

It was Suzanne who came, posthumously, to the rescue. Claude learned that if Suzanne was officially recognized as a casualty of the Resistance—*Morte pour la France*—he would receive tax benefits on her estate. He submitted the petition, and it was done. The phrase was added to the cross marking her grave, although Suzanne would have protested that she hadn't died for France; she was serving humanity.

Another asset was the art collection purchased with Suzanne's fortune. This included two dozen Magrittes, some of them masterworks, and an equal number of Delvauxs. Claude lived off the collection for years, selling a painting whenever he needed to raise some cash.

Claude couldn't deny that Suzanne's death financed his life with Ruth. One day when Bazou was in his teens, Claude mused, "I really don't know what I would have done if your mother had come back." Bazou never forgave his father for that remark.

Claude's precise relationship to Leopold Trepper and Soviet intelligence has remained a mystery. After the war, British and US intelligence agencies conducted investigations of Trepper's network from their new Cold War footing. The CIA, noting Paul-Henri's alliance with the British, observed "an unusual thing among the Belgians which was that one side of the family would have Western sympathies and the other was inclined toward Moscow. This was a form of re-insurance for the family."[19]

The CIA report limited Suzanne's connection to Trepper to aiding his escape and introducing him to someone who had radio contact with London.

The British Study places all emphasis on Claude Spaak as Trepper's assistant. The Personality Index of the Study under Claude Spaak has the following: "The confidence which Trepper reposed in Spaak suggests that he was a well-known and well-tried friend of the USSR if not of the GRU [Soviet military intelligence]." . . . Ruth Peters, who was living with

Claude Spaak, became Mme. Claude Spaak No. 2 and was working with him in assisting Trepper during the time Suzanne Spaak was in prison according to the Study.*

The CIA officer added a chilling speculation based on the British research:

> The British should have fairly positive information regarding Suzanne Spaak's execution unless Claude Spaak, wanting Suzanne out of the way in order to marry Ruth Peters, and [Gestapo agent Horst] Kopkow, to protect himself, did not give the facts.[20]

As intriguing as they were, the intelligence reports were far from authoritative. Heinz Pannwitz's testimony reflected his self-interest, just as Leopold Trepper shaped his version to his. The various accounts created a patchwork fraught with errors.

Pilette and Bazou grew up and pursued independent lives. Through her uncle the prime minister, Pilette met a handsome Moroccan who was an adviser to the king of Morocco. After they married, he pursued political ambitions that played out on three continents but left him disappointed in the end. He spent much of her sizable inheritance chasing his dreams. However, the couple shared some happiness and produced a fine son along the way.

Bazou went to the Sorbonne and decided to study a dead language. He became an eminent Sanskrit scholar who divided his time between Paris and India, marrying an Indian wife and fathering two accomplished sons.

Pilette and Bazou nursed a lasting ache for their mother and a

---

* Pilette considered this theory "ludicrous."

simmering anger toward their father. As Claude sold off the family's art collection, the luminous Magrittes and Delvauxs took their places on the walls of Hollywood mansions and leading museums. Bazou still owns the Magritte painting of the two children, and Pilette his portrait of their mother.

It is impossible to say exactly how many Jewish children were rescued over the course of the occupation, or to assign specific roles to the rescuers. Suzanne's networks included the MNCR, Entr'aide Temporaire, the Oratoire, and the underground UGIF, as well as their partners, including the Jewish charities OSE and the Amelot Committee, the Catholic network, and the Protestant relief group Cimade. Their combined reach was considerable.

Roughly eleven thousand Jewish children were deported from France between the Vel d'Hiv arrests in July 1942 and the liberation in August 1944. It is estimated that the rescue networks saved over one thousand. Suzanne Spaak established bonds of trust and promoted cooperation. She was not the only person who served this purpose, but her contribution was extraordinary.

At the end of the occupation, the hidden children were scattered across the countryside. Suzanne's colleagues gradually collected them and set about reuniting them with their family members wherever possible. Eventually the surviving parents and relations came out of hiding or returned from the camps and found their children.

A group of them remained unclaimed. The MNCR assembled fifty children hidden by its network and prepared to care for them. Suzanne's friends, including Peggy Camplan, located a large villa in the suburb of Montmorency that had been requisitioned for the German military during the occupation. Now the French state offered it as a home for the children. The cofounders included Jewish Communists and members of the Oratoire's congregation, which continued to take up collections to support the children. Pastor Vergara and Marcelle Guillemot were named to the board of directors.

The children called their new home Renouveau ("Renewal"). It was said that most of them had been "saved by Suzanne Spaak," and a room was named after her.[21] Several of the orphans had been rescued at La Clairière in February 1943, though they were young children at the time and their memories of the event were foggy.

The director of Renouveau was Madame Claude François-Unger, whose first husband had died in Auschwitz in 1942.[*] François-Unger's motto was "Don't look back." The children were urged to bury the past, study hard, and think of each other as family. In many respects the program was a success; the orphans grew up to become successful professors, engineers, and business leaders.

But as they reached their later years, the past resurged, along with its pain. One of the rescued children, Jacques Alexandre, pieced together elements of the hidden history, aided by Peggy Camplan. She told him she and other members of Suzanne's rescue network had also gathered intelligence for the Red Orchestra—small things, such as counting the German uniforms in a bar. Alexandre's friend Sami Dassa wrote a moving memoir called *Vivre, aimer avec Auschwitz au cœur* (*To Live and Love with Auschwitz in Your Heart*). When the two learned of Suzanne Spaak's role in their rescue, they made a ritual of placing flowers on her grave, but they had no idea she'd had children of her own.

Suzanne Spaak was both honored and forgotten. On March 9, 1945, Adam Rayski's newspaper, the *Naïe Presse*, published an article about her, praising her as a woman "who was not content with just words." A 1947 Paris exhibition included a display highlighting "some noble figures from the French people who braved every danger to save Jewish children from deportation." Four of the seven subjects were members of Suzanne Spaak's network: the Countess

---

[*] Their son, Fred Kupferman, lived in the orphanage and grew up to become a prominent historian of the Vichy period.

de la Bourdonnaye, Paul Vergara, Marcelle Guillemot, and Suzanne herself.[22]

More recognition followed, but as a by-product of politics. In the early 1960s, Israel began a program to recognize non-Jews who had risked or sacrificed their lives on behalf of Jews. Known as the "Righteous Among the Nations," it was administered by the Yad Vashem memorial in Jerusalem.

In April 1963, the director of Yad Vasham learned that Paul-Henri Spaak was planning to visit Israel. Aware of the article about Suzanne, the director decided to conduct a ceremony to honor her in conjunction with her brother-in-law's visit. He wrote to Claude and asked him to help assemble the documentation regarding his wife. Claude confirmed that Suzanne had organized rescues, but he specified that the reasons for her arrest and execution had been "classic" acts of resistance.[23] Yad Vashem named Suzanne Spaak "Righteous Among the Nations" on April 21, 1985.

But her story went cold. After the war, each movement involved in the rescues wrote its own history. Suzanne's name appeared in many of them: Denise Milhaud's account of Entr'aide Temporaire; Adam Rayski's histories of Solidarité and the MNCR; the Oratoire's story of La Clairière. But inasmuch as Suzanne didn't belong to any party or a religion, she was always a footnote. As a woman without a business or profession, she left few papers for archives, and her husband burned what little she had. She was always an outlier: a Belgian amid the French, an atheist amid the believers, an independent among the militants.

These were the vital components of her story: as a member of the ruling class, she had the means to help others. As a humanitarian, she chose to do so. As a political independent, she was overlooked in the institutional histories, and as a shunned wife, she was almost erased by her husband.

The deportations marked a moment when anti-Semitism and

xenophobia converged, among the French as well as the Germans.*
Most of the population was not motivated by hatred or cruelty;
people simply acted out of self-interest, and found it convenient to
look the other way. This is human nature, and such behavior tends
to be the norm when societies are confronted with injustice on an
epic scale.

It was laudable but not surprising when brave members of the
immigrant Jewish community—including Sophie Schwartz, Léon
Chertok, Charles Lederman, and Adam Rayski—defended their
own. But Suzanne Spaak, along with her small army of outliers, belonged to a different category. Suzanne Spaak was capable of seeing
and serving the "alien other" because, in her clear gaze, no fellow
human was alien, or other. *Il faut faire quelque chose.* "Something
must be done."

---

* Forty-one percent of France's foreign Jews were deported, compared with
  13 percent of the French Jews, and even this lopsided figure is misleading. Serge Klarsfeld shows that those described as "French citizens" among
  the deported included some eight thousand naturalized citizens and eight
  thousand children born in France of immigrant parents—culturally, if not
  legally, "foreign Jews." Adjusted for these factors, 52 percent of France's
  immigrant Jews were deported, compared with 7.5 percent of the French
  Jews of old stock.

17

the aftermath

Bazou and Pilette

As of 2017, the Spaak siblings live near Paris, close to their grown children and grandchildren. Pilette is an accomplished knitting instructor who offers classes and instructional videos. Bazou spends part of the year with his wife in his ashram in India.

Claude Spaak

Claude continued to write and produce plays, but none of them achieved the success of *The School for Scandal* in 1940. Suzanne haunted his work. In 1959 he wrote *Soleil de Minuit* (*Midnight Sun*), set in occupied Norway in February 1944. In it, a German officer has arrested five men accused of resistance activities. The officer interrogates the prisoners' families, falling deeper and deeper into a moral quandary. One couple, the same age as the Spaaks during the occupation, reverse their roles. The husband is in German custody facing execution, and his wife, at liberty, must decide how to respond. The German officer finally releases all five suspects, concludes that he is the only true criminal, and presents himself for court-martial.[1]

In *Les Survivants* (*The Survivors*, 1963) a couple wanders the ruins of postwar Germany. "They both fiercely opposed the regime that destroyed the country, and their spouses paid with their lives. They have everything they need to rebuild their lives, but they cannot."[2]

Claude and Ruth were by all accounts a devoted couple, and lived well on a combination of the Spaaks' art collection and Ruth's eventual inheritance. Claude died in 1990 at the age of eighty-five, and Ruth died shortly after.

Charles Spaak

After the war, critics excoriated Claude's brother Charles for writing screenplays for the German-owned Continental Films. Some artists in his situation were barred from working due to their collaborationist histories, but Charles's support for Suzanne's activities exonerated him. His daughters Catherine and Agnès became well-known movie actresses in the 1960s.

René Magritte

Claude Spaak and Magritte never resumed their friendship and creative partnership. Magritte struggled to recapture his earlier spark. For a while he survived by painting forgeries of the works of Paul Klee, Titian, and Max Ernst (Ernst liked the forgery so much that he signed it), then drifted into painting soft-focus nudes.[3] By 1960 his reputation rebounded. He bought Georgette an elegant new home and died a prosperous man. A major museum in Brussels is dedicated entirely to him. His portrait of Suzanne is considered an important work, but the subject has generally been described as "Claude Spaak's wife."

Leopold Trepper and Heinz Pannwitz

Leopold Trepper's life continued to veer between the terrifying and the picaresque. With the liberation of Paris, he emerged from hiding and reported to Moscow, but he met a chilly reception. The directors of Soviet intelligence were deeply suspicious of Trepper and his "Great Game." Trepper claimed that he had tricked the Gestapo into believing that he was serving as its double agent, when he was actually working as Moscow's triple agent. His minders in Moscow were unconvinced. In September 1944 Trepper showed up on the Spaaks' doorstop. He asked Claude to verify his story, and Claude wrote out a report. He placed it in a yellow envelope and dispatched Pilette to drop it off at the Soviet embassy near Invalides.

But to no avail. In 1945 the Soviets bundled Trepper and a dozen other agents onto a plane to Moscow. Shortly after he arrived, he was ordered to write out a detailed description of his wartime activities. Then he was hauled off to the notorious Lubianka Prison.

A few months later, his interrogator came into his cell and announced that a Gestapo officer, Heinz Pannwitz, had just landed at the Moscow airport, proposing to cast his lot with the Soviets. He offered his expertise to break the codes of the British and the Americans, but the Soviets had other ideas and placed him under arrest.

Trepper was startled. "That same night, Pannwitz and his accomplices slept in Lubianka," he wrote. "History had played an enormous joke: the head of the Red Orchestra and the head of the Gestapo task force, a few meters apart, in the same prison."[4] The two men passed the time comparing notes on their wartime contest. Heinz Pannwitz would be imprisoned by the Soviets until 1955; Leopold Trepper walked out of Lubianka only a year earlier. Trepper rejoined his long-suffering wife, Luba, and their two sons, and they returned to their native Poland. But it was an unhappy choice. In the early 1970s the Polish Communist government carried out a massive anti-Semitic campaign, and Trepper was barred from leaving the country. An international campaign was launched to win his freedom with the support of Red Orchestra survivors, enlisting Claude Spaak, Charles Lederman, and Harry Sokol's brother Jacques.[5] Trepper was allowed to emigrate to Israel in 1974 and died there eight years later. He was given a hero's burial that was attended by a host of high-ranking Israeli officials, including Ariel Sharon.

Suzanne's Children

Rudolf Rathke

British intelligence files dated March 1945 recorded Rathke's surrender. "A 42-year-old native of Stettin. He was a member of the Gestapo, but deserted to the American troops in the hope of saving his skin. He talked willingly, without, of course, compromising himself. However, he gave the impression of a man with a burdened conscience, his attitude having been one of constant fear. At times he seemed to regret his surrender and voiced intentions of escaping or committing suicide."

Theodor Dannecker

Dannecker, the SS officer who ordered the Vel d'Hiv arrests, expanded his mandate to include Jewish children. His superiors recalled him from Paris in late 1942 under charges of corruption and misconduct. He organized deportations from several other countries until the end of the war, and was captured by American forces. He committed suicide in an American prison camp on December 10, 1945, at the age of thirty-two.

Alois Brunner

In July 1943, the thirty-one-year-old SS commander was placed in charge of the internment camp at Drancy and instructed to expedite the deportations from Paris. He escaped after the war and eventually made his way to Syria, where he instructed security services in the use of electrical torture devices. His whereabouts were a mystery until 2017, when reports emerged that he had spent his final years incarcerated in a Damascus basement, where he died in 2001 at the age of eighty-nine.

Helmut Knochen

Knochen was the thirty-year-old SS officer placed in charge of security in Paris in 1940, and his jurisdiction was later expanded across northern France. He oversaw the pursuit of thousands of Jews, as well as members of the French resistance and British SOE agents. After the war he was tried and sentenced to death (sequentially) in British and French courts, but the sentences were commuted. In 1962, he was released by President Charles de Gaulle. He died in Germany in 2003 at the age of ninety-three.

Klaus Barbie

In November 1942, the twenty-nine-year-old SS officer was placed in charge of the Gestapo office in Lyon. There he oversaw the torture and murder of members of the French resistance, including Jean Moulin, and the deportation of numerous Jews, including forty-four children from the orphanage at Izieu. In 1947, he was recruited by the US Army Counterintelligence Corps (CIC). The French attempted to extradite him, but he escaped, allegedly with the help of US intelligence. In 1983, he was finally extradited from Bolivia to France, where he was tried, convicted, and sentenced to life imprisonment. He died of cancer in a Lyon prison in 1991.

Robert Debré and Elisabeth de la Panouse, Countess de la Bourdonnaye ("Dexia")

Robert Debré was widely recognized as the foremost French pediatrician of his time. The couple married in 1956, and the countess continued to support his medical work. She suffered terrible losses in the final months of the war in Europe. Her son Geoffroy, the gallant tank commander, was killed in January 1945 in a battle in Alsace. Later she learned that her younger son Guy, who had been captured on his way to join the Free French, had died in a German concentration camp the same month.

Robert Debré was luckier. His children not only survived the war but his son Michel triumphed in peacetime. He became the principal author of the new French Constitution in 1958, and was named prime minister shortly afterward. Michel moved into the Hôtel Matignon on the Rue de Varennes—the official residence, next door to the apartment where the countess, his new stepmother, had hidden a dozen Jewish children from La Clairière.

The countess died in 1972 at the age of seventy-four, and Robert Debré died five years later at the age of ninety-five. The Hôpital Universitaire Robert-Debré, the leading pediatric hospital in France, was named after him, and the Centre Elisabeth de la Panouse-Debré children's clinic was named after her.

Paul Vergara and Marcelle Guillemot

Pastor Vergara and Marcelle Guillemot returned to their callings at the Oratoire and La Clairière after the war. The pastor's family paid a heavy price for their commitment to the Resistance. His son Sylvain returned from Buchenwald bearing the physical and psychological scars of his ordeal. He married his twin sister's best friend, a Jewish girl who had been hidden by his family—but he lived in fear that Nazis would reappear and arrest his half-Jewish children. Vergara's son-in-law, Jacques Bruston, who was arrested after picking up an airdrop from London, died in the Mauthausen concentration camp in March 1944 at the age of thirty-five.

After the war the MNCR emerged as a legal organization, and Pastor Vergara and Marcelle Guillemot joined its board. The group's leaders took an active role in aiding France's shell-shocked Jewish population.

Charles Lederman

The Communist lawyer became a prominent politician in the postwar era, benefiting from the prestige the Communist Party had won with its resistance efforts. He served for many years as a senator and judge on the High Court of Justice (Haute cour de justice).

Adam Rayski

Like many of his counterparts, Rayski returned to Poland after the war to help build a new Communist Poland. But he soon ran afoul of

the Communist Party and returned to France, where he was implicated in a Polish espionage case. He later became a leading historian
of the Jewish resistance. He called his 1985 memoir *Our Lost Illusions*. Rayski died in 2008 at the age of eighty-five. His son, Benoît,
the hidden child, became a noted author and critic who published
a controversial 2012 article describing himself as an "Islamophobe."

Léon Chertok

The handsome psychiatrist moved to New York in 1947 and worked
at Mount Sinai Hospital in New York, where he became an early
advocate of the use of hypnosis in American psychiatry. Then he returned to France and developed a reputation as a renegade theorist.
Chertok died in 1991 at the age of eighty. His son Grégoire became
a managing partner at a Rothschild merchant bank.

Sophie Schwartz

Sophie Schwartz, Peggy Camplan, and the Milhauds devoted years
of their lives to caring for the Jewish orphans. Sophie took many
of them under her wing, and remained especially close to Larissa
Gruszow. Sophie died in 1999 at the age of ninety-five.*

Hélène Berr

Hélène and her parents, Raymond and Antoinette, were arrested
on March 7, 1944, held in Drancy for two weeks, then deported to
Auschwitz. Antoinette was gassed on April 30, 1944, and Raymond
was murdered in September. Hélène was transferred to Bergen-
Belsen, where she died of typhus in April 1945, a few weeks after
Anne Frank died of the same cause in the same camp, and a few days
before the camp's liberation.

---

* The US Holocaust Memorial Museum's online archives contain a video
  interview with her under the name of "Sophie Micnik."

Suzanne's Children

Larissa Gruszow

Larissa's father returned from his POW camp after the war and took her to Poland with his second wife, but she was unhappy there. She received an engineering degree and returned to Belgium, where she lived with her husband and two children. She and Pilette and Bazou Spaak remain close friends.

The Children

After the war, Peggy Camplan told her charges at Renouveau that the master list of rescued children had been buried under a tree at Suzanne's country house in Choisel. That list has not been found. The available evidence suggests that all of the children rescued by the network survived the occupation.

Righteous Among the Nations

The Yad Vashem memorial in Israel is charged with identifying non-Jews who risked their safety or their freedom to save Jewish lives from the Holocaust, with no expectation of personal gain. The process requires rigorous documentation. Suzanne Spaak was designated Righteous Among the Nations in 1985. Since then, at least fourteen members of her network have been so honored. Others include: Fernand and Odette Béchard (Oratoire parishioners); Marguerite Camplan (MNCR); Louis and Hélène Cardon (sheltered Larissa Gruszow); Simone and Adrien Chaye (sheltered children from the La Clairière rescue); Lucie Chevalley-Sabatier (founder of Entr'aide Temporaire); Noémie Fradin (sheltered Benoît Rayski and others); Marcelle Guillemot (social worker at La Clairière); Marie Marteau (ran the Hotel Stella, used as a way station for the network); and Paul and Marcelle Vergara (pastor of the Oratoire and his wife).

acknowledgments

Some years ago, in the course of researching *Red Orchestra*, I came across a crudely retouched photo of Suzanne Spaak in the memoirs of Soviet agent Leopold Trepper. I was struck by her haunting gaze and tried to learn more about her, without success. I found an occasional sentence or paragraph in various histories of the Occupation, but no major articles or books, in French or English, that told her story.

In 2009, I tracked down her daughter, Pilette, in suburban Maryland. She was glad to hear from me. "Everyone said Mama was a Soviet spy," she told me. "I wouldn't care if she was, but she was something completely different." That conversation set off a series of three dozen interviews, conducted over seven years in Washington, DC's Union Station, her Maryland living room, and finally her apartment outside Paris. The story revealed how principled individuals of many different nationalities and religious backgrounds worked together in the name of compassion and decency.

Pilette was unfailingly generous in sharing her story with me. She introduced me to her brother, Paul-Louis ("Bazou"), who added

acknowledgments

to her recollections, and to members of the Lorge and Spaak clans, who offered their perspectives. My deepest thanks go to Pilette and Bazou, as well as to Tommy Happé, Anthony Palliser, and Antoinette Spaak. I also thank the "hidden children" who shared their memories and archival materials: Jacques Alexandre, Sami Dassa, and Larissa Gruszow. I could not have written this book without them. I am very grateful for the assistance of now-grown children of the rescue network: Claude Bassi-Lederman, Oriane de la Bourdonnaye Guéna, Richard Bruston, and Michèle Meunier. I thank Lillie Paquette for her artful and sensitive video recording of interviews with many of these individuals and the sites they inhabited.

Two distinguished historians, my Columbia colleague Volker Berghahn and the late Allan Mitchell, read a long manuscript and helped me find the book within, and encouraged me when I most needed it.

In Paris, I received assistance from the Mémorial de la Shoah and the Archives du Centre de Documentation Juive Contemporaine, as well as from the Musée du Général Leclerc de Hautecloque et de la Libération de Paris–Musée Jean Moulin. I am grateful to the clergy and congregation of l'Oratoire du Louvre, in addition to the staffs of La Clairière and the Centre Israélite de Montmartre at 16 Rue Lamarck, both of which continue to serve immigrant communities. Guillaume Bourgeois shared his insights on the strange history of Leopold Trepper. In New York, I benefited from the unparalleled resources of the Butler Library at Columbia University and the Dorot Jewish Division of the New York Public Library, and in Washington, DC, from the archives of the US Holocaust Memorial Museum. I offer my appreciation to the Bibliothèque nationale de France and its superb online resource Gallica, as well as Google Books, which was indespensable in tracing obscure sources in several languages.

I thank my fine research assistant, Avery Curran, for her help in analyzing contemporary press accounts and the role of activists in

Lyon. Kristen Frederickson did me a great favor in tracking down Magritte's *La ligne de la vie* in London. David Armstrong also shared insights on research.

Friends, including Lauren Belfer, Sharon Isbin, Tommy Kail, Jack Snyder, and Lauren Westbrook, have advised and cheered me along the way. The Twelfth Night Players have lifted my spirits, and D. F. Sharp has given me wise counsel. My parents, Ted and Gerada Nelson, sowed the seeds of my interest in this period. George Black and David Nelson Black have shared that interest, and Julia Nelson Black has lent her editorial perspective at critical junctures.

The Salzmann Institute for War and Peace Studies at Columbia University has given me the valuable opportunity to pursue my research as a fellow there. Some of this work was conceived during a Bellagio Fellowship, and I offer my warm appreciation to the Rockefeller Foundation and the other fellows. My 2005 Guggenheim fellowship nurtured this book as well as my last one.

I thank my legendary editor, Alice Mayhew, at Simon & Schuster, for her enthusiasm for this book and for her keen editorial eye in guiding it to completion. Her assistant, Stuart Roberts, has provided ongoing support. My editor at Robert Laffont in Paris, Dorothée Cuneo, offered valuable research assistance. I am very lucky to have Ethan Bassoff as my agent. He has been a joy to work with every step of the way.

appendix

Suzanne Spaak sent these letters to her children from the prison at Fresnes two months before she was executed.

Fresnes on 12 June 1944

My darling little Pilette,

Despite the purpose of my letter, I am still very happy to be able to write to you, to be able to tell you, my little darling, how much I love you, how my thoughts are constantly with you all even at night, for it is then that I dream about you. I never felt as if I were completely alone, it seems to me that you all surround me, and your dear presence makes the hours fly quickly. Seven months are not much to think about everyone you love, to evoke all the good memories they have given you.

Since I have permission to do so, I will tell you a lot about my life here and you will see that there is a way, even in prison, to say with Goethe: "Whatever is LIFE is a good thing."

appendix

Fresnes does not resemble Saint-Gilles at all, it is a "beautiful" prison, which is next to Antony, almost in the country, and a wonderful number of birds sing around me. I recognize the finch, the blackbird, the swallow, the robin, and a few times I heard a cuckoo. The cells are large, lit by a huge window (on the days when the weather is nice I have sun all afternoon). The bed doesn't fold up and I have a good woolen mattress. A board fixed to the wall serves as a table. There's a wooden floor and a real toilet.

The disciplinary and food regime is really tolerable, and the two guards in charge of me are particularly kind. (For example, they let me lie on my bed during the day as long as I want, which is my favorite position.) I get up at 8am and make my bed, sweep, and do ten minutes of gymnastics. After my toilette I have lunch (coffee and bread, and I always have something to put on it). At noon we have a bowl of very good soup, so much that I always have some left for supper. At 4 o'clock coffee again—with the bread I get some butter and often cheese, and on Sunday a piece of meat.

On average I receive two parcels from the Red Cross per month, a large one (one pound of sugar, jam, fruit paste, some shortbread, apples, a quarter pound of butter, two packages of Gruyère, and five bars of milk chocolate), and a small one (one pound of prune jam, gingerbread, cookies, cremosine, and five bars of chocolate). You see that is enough. The proof is that I never eat my entire bread ration, and I assure you that I am rather less thin than before. "But Maman, what do you do all day?" Well, my dear, it's incredible what you can do when you're not allowed to do ANYTHING! First of all, we think of those we love and I have already told you, it is a great comfort. Then I shine my floor, it's good exercise and when it's very bright I am very proud! Then I "walk" (once a week a "real" walk outside). Finally, one becomes very ingenious and I knit with small bits of straw and I embroider during the day with a tooth of my comb.

I made myself a game of dominoes by cutting letters from the newspaper that we are given as toilet paper (which also serves me to practice in German) and finally, I wrote several little poems for you (don't make fun of me!) that I do not find bad at all. I send you, my dear, something that is very precious to me and whose story is here: one day, my guard brought me a very small bouquet, and imagine, it was March 27th! The day of our wedding anniversary! I kept these flowers (you see that I am also a framer) and they have been on my table ever since. I am glad to think that they will now go to be near you. Hang them near your bed and every night and every morning, it's a little bit of your maman who will bid you goodnight and good morning.

I assure you that I am <u>very well</u> and I have not even had a cold all winter.

Believe that all I have told you is strictly correct and that I do not embellish anything. I believe that I have been given a character that easily adapts to everything. I especially believe that when your CONSCIENCE IS AT PEACE you can always find joy in life.

Of course, the first two weeks were painful, but by the end of November I had already found the rhythm I described to you. And even with their monotony, after some time the days seem to pass quickly despite everything.

For the past three weeks I've had the right to have books (what a delight!). And a guard has provided me what I need to knit and crochet. But for a long time I have had permission to have a New Testament, which is a very fortifying reading, I would like you to read a few verses from time to time, my darling, and <u>reflect on them</u> well. Even if you don't believe in God, you can try to exercise Christian morality, which seems to me admirable from every point of view. (My darling, be patient with your brother and tell him that you must replace me at his side.)

appendix

Now my big girl, my darling little Pilette, I will see you SOON and I will say goodbye very quickly so I have the strength to do it. I won't speak of all the kisses, all the tenderness, there's too much!

My beloved little Bazou. Yesterday was your birthday and by a fortunate coincidence I had permission to write to you today! Naturally, everything I say to Pilette is for you as well (as for all those who love me) and I only want to speak of your thirteen years, darling, which you have celebrated without your mother being able to embrace you. But a little more patience, my little man, and we will soon be all together. I also have a small gift for you! And I believe that you have never received one that is so ugly and poorly made, but I am sure you never received one made with more love. This poor little necktie (I am also sending you my "needles" to knit) took me almost two months to make, and each stitch contains a tender thought, and more kisses than I have ever given you. I hope you are working well and that you do not forget that after the war you should go back to Henri IV with the boys your age. I also hope that you will have plenty of poems and plays to show me. My darling, it is difficult to choose from all I want to tell you, there is so little room! Are you careful not to eat too fast and to chew well? Do you avoid quarrelling with your sister? Do you still like "hist"? Am I still your "Tigrimounette"? I would like to go on for a long time, but all the good things have an end, and since I left Pilette very quickly I will do the same for you, but my dear, HAVE FAITH and À BIENTÔT.

notes

| CHAPTER 1 | strangers

1. Interview, Anthony Palliser, Paris, March 8, 2015.
2. *La découverte de feu,* 1935, and *Le modèle rouge,* 1935, currently in the Moderna Museet in Stockholm. Claude's acquisitions were not to everyone's taste. His brother-in-law, Milo Happé, consigned his Magrittes to the attic, but they would eventually contribute to his family fortune. Interview, Tommy Happé, December 3, 2014.
3. The *Comité Mondial des Femmes contre la Guerre et le Fascisme* (Women's Committee against War and Fascism), which had ties to the Communist Party.
4. Pirotte gained renown for documenting the French Resistance in Marseille. She used Bunny's Leica until her death in 2000. See "Julia Pirotte," International Center for Photography, https://www.icp.org/browse/archive/constituents/julia-pirotte?all/all/all/all/0.
5. Gilles Perrault, *The Red Orchestra* (New York: Pocket Books, 1970), 101.

6. Ibid.

7. Ibid., 103.

8. Esther Benbassa, *The Jews of France* (Princeton, NJ: Princeton University Press, 1999), 134.

9. See the Immigration Act of 1924 (the Johnson-Reed Act), n.d., Office of the Historian, Bureau of Public Affairs, US Department of State, http://history.state.gov/milestones/1921-1936/immigration-act.

10. The French tended to use the terms *litwak* (Lithuanian) or, less frequently, *polonais* (Polish) as general designations for persons from regions that included parts of Russia, Ukraine, Poland, and the Baltic region.

| CHAPTER 2 | the real war

1. Major D. Barlone, *A French Officer's Diary* (New York: Cambridge University Press, 2011), 4.

2. Douglas Porch, *The French Foreign Legion* (New York: Skyhorse Publishing, 2010), 451.

3. Renée Poznanski, *Jews in France during World War II*, trans. Nathan Bracher (Hanover, NH: Brandeis University Press, University Press of New England in association with the United States Holocaust Memorial Museum, 2001), 19.

4. These "special units" included the Twenty-First, Twenty-Second, and Twenty-Third Foreign Infantry Battalions and the Foreign Legion's Half-Brigade No. 13. See Poznanski, *Jews in France during World War II*, 20.

5. Marie-France Pochna, *Christian Dior: The Man Who Made the World Look New* (New York: Arcade, 1996), 63.

6. Paul Belien, *A Throne in Brussels: Britain, the Saxe-Coburgs and the Belgianization of Europe* (Charlottesville, VA: Imprint Academic, 2005), 199–200.

7. Michel Dumoulin, *Spaak* (Brussels: Éditions Racine, 1999), 159.

8. Belien, *A Throne in Brussels*, 201.

9. Ibid.

10. René Magritte, *Catalogue raisonnée*, vol. 2 (Brussels: Fonds Mercator, 1997), 8.

11. René Magritte, *La ligne de la vie*, manuscript, National Art Library, London, 1938, 8.

12. Magritte, *Catalogue raisonnée*, vol. 2, 81–82; interview with Pilette Spaak, June 16, 2012.

13. Magritte, *Catalogue raisonnée*, vol. 2, 81.

14. Julian Jackson, *The Fall of France: The Nazi Invasion of 1940* (New York: Oxford University Press, 2003), 180.

15. Richard Vinen, *The Unfree French: Life under the Occupation* (New Haven, CT: Yale University Press, 2007), 30.

16. The account of Suzanne and Claude Spaak's flight from Paris is drawn from interviews with Pilette and Bazou Spaak, and from Dumoulin, *Spaak*.

17. Poznanski, *Jews in France during World War II*, 20–21.

18. "Maréchal Petain's Speech of 17 June 1940," Vichy Web, maintained by Simon Kitson, French Studies, University of Birmingham, United Kingdom, http://artsweb.bham.ac.uk/vichy/english.htm.

19. Sherry Mangan, "Paris under the Swastika," *Life*, September 16, 1940, 78.

20. Léon Blum's brother René, the impresario of the Ballet Russes de Monte Carlo, was in New York at the time of the invasion. He returned to France to be with his family, and would perish in a gas chamber in Auschwitz two years later. Léon Blum himself miraculously survived a show trial, Buchenwald, and Dachau.

21. Susan Zucotti, *The Holocaust, the French, and the Jews* (Lincoln: University of Nebraska Press, 1999), 47.

22. Hanna Diamond, *Fleeing Hitler: France 1940* (New York: Oxford University Press, 2008), 145–46.

23. Zucotti, *The Holocaust, the French, and the Jews*, 52.

24. Michael R. Marrus and Robert O. Paxton, *Vichy France and the Jews* (New York: Schocken Books, 1983), 13.

25. Thomas Laub, *After the Fall: German Policy in Occupied France, 1940–1944* (New York: Oxford University Press, 2009), 89.

26. Robert O. Paxton, *Vichy France: Old Guard and New Order, 1940–1944* (New York: Columbia University Press, 2001), 171.

27. Zucotti, *The Holocaust, the French, and the Jews,* 53.

28. Ibid., 54.

29. Adam Rayski, *The Choice of the Jews under Vichy: Between Submission and Resistance* (South Bend, IN: Notre Dame Press in association with the United States Holocaust Memorial Museum, 2005), 27–29.

30. Robert Gildea, *Fighters in the Shadows* (London: Faber & Faber, 2015), 220.

| CHAPTER 3 | paris by night

1. Paxton, *Vichy France,* 45.

2. Central Intelligence Agency, *The Rote Kapelle: The CIA's History of Soviet Intelligence and Espionage Networks in Western Europe, 1936–1945* (Washington, DC: University Publications of America, 1979), 39. See also Perrault, *The Red Orchestra,* 102. According to the CIA's account, Mira Sokol may have received a payment from a suspected Soviet agent as early as 1939 (*The Rote Kapelle,* 357).

3. Poznanski, *Jews in France during World War II,* 56–57.

4. David Diamant, *Le billet vert* (Paris: Renouveau, 1977), 87.

5. Ibid., 89, 96.

6. Poznanski, *Jews in France during World War II,* 56–57.

7. Léon Chertok, *Memoires: Les résistances d'un psy* (Paris: Odile Jacob, 2006), 80–81.

8. Ibid., 81.

9. Jacques Bielinky, *Journal, 1940–1942: Un journaliste juif à Paris sous l'Occupation* (Paris: Éditions du Cerf, 1992), cited in Poznanski, *Jews in France during World War II,* 59.

10. Poznanski, *Jews in France during World War II*, 60.

11. Perrault, *The Red Orchestra*, 103–5.

12. Ibid.

13. "B. Aronson," "Suzanne Spaak, sauveteur d'enfants Juifs," *Naïe Presse*, March 9, 1945, Archives du Centre de Documentation Juive Contemporaine, Paris, CCXVIII-88a.

14. Chertok, *Memoires*, 86.

15. Adam Rayski, *Nos illusions perdues* (Paris: Éditions Balland, 1985), 99.

16. Chertok, *Memoires*, 117.

17. Jeremy Josephs, *Swastika over Paris: The Fate of the French Jews* (London: Bloomsbury, 1989), 37.

18. Rayski, *The Choice of the Jews under Vichy*, 23.

19. Ibid., 45.

20. Christopher Browning, *The Origins of the Final Solution: The Evolution of Nazi Jewish Policy, September 1939–March 1942* (Lincoln: University of Nebraska Press, 2007), 281.

21. Matthew Cobb, *The Resistance: The French Fight Against the Nazis* (London: Pocket Books, 2009), 77.

22. Adam Rayski, "Testimony," Archives du Centre de Documentation Juive Contemporaine, DLXI_84, 6. Rayski's undated statement begins, "A. Raisky, who is no longer in agreement with certain ideas of the Communist Party, has preferred to reclaim his independence. Nonetheless he maintains a faithful memory of the past, which allows him to evoke with great honesty the actions of resistance of Communist Jews. He directed the UJRE [the successor organization to Solidarité] until 1949."

23. R. Cardinne-Petit, *Les secrets de la Comédie Française: 1936–1945* (Paris: Nouvelles Éditions Latines, 1958), 220.

24. Francis Steegmuller, *Cocteau* (Boston: Little, Brown & Company, 1970), 436.

25. Jean Cocteau, *L'Impromptu du Palais-Royal* (Paris: Éditions Gallimard, 1962), quoted in Claude Bourgelin and Marie-Claude Shapira, *Lire Cocteau* (Lyon: Presses Universitaires Lyon, 1992), 66.

26. Judith Thurman, *Secrets of the Flesh: A Life of Colette* (New York: Ballantine Books, 1999), 468–69.

27. *Colette*, directed by Yannick Bellon, 1951, available at https://www .youtube.com/watch?v=lqEa9cVRGlk.

28. Thurman, *Secrets of the Flesh*, 422–23.

29. Michel Lincourt, *In Search of Elegance: Towards an Architecture of Satisfaction* (Liverpool: Liverpool University Press, 1999), 162.

30. Margaret Mitchell's 1936 novel was wildly popular in occupied France. The Nazis banned it in response, and prices for illegal copies shot up. Mitchell was amused at the idea of Scarlett's flinty Irish father, Gerald O'Hara, exclaiming, "*Oo la la.*" See Anita Price, *The Margaret Mitchell Encyclopedia* (Jefferson, NC: McFarland, 2013), 78.

31. Patricia Volk, *Shocked: My Mother, Schiaparelli, and Me* (New York: Alfred A. Knopf, 2013), 123.

32. In early 1942, Feferman and his partners joined the FTP-MOI, but their days were numbered. In May, Feferman and another youth were apprehended by police. He swallowed a tablet of cyanide and shouted "Vive la France et le Communisme" and, as a guarantee, fired his last bullet into his head. He was twenty-one years old. See David Diamant, *Jeune combat: La jeunesse juive dans la Résistance* (Paris: Éditions L'Harmattan, 1993), 39.

33. See Cobb, *The Resistance*, 77–84.

34. Jean-Jacques Bernard, *Le Camp de la morte lente* (Paris: Éditions le Manuscrit, 2006).

35. Maurice Goudeket, *Près de Colette* (Paris: Flammarion, 1956), 203.

36. *Le Petit Parisien*, December 31, 1941, 1.

37. Rayski, *The Choice of the Jews under Vichy*, 49.

| CHAPTER 4 | *la plaque tournante*

1. Interview, Antoinette Spaak, Brussels, November 2014.

2. Charles Lederman, unpublished memoirs, collection of Claudie Bassi-Lederman, 144.

3. *Radio Paris ment* and *Messages personnels*, BBC, Jalons, http://fresques.ina.fr/jalons/fiche-media/InaEdu00282/bbc-radio-paris-ment-et-messages-personnels.html.

4. Jacques Adler, *The Jews of Paris and the Final Solution: Communal Response and Internal Conflicts, 1940–1944* (New York: Oxford University Press, 1989), 177.

5. Vinen, *The Unfree French*, 118–22.

6. United States Holocaust Memorial Museum, "Polish Victims," in *Holocaust Enyclopedia*, www.ushmm.org/wlc/en/article.php?ModuleId=10005473.

7. Christopher Browning, *Ordinary Men: Reserve Police Battalion 101 and the Final Solution in Poland* (New York: HarperPerennial, 1998), xv.

8. Robert Belleret, "Premier convoi pour Auschwitz," *Le Monde*, March 26, 2002, www.lemonde.fr/idees/article/2002/03/26/premier-convoi-pour-auschwitz_268264_3232.html.

9. Bernhard Blumenkranz, *Histoire des Juifs en France* (Toulouse: Privat, 1972), 405.

10. Rayski, "Testimony," 10. See also Jonathan Frankel and Dan Diner, eds., *Dark Times, Dire Decisions: Jews and Communism* (New York: Oxford University Press, 2004).

11. Rayski, "Testimony," 12.

12. Ibid., 13.

13. Jeanne List-Pakin, "Testimony," Archives du Centre de Documentation Juive Contemporaine, Paris, Document DLXXXVII-7, 2.

14. Stéphane Courtois, Denis Peschanski, and Adam Rayski, *L'Affiche Rouge: Immigranten und Juden in der französischen Résistance* (Berlin: Schwarze Risse Verlag, 1994), 107.

15. See Chertok, *Memoires*, and Rayski, *Nos Illusions Perdues*, for descriptions of their clandestine life.

16. Renée Poznanski, *Propagandes et persécutions: La Résistance et le "problème juif," 1940–1944* (Paris: Librairie Arthème Fayard, 2008), 225–26. Poznanski records that *J'Accuse* was launched in April

1942 under Mouni Nadler but modified its subtitle several times that year. The MNCR archives begin with an edition identified as "No. 1," dated October 10, 1942: http://archives.mrap.fr/images /c/c0/Jaccuse_1opt.pdf.

17. Adler, *The Jews of Paris and the Final Solution*, 190–91.
18. Cédric Gruat and Cécile Leblanc, *Amis des Juifs: Les résistants aux étoiles* (Paris: Éditions Tirésias, 2005), 45, quoted in Ronald Rosbottom, *When Paris Went Dark: The City of Light under German Occuption, 1940–1944* (New York: Little, Brown, 2014), chapter 7.

| CHAPTER 5 | monsieur henri

1. Perrault, *The Red Orchestra*, 130.
2. Guillaume Bourgeois, *L'Orchestre rouge* (Paris: Nouveau Monde Éditions, 2015), 136.
3. W. F. Flicke, *Rote Kapelle: Spionage und Widerstand* (Augsburg, Germany: Weltbild Verlag, 1990), 161–62.
4. Harry's brother Jacques, a Communist architect based in Brussels, was also arrested on suspicion of involvement in his brother's activities. Jacques survived the war. See Central Intelligence Agency, *The Rote Kapelle*, 356.
5. Betty Depelsenaire, *Symphony Fraternelle* (Brussels: Lumen, 1942).
6. Ibid.
7. Ibid., 22.
8. V. E. Tarrant, *The Red Orchestra: The Soviet Spy Network Inside Nazi Europe* (London: Arms & Armour Press, 1995), 39–41. See also Leopold Trepper, *The Great Game: Memoirs of the Spy Hitler Couldn't Silence* (New York: McGraw-Hill, 1977), and Flicke, *Rote Kapelle*.
9. Leopold Trepper, with Patrick Rotman, *Le Grand Jeu* (Paris: Éditions Albin Michel, 1975), 240.
10. Trepper, *The Great Game*, 164.

| CHAPTER 6 | spring wind, winter stadium

1. Hélène Berr, *Journal*, trans. David Bello (New York: Weinstein Books, 2008), 51.
2. Poznanski, *Jews in France during World War II*, 250.
3. Adler, *The Jews of Paris and the Final Solution*, 159.
4. Claudie Bassi-Lederman and Roland Wlos, "La rafle du Vel' d'Hiv, ou le 'sombre jeudi,'" *L'Humanité*, July 6, 2012. See also Rayski, *The Choice of the Jews under Vichy*, 86.
5. Rayski, *Nos illusions perdues*, 128.
6. Carmen Callil, *Bad Faith: A Forgotten History of Family, Fatherland and Vichy France* (New York: Knopf Doubleday, 2008), 265.
7. Rayski, *The Choice of the Jews under Vichy*, 86.
8. Michel Laffitte, "The Velodrome d'Hiver Round-up: July 16 and 17, 1942," SciencesPo, http://www.sciencespo.fr/mass-violence-war-massacre-resistance/en/document/va-lodrome-da-hiver-round-july-16-and-17-1942.
9. Israel Gutman, *Encyclopedia of the Holocaust*, volume 2 (New York: Macmillan Library Reference, 1995), 1079.
10. US diplomat Tyler Thompson, August 1942, cited in Marrus and Paxton, *Vichy France and the Jews*, 228.
11. Marrus and Paxton, *Vichy France and the Jews*, 225.
12. De Brinon was executed at the end of the war as a collaborator. His wife lived another forty years before she died in a nursing home in Montmorency.
13. Laffitte, "The Velodrome d'Hiver Round-up."
14. Marrus and Paxton, *Vichy France and the Jews*, 241–42.
15. Serge Klarsfeld, *French Children of the Holocaust: A Memorial*, trans. Glorianne Depondt and Howard M. Epstein (New York: New York University Press, 1996), 35.
16. Berr, *Journal*, 85–87.
17. Ibid., 93.
18. Memorandum reproduced in Gilles Perrault, *Paris under the Occupation*,

trans. Allison Carter and Maximilian Vos (New York: Vendome Press, 1987), 177.

19. Klarsfeld, *French Children of the Holocaust*, 37.

20. Ibid., 40.

21. There is disagreement as to the total number of police deployed over the two days. Susan Zucotti uses the figure 4,500 in *The Holocaust, the French, and the Jews*, 104.

22. Sarah Litmanovitch, "Juillet 1942, la rafle des juifs dans le 18e, témoignages," Dixhuitinfo.com, March 10, 2010, www.dixhuit info.com/societe/histoire/article/juillet-1942-la-rafle-des-juifs.

23. Zucotti, *The Holocaust, the French, and the Jews*, 107.

24. Rayski, *Nos illusions perdues*, 99–100.

25. Chertok, *Memoires*, 84.

26. Zucotti, *The Holocaust, the French, and the Jews*, 107.

27. Chertok, *Memoires*, 85.

28. Ibid. See also Adam Rayski, *16 et 17 juillet 1942: La rafle du Vélodrome d'Hiver* (Paris: Mairie de Paris, 2012), 29.

29. Alain Pierret, "La Rafle, le film: Le vrai capitaine Pierret raconté par son fils Alain," Dixhuitinfo.com, March 10, 2010, www.dix huitinfo.com/culture/cinema/article/la-rafle-le-film-le-vrai-cap itaine.

30. David Lees, "Remembering the Vel d'hiv Roundup," University of Warwick Knowledge Centre, July 2012, www2.warwick.ac.uk /knowledge/arts/roundups.

31. Klarsfeld, *French Children of the Holocaust*, 42.

32. Josephs, *Swastika over Paris*, 64. See also Klarsfeld, *French Children of the Holocaust*, 68.

33. Fred and Denise Milhaud, *L'Entraide temporaire: sauvetage d'enfants juifs sous l'occupation* (Paris: Alliance Israelite Universelle, 1984), http://www.europeana.eu/portal/en/record/09305/C67A0AF 1D7E0EB7CC4A923753431A15BEEADBFB6.html.

| CHAPTER 7 | the ragged network

1. Klarsfeld, *French Children of the Holocaust*, xxi and 119. See also "Plus qu-un nom dans une liste: Israël Knaster," Jewish Traces, http://jewishtraces.org/israelknaster/.
2. Klarsfeld, *French Children of the Holocaust*, 119–25.
3. Ibid., 43.
4. See Lucien Lazare, *Rescue as Resistance: How Jewish Organizations Fought the Holocaust in France*, trans. Jeffrey M. Green (New York: Columbia University Press, 1996), 76.
5. Author's interview with Oriane de la Bourdonnaye Guéna, Paris, June 2015.
6. Robert Debré, *L'Honneur de vivre* (Paris: Hermann et Stock, 1974), 333–40.
7. "Activité du Groupe Medical du Mouvement National Contre le Racisme," tract, MNCR Archives, Paris, http://archives.mrap.fr/index.php/Accueil.
8. "Aronson," "Suzanne Spaak, sauveteur d'enfants Juifs."
9. "Activité du Groupe Medical du Mouvement National Contre le Racisme."
10. Quoted in Serge Klarsfeld, *Le calendrier de la persécution des Juifs de France, Septembre 1942–Août 1944* (Paris: Fayard, 2001), 575.
11. See Michael Curtis, *Verdict on Vichy: Power and Prejudice in the Vichy France Regime* (New York: Skyhorse Publishing, 2015), chapter 13, "The Churches and Anti-Semitism."
12. Lederman, unpublished memoirs.
13. Ibid. See also Nancy Levenfeld, "Unarmed Combat: Jewish Humanitarian Resistance in France during the Shoah," in Patrick Henry, ed., *Jewish Resistance Against the Nazis* (Washington, DC: Catholic University of America Press, 2014), 112.
14. "Lettre pastorale de Monseigneur Saliège du 23 Août 1942," Musée de la Résistance en ligne, http://museedelaresistanceenligne.org

/media6523-Lettre-pastorale-de-Monseigneur-SaliA. See also Yad Vashem, http://www.yadvashem.org/righteous/stories/saliege.

15. Lederman, unpublished memoirs, 133.

16. Klarsfeld, *French Children of the Holocaust*, 46.

17. Ibid., 52.

18. Poznanski, *Jews in France during World War II*, 265.

19. Quoted in Jean-Pierre Levy, *Mémoires d'un franc-tireur: Itinéraire d'un résistant (1940–1944)* (Paris: Éditions Complexe, 2000), 157.

20. "Hommes de coeur," tract, MNCR archives, Paris, http://archives .mrap.fr/images/b/b4/MNCR_tract_1opt.pdf.

21. "Madame, Monsieur," tract, MNCR archives, http://archives .mrap.fr/images/4/40/MNCR_tract_2.pdf.

22. *Défense de la France*, July 30, 1942. Quoted in Cobb, *The Resistance*, 137.

23. Lazare, *Rescue as Resistance*, 176.

24. Ibid., 177.

25. List-Pakin, "Testimony," 2.

| CHAPTER 8 | suzanne and sophie

1. Lederman, unpublished memoirs, 148.

2. "Enregistrement de Sophie Micnik [Schwartz], lors de son séjour à Munich en mars 1985," unpublished interview conducted by Larissa Gruszow, March 1985, 29.

3. Ibid.

4. Sholem Aleichem, *Tevye the Dairyman and the Railroad Stories* (New York: Knopf Doubleday, 2011).

5. See *16 rue Lamarck, 1938, Paris*, Framepool, http://footage.frame pool.com/fr/shot/943433765-16-rue-lamarck-hostel-montmar tre-entrer.

6. Annette Muller, *La petite fille du Vel d'Hiv* (Paris: Hachette Livre, 2012).

7. "Enregistrement de Sophie Micnik," 27.

8. René Goldman, *Une femme juive dans les tourmentes du siècle passé: Sophie Schwartz-Micnik* (Paris: AGP, 2006), 21.

9. Rayski, *The Choice of the Jews under Vichy*, 94–95.

10. "Enregistrement de Sophie Micnik," 23.

11. Goldman, *Une femme juive dans les tourmentes du siècle passé*, 29.

12. Poznanski, *Jews in France during World War II*, 308.

13. Adler, *The Jews of Paris and the Final Solution*, 201.

14. Zucotti, *The Holocaust, the French, and the Jews*, 157–59.

15. Ibid., 162.

16. Goldman, *Une femme juive dans les tourmentes du siècle passé*, 26.

17. Ibid., 29.

18. David Diamant, *250 combattents de la Résistance témoignant* (Paris: Éditions L'Harmattan, 1991), 86–88.

| CHAPTER 9 | the unimaginable

1. Rayski, *Nos illusions perdues*, 125.

2. *J'Accuse*, October 10, 1942, http://gallica.bnf.fr/ark:/12148/bpt6k874090h/f2.item.zoom.

3. *J'Accuse*, October 20, 1942, http://gallica.bnf.fr/ark:/12148/bpt6k874091w/f1.item.zoom.

4. Anne Nelson, "Nur seinem Gewissen verpflichtet: Rudolf von Scheliha," in *Widerstand und Auswärtiges Amt: Diplomaten gegen Hitler*, edited by Jan Erik Schulte and Michael Wala (Munich: Seidler, 2013).

5. Marrus and Paxton, *Vichy France and the Jews*, 348.

6. Marcelle Guillemot, "Testimony," in "Témoignage de Melle [*sic*] GUILLEMOT, assistant sociale et Directrice de l'Oeuvre du Temple l'Oratoire du Louvre—La Clairière, 60 ru Greneta, recueilli par Mme GAUDELETTE le 22 février 1946," Archives du Centre de Documentation Juive Contemporaine, Paris, Document CDLXVIII-17.

7. See Céline Marrot-Fellag Ariouet, "Les enfants cachés pendant la seconde guerre mondiale aux sources d'une histoire clandestine," http://lamaisondesevres.org/cel/cel3.html.

8. Milhaud and Milhaud, *L'Entraide temporaire*, 18.

9. Bourgeois, *L'Orchestre rouge*, 85.

10. Ibid., 475.

11. Cobb, *The Resistance*, 117–18.

12. Heinz Pannwitz, "CARETINA's History of the Sonderkommando Rote Kapelle," EGMA-44213/42334/43172, 20.

13. Henri Calet, *Les Murs de Fresnes* (Paris: Éditions Viviane Haly, 1993), 99.

| CHAPTER 10 | la clairière

1. Adler, *The Jews of Paris and the Final Solution*, 208.

2. These institutions included the centrist Amelot Committee, which received funding from both the UGIF and the American Joint Distribution Committee (the "Joint"), a US-based Jewish charity that aided many European Jews during the war. The Amelot Committee shared its funding with Solidarité and cooperated with Entr'aide Temporaire. See Adler, *The Jews of Paris and the Final Solution*, 208.

3. Klarsfeld, *French Children of the Holocaust*, 67.

4. Ibid., 69.

5. Some categories were exempted, including Jews of Turkish, Anglo-Saxon, and a few other nationalities; foreign Jews with non-Jewish spouses; those with a UGIF pass; ill, blind, or paralyzed "untransportable" persons; and mothers of children under two and the children themselves. See Klarsfeld, *French Children of the Holocaust*, 67.

6. Ibid., 70.

7. The testimonies of Simone and Armand Boruchowicz, quoted in Sami Dassa, *Vivre, aimer avec Auschwitz au cœur* (Paris: Éditions L'Harmattan, 2002), 96; see also Dassa's speech at Rue Guy-Patin, February 10, 2013, in J. Laloum, "Les maisons d'enfants de l'UGIF: Le centre de Saint-Mandé," *Revue d'Histoire de la Shoah* 1555 (September–December 1995): 89–90.

8. Quoted in Dassa, *Vivre, aimer avec Auschwitz au cœur*, 98, and speech of February 10, 2013, at Rue Guy-Patin.

9. As of 1944, Thérèse Cahen was directing the UGIF home in Saint-Mandé. She was deported with the girls from the home in July 1944 on Convoy 77, a month before liberation. She was selected to work, but chose to go to the gas chamber with her charges. See "Thérèse Cahen," Anonymes, Justes et Persécutés durant la période Nazie dans les communes de France (AJPN), http://www.ajpn.org/personne-Therese-Cahen-8532.html.

10. Rayski, *The Choice of the Jews under Vichy*, 243.

11. The five detailed accounts are from Marcelle Guillemot, recorded in a 1946 interview in the Archives du Centre de Documentation Juive Contemporaine; the testimony of Marguerite Camplan, recorded in the *Renouveau* pamphlet and reproduced in Dassa, *Vivre, aimer avec Auschwitz au cœur*; the recollections of Fred and Denise Milhaud, *L'Entraide Temporaire*, recorded in the 1980s and also found in the Archives du Centre de Documentation Juive Contemporaine; the recollections of Sophie Schwartz, published by Goldman in *Une femme juive dans les tourmentes du siècle passé*; and the memories of Pilette Spaak, recorded by Anne Nelson in various interviews.

12. Goldman, *Une femme juive dans les tourmentes du siècle passé*, 31.

13. "Aronson," "Suzanne Spaak, sauveteur d'enfants Juifs."

14. Interview, Michèle Meunier, Paris, June 22, 2015.

15. Camplan, *Renouveau*, document, quoted in Dassa, *Vivre, aimer avec Auschwitz au cœur*, 116.

16. Goldman, *Une femme juive dans les tourmentes du siècle passé*, 31.

17. Interview, Sami Dassa, Paris, September 30, 2014.

18. Camplan, *Renouveau*, in Dassa, *Vivre, aimer avec Auschwitz au cœur*, 116.

19. Ibid., 117.

20. Guillemot, "Testimony," 2.

21. Ibid., 3.

22. Camplan, *Renouveau*, in Dassa, *Vivre, aimer avec Auschwitz au cœur*, 117.

23. See Perrault, *The Red Orchestra*, 391.

24. Guillemot, "Testimony."

25. Meunier interview.

26. Dassa, *Vivre, aimer avec Auschwitz au cœur*, 96.

27. Interview, Oriane de la Bourdonnaye Guéna, Paris, June 23, 2015. There were some attempts to convert the hidden children to Christianity by certain individuals and institutions (but there is no suggestion that the Bourdonnayes were among them). In most cases, if Jewish children were instructed to learn the catechism, it was in support of their cover stories.

28. Camplan, *Renouveau*, quoted in Dassa, *Vivre, aimer avec Auschwitz au cœur*, 119.

29. Milhaud and Milhaud, *L'Entraide Temporaire*.

30. Ibid.

31. Patrick Cabanel, "La tentation d'une église confessante?" in Philippe Braunstein, ed., *L'Oratoire du Louvre et les Protestants Parisiens* (Geneva: Labor et Fides, 2011), 251–52. "Nosley" makes an appearance in Hélène Berr's diary in August 1942.

32. This figure is cited by both Jeanne List-Pakin and Marcelle Guillemot. See List-Pakin, "Testimony," 3, and Guillemot, "Testimony," 3.

33. List-Pakin, "Testimony," 2.

| CHAPTER 11 | *le grand livre*

1. Dassa, *Vivre, aimer avec Auschwitz au cœur*, 152.

2. Pilette Spaak interview.

3. Camplan, *Renouveau*, quoted in Dassa, *Vivre, aimer avec Auschwitz au cœur*, 121.

4. Lederman, unpublished memoirs, 152.

5. Goldman, *Une femme juive dans les tourmentes du siècle passé*, 27.

6. Interview, Larissa Gruszow, Brussels, December 2, 2014, and e-mails, Richard Bruston, 2015–16.

7. Patrick Cabanel, *Histoire des Justes de France* (Paris: Armand Colin, 2012), 295.

8. Trocmé and his deputy, pastor Éduoard Theis, were arrested by French police on February 13, 1943, the same week as the rescue at La Clairière. After a month they were released, and they returned to their rescue work until the end of the year, when they went into hiding. Trocmé's wife, Magda, oversaw the rescue efforts in their absence.

9. Debré, *L'Honneur de vivre*, 342.

10. "Fradin Noémie," Comité Français pour Yad Vashem, https://yadvashem-france.org/les-justes-parmi-les-nations/les-justes-de-france/dossier-3238/.

11. Debré, *L'Honneur de vivre*, 355.

12. Ibid., 357.

13. Camplan, *Renouveau*.

14. "Aronson," "Suzanne Spaak, sauveteur d'enfants Juifs."

15. Rayski, *Nos illusions perdues*, 127.

16. Rayski's memoirs state that "Jouvenel, the husband of Colette, was half-Jewish." But Colette had been divorced from Henry de Jouvenel (who was not Jewish) since 1924. Her Jewish husband in hiding was Maurice Goudeket. According to Colette's biographer, Judith Thurman, Goudeket spent most of the eighteen months following December 1942 in hiding at the Palais Royal. See Thurman, *Secrets of the Flesh*, 460.

17. Ibid., 457.

18. Jean-Louis Debré, *Les Femmes qui ont reveillé La France* (Paris: Fayard, 2013), 264.

19. Schloesing was shot down and killed August 26, 1944—the day after the liberation of Paris—having completed eighty-five combat missions. See Pierre Mergier, *Itineraire d'un français libre* (Paris: Librairie Harmattan, 2010).

20. Gildea, *Fighters in the Shadows*, 123.

21. "Hugues Limonti," Musée de l'Ordre de la Libération, http://www.ordredelaliberation.fr/fr/les-compagnons/598/hugues-limonti.

22. Goldman, *Une femme juive dans les tourmentes du siècle passé*, 39.

| CHAPTER 12 | the unraveling

1. See Rita Kramer, *Flames in the Field: The Story of Four SOE Agents in Occupied France* (New York: Penguin, 2011).

2. SOE officer F. F. E. Yeo-Thomas believed that some of his colleagues' execrable French might have contributed to their arrest.

3. Guillemot, "Testimony," 6.

4. Hugues Limonti was arrested on December 24, 1943, and interrogated in the prison at Fresnes. He was deported on January 24 and imprisoned in the concentration camps at Buchenwald, Bergen-Belsen, and Drutte. He was awarded the Legion of Honor, among other decorations, and lived until 1988. See "Hugues Limonti," Musée de L'Ordre de la Libération.

5. Dassa, *Vivre, aimer avec Auschwitz au cœur*, 127–29.

6. Lucienne/Katia eventually became a leading Paris madame. She protested her innocence of the collaboration charges, but the matter was never resolved; see Josephs, *Swastika over Paris*, 76–78. See also Laurent Joffrin, *Les Résistants: Témoignages 1940–1945* (Paris: Omnibus, 2013), 140.

7. See Goldman, *Une femme juive dans les tourmentes du siècle passé*, 40.

8. Rayski, *The Choice of the Jews under Vichy*, 235.

9. When Sophie left the hospital in November, she fled to Lyon, where she worked alongside Adam Rayski to rebuild the organization.

10. Dassa, *Vivre, aimer avec Auschwitz au cœur*, 134.

11. Debré, *L'Honneur de vivre*, 369.

12. Ibid., 367–73.

13. See Gérard Streiff, *Un soldat allemand dans la résistance française: Le courage de désobéir* (Paris: Oskar Éditeur, 2011). See also Mathias Meyers, "Résistance statt Wehrmacht," Kreisvereinigung Tübingen-Mössingen, July 17, 2012, http://tuebingen.vvn-bda.de /2012/07/17/resistance-statt-wehrmacht.

14. Karlen Vesper, "Ich wollte kein Komplize sein," Neues Deutschland, March 6, 2012, www.neues-deutschland.de/artikel/220381 .ich-wollte-kein-komplize-sein.html.

15. There was strikingly little interest among the Communists in attacking German officials overseeing the Jewish deportations. It appears that the group chose Ritter as a target in an attempt to win over the non-Jewish French public based on their objections to the STO.

16. Rayski, *The Choice of the Jews under Vichy*, 235.

17. Leroux, Malassis, and Vast, "Une dénonciation par l'image de la répression et des crimes nazis."

18. Ibid.

19. See Jacques Vistel, "Discours de Monsieur Jacques Vistel, Président de la Fondation de la Résistance, www.fondationresistance.org /pages/actualites/une-plaque-memoire-defense-france-sorbonne _actu443.htm.

| CHAPTER 13 | flight

1. Pilette Spaak, interview.

2. Donal O'Sullivan, *Dealing with the Devil: Anglo-Soviet Intelligence Cooperation in the Second World War* (New York: Peter Lang, 2010), 28.

3. Perrault, *The Red Orchestra*, 371.

4. Bourgeois, *L'Orchestre rouge*, 466. See also Perrault, *The Red Orchestra*, 391, and Trepper, *The Great Game*, 282.

5. SEO agent F. F. E. Yeo-Thomas used the cardboard trick. See Bruce Marshall, *The White Rabbit: The Secret Agent the Gestapo Could Not Crack* (London: Cassell, 2002), 44.

6. Bourgeois, *L'Orchestre rouge*, 474.
7. Gilles Perrault, *L'Orchestre rouge* (Paris: Fayard, 1989), 386.
8. Ibid., 388.
9. Bourgeois, *L'Orchestre rouge*, 467. Claude tried to find connections for Trepper in the Southern Zone and thought of Ruth Peters's fifteen-year-old relation, Antonia Lyon-Smith, a British girl who had been stranded in occupied France. Antonia wrote a note of introduction to a friend. The Gestapo discovered the note in Georgie de Winter's possession, which led to Lyon-Smith's arrest. She gave a colorful account of her time in Gestapo detention in her 1982 memoir, *A Little Resistance* (written under her married name, Antonia Hunt).
10. Pilette Spaak interview.
11. Trepper, *The Great Game*, 286.
12. Cabanel, "La tentation d'une église confessante?" in Braunstein, ed., *L'Oratoire du Louvre et les Protestants Parisiens*, 251.
13. Perrault, *L'Orchestre rouge*, 390.
14. Trepper, *The Great Game*, 288.
15. Perrault, *L'Orchestre rouge*, 393.
16. Ibid., 388.
17. Chertok, *Memoires*, 131.
18. Ibid., 112.
19. Ibid.
20. Pannwitz, "CARETINA's History of the Sonderkommando Rote Kapelle," 32–33.
21. Perrault, *L'Orchestre rouge*, 399.
22. Camplan, *Renouveau*, 3.
23. Pilette Spaak interview.
24. Chertok, *Memoires*, 113–14. See also Perrault, *L'Orchestre rouge*, 401.

| CHAPTER 14 | all saints' day

1. Milhaud and Milhaud, *L'Entraide Temporaire*, 25.
2. Pilette Spaak interview.

3. Paul (Bazou) Spaak, e-mail interview, February 21, 2012.

4. Madeleine Legrand (Madeleine Grou-Radenez), *À Fresnes* (Paris: Éditions Stock, 1944), 11–12.

5. Janine Spaak, *Charles Spaak, mon mari* (Paris: Éditions France-Empire, 1977), 124.

6. Ibid., 129.

7. Perrault, *L'Orchestre rouge*, 410.

8. Pannwitz, "CARETINA's History of the Sonderkommando Rote Kapelle," 38.

9. Henri Calet, *Les Murs de Fresnes* (Paris: Éditions Viviane Haley, 1993), 15.

10. Ibid., 115.

11. Thomas Childers, *In the Shadows of War: An American Pilot's Odyssey Through Occupied France and the Camps of Nazi Germany* (New York: Henry Holt, 2002), 220.

12. Legrand, *À Fresnes*, 25–26.

13. Ibid., 32.

14. Calet, *Les Murs de Fresnes*, 119.

15. Perrault, *L'Orchestre rouge*, 330.

16. Bourgeois, *L'Orchestre rouge*, 496.

17. Perrault, *L'Orchestre rouge*, 423.

18. Bourgeois, *L'Orchestra rouge*, 496.

| CHAPTER 15 | the last train

1. Ariouet, "Les enfants cachés pendant le seconde guerre mondiale aux sources d'une histoire clandestine."

2. "Interrogation of Honore," SOE memorandum, November 20, 1943, National Archives, Kew, UK, HS9/94/7 C663083.

3. Camplan, quoted in Dassa, *Vivre, aimer avec Auschwitz au cœur*, 123.

4. M. R. D. Foot, *SOE in France: An Account of the Work of the British Special Operations Executive in France, 1940–1944* (London: Frank Cass Publishers, 2004), 360. See also Pierre Tillet, "Tentative

History of In/Exfiltrations into/from France during WWII from 1940 to 1945," www.plan-sussex-1944.net/anglais/infiltrations_into_france.pdf.

5. Pannwitz, "CARETINA's History of the Sonderkommando Rote Kapelle," 39.

6. Pilette states that she never received such a doll from her mother. Pilette Spaak interview.

7. Ibid.

8. Perrault, *L'Orchestre rouge*, 439.

9. Ibid., 432.

10. Ibid., 435.

11. Trepper wrote a highly dramatic account of the "great day" of the attack on the Rue de Courcelles in his memoirs. See Trepper, *The Great Game*, 325.

12. Klarsfeld, *French Children of the Holocaust*, 89–91.

13. Dassa, *Vivre, aimer avec Auschwitz au cœur*, 205–6.

14. Ibid., 208.

15. Paula Hyman, *The Jews of Modern France* (Berkeley: University of California Press, 1998), 184.

16. See Katy Hazan, "Les réseaux de sauvetage d'enfants, la face clandestine de l'UGIF," www.ose-france.org/wp-content/uploads/2013/05/Sauvetage-UGIF.pdf.

17. Perrault, *L'Orchestre rouge*, 433.

18. Ellie Pithers, "Who Was the Original Miss Dior?" *Telegraph*, November 12, 2013, http://fashion.telegraph.co.uk/beauty/news-features/TMG10443967/Who-was-the-original-Miss-Dior.html.

19. Klarsfeld, *French Children of the Holocaust*, 92. See also Josephs, *Swastika over Paris*, 129.

20. Marshall, *The White Rabbit*, 40, 48.

21. "Activité du Groupe Medical du Mouvement National Contre le Racisme."

| CHAPTER 16 | liberation

1. Perrault, *L'Orchestre rouge*, 436.
2. Pilette Spaak interview.
3. Perrault, *L'Orchestre rouge*, 437.
4. Ibid.
5. Pilette Spaak interview.
6. Ibid.
7. Dumoulin, *Spaak*, 256–57.
8. Ibid., 258.
9. Lauren Faulkner Rossi, *Wehrmacht Priests* (Cambridge, MA: Harvard University Press, 2015), 140, 309n52. See also "Franzosen geholfen: Ein Buch über Pfarrer Theodor Loevenich," *Rhein-Erft Rundschau*, March 17, 2013, http://www.rundschau-online.de /region/rhein-erft/franzosen-geholfen-ein-buch-ueber-pfarrer -theodor-loevenich-5282192.
10. René Closset, *L'Aumonier de l'enfer: Franz Stock* (Mulhouse, France: Éditions Salvator, 1965), 158–59.
11. Jean-Pierre Guéno, *Paroles des femmes: La liberté du regard* (Paris: Radio France, 2007), 58–59.
12. Childers, *In the Shadows of War*, 227.
13. Pannwitz, "CARETINA's History of the Sonderkommando Rote Kapelle," 39.
14. Dassa, *Vivre, aimer avec Auschwitz au cœur*, 135.
15. Perrault, *L'Orchestre rouge*, 438.
16. Trepper, *Le Grand Jeu*, 577. See also Trepper, *The Great Game*, 418.
17. Perrault, *L'Orchestre rouge*, 439.
18. Palliser interview.
19. Pannwitz, "CARETINA's History of the Sonderkommando Rote Kapelle," 18.
20. Ibid., 36.
21. José Ainouz, *Attention aux enfants! Les Orphelins de la Shoah de Montmorency*, www.orphelins-shoah-montmorency.com/Site_Attention

_aux_enfants/Note_dintention.html. See also Mordecai Paldiel, *The Path of the Righteous: Gentile Rescuers of Jews during the Holocaust* (Hoboken, NJ: KTAV Publishing House, 1993), 44.

22. Cabanel, *Histoire des Justes de France*, 24.
23. Ibid., 33.

| CHAPTER 17 | the aftermath

1. Claude Spaak, *Théatre*, volume 1 (Paris: Éditions la Tête de Feuilles, 1973). See also Robert Frickx and Raymond Trousson, *Lettres Françaises de Belgique: Dictionnaire des Œuvres* (Paris: Duculot, 1989), 214. The play also includes a young female character whose experience echoes the story of Ruth Peters's teenage relation, Antonia Lyon-Smith. The conditions of her detention were particularly mild, thanks in large part to the German guard who fell in love with her.
2. Jacques Decker, "'Les Survivants' de Claude Spaak, au Théâtre du Parc, une Insistante Sonate," *Le Soir*, June 2, 1995, http://archives .lesoir.be/-les-survivants-de-claude-spaak-au-theatre-du -parc-une-_t-19950602-Z09LFN.html.
3. Mia Vandekerckhove, interview, Brussels, November 2014.
4. Trepper, *Le Grand Jeu*, 475.
5. Ibid., 548.

bibliography

Adler, Jacques. *The Jews of Paris and the Final Solution: Communal Response and Internal Conflicts, 1940–1944.* New York: Oxford University Press, 1989.

Aleichem, Sholem. *Tevye the Dairyman and the Railroad Stories.* New York: Knopf Doubleday, 2011.

Ariouet, Céline Marrot-Fellag. "Les enfants cachés pendant la seconde guerre mondiale aux sources d'une histoire clandestine," http://lamaisondesevres.org/cel/cel3.html.

"Aronson, B." "Suzanne Spaak, sauveteur d'enfants Juifs." *Naïe Presse,* March 9, 1945, Archives du Centre de Documentation Juive Contemporaine, Paris, Document CCXVIII-88a.

Barret, Dennis John. "Lt. D. J. Barrett Files." National Archives, Kew, UK, HS9/94/7 C663083.n.

Barrot, Olivier, and Raymond Chirat. *La vie culturelle dans la France occupée.* Paris: Gallimard, 2009.

Bassi-Lederman, Claudie, and Roland Wlos. "La rafle du Vel' d'Hiv, ou le 'sombre jeudi.'" *L'Humanité,* July 6, 2012.

Bauer, Yehuda. *American Jewry and the Holocaust*. Detroit: Wayne State University Press, 1982.

Beevor, Antony, and Artemis Cooper. *Paris After the Liberation, 1944–1949*. New York: Penguin, 2004.

Belien, Paul. *A Throne in Brussels: Britain, the Saxe-Coburgs and the Belgianization of Europe*. Charlottesville, VA: Imprint Academic, 2005.

Belleret, Robert. "Premier convoi pour Auschwitz." *Le Monde*, March 26, 2002, www.lemonde.fr/idees/article/2002/03/26/premier-convoi-pour-auschwitz_268264_3232.html.

Benbassa, Esther. *The Jews of France*. Princeton, NJ: Princeton University Press, 1999.

Bernard, Jean-Jacques. *Le Camp de la morte lente*. Paris: Éditions le Manuscrit, 2006.

Berr, Hélène. *Journal*. Translated by David Bello. New York: Weinstein Books, 2008.

Block, Gay, and Cynthia Ozick. *Rescuers: Portraits of Moral Courage in the Holocaust*. New York: Holmes & Meier, 1992.

Blumenkranz, Bernhard. *Histoire des Juifs en France*. Toulouse: Privat, 1972.

Bober, Robert. *What News of the War?* Translated by Robin Buss. London: Hamish Hamilton, 1998.

Bourgelin, Claude, and Marie-Claude Shapira. *Lire Cocteau*. Lyon: Presses Universitaires Lyon, 1992.

Bourgeois, Guillaume. *L'Orchestre rouge*. Paris: Nouveau Monde Éditions, 2015.

Braunstein, Philippe, ed. *L'Oratoire du Louvre et les Protestants Parisiens*. Geneva: Labor et Fides, 2011.

Breitman, Richard, Norman J. W. Goda, Timothy Naftali, and Robert Wolfe. *U.S. Intelligence and the Nazis*. New York: Cambridge University Press, 2005.

Brown, Frederick. *The Embrace of Unreason: France, 1914–1940*. New York: Alfred A. Knopf, 2014.

Browning, Christopher. *Ordinary Men: Reserve Police Battalion 101 and the Final Solution in Poland*. New York: HarperPerennial, 1998.

———. *The Origins of the Final Solution: The Evolution of Nazi Jewish Policy, September 1939–March 1942.* Lincoln: University of Nebraska Press, 2007.

Burney, Christopher. *Solitary Confinement and the Dungeon Democracy.* London: Macmillan, 1984.

Cabanel, Patrick. *Histoire des Justes de France.* Paris: Armand Colin, 2012.

"Cahen, Thérèse." Anonymes, Justes et Persécutés durant la période Nazie dans les communes de France (AJPN), http://www.ajpn.org/personne-Therese-Cahen-8532.html.

Calet, Henri. *Les Murs de Fresnes.* Paris: Éditions Viviane Haley, 1993.

Callil, Carmen. *Bad Faith: A Forgotten History of Family, Fatherland, and Vichy France.* New York: Knopf Doubleday, 2008.

Camplan, Marguerite. *Renouveau.* Rare Book Collection, US Holocaust Memorial Museum.

Cardinne-Petit, R. *Les Secrets de la Comédie Française: 1936–1945.* Paris: Nouvelles Éditions Latines, 1958.

Central Intelligence Agency. *The Rote Kapelle: The CIA's History of Soviet Intelligence and Espionage Networks in Western Europe, 1936–1945.* Washington, DC: University Publications of America, 1979.

Cesarani, David, ed. *The Final Solution: Origins and Implementation.* London: Routledge, 1994.

Chaigneau, Jean-François. *Le Dernier wagon.* Paris: France Loisirs, 1982.

Chertok, Léon. *Memoires: Les résistances d'un psy.* Paris: Odile Jacob, 2006.

Childers, Thomas. *In the Shadows of War: An American Pilot's Odyssey Through Occupied France and the Camps of Nazi Germany.* New York: Henry Holt, 2002.

Closset, René. *L'Aumonier de l'enfer: Franz Stock.* Mulhouse, France: Éditions Salvator, 1965.

Cobb, Matthew. *The Resistance: The French Fight Against the Nazis.* London: Pocket Books, 2009.

Cohen, Richard I. *The Burden of Conscience: French Jewish Leadership during the Holocaust.* Bloomington: Indiana University Press, 1987.

Colette. *Belle Saisons: A Colette Scrapbook*. New York: Farrar, Straus and Giroux, 1978.

———. *Looking Backwards*. Translated by David Le Vay. Bloomington: Indiana University Press, 1975.

———. *Paris de ma fenêtre*. Paris: Hachette, 1976.

Cordier, Daniel. *Alias Caracalla*. Paris: Gallimard, 2009.

Courtois, Stéphane, Denis Peschanski, and Adam Rayski. *L'Affiche Rouge: Immigranten und Juden in der französischen Résistance*. Berlin: Schwarze Risse Verlag, 1994.

———. *Le Sang de l'étranger: Les immigrés de la MOI dans la Résistance*. Paris: Fayard, 1989.

Courtois, Stéphane, and Adam Rayski. *Qui savait quoi? L'extermination des Juifs, 1941–1945*. Paris: Éditions la Découverte, 1987.

Cowburn, Benjamin. *No Cloak, No Dagger: Allied Spycraft in Occupied France*. London: Folio Society, 2011.

Curtis, Michael. *Verdict on Vichy: Power and Prejudice in the Vichy France Regime*. New York: Skyhorse Publishing, 2015.

Dassa, Sami. *Vivre, aimer avec Auschwitz au cœur*. Paris: Éditions L'Harmattan, 2002.

Deak, Istvan. *Europe on Trial*. Boulder, CO: Westview Press, 2015.

Debré, Jean-Louis. *Les Femmes qui ont reveillé la France*. Paris: Fayard, 2013.

Debré, Robert. *L'Honneur de vivre*. Paris: Hermann et Stock, 1974.

Decker, Jacques. "'Les Survivants' de Claude Spaak, au Théatre du Parc, une Insistante Sonate." *Le Soir*, June 2, 1995. http://archives.lesoir.be/-les-survivants-de-claude-spaak-au-theatre-du-parc-une-_t-19950602-Z09LFN.html.

Depelsenaire, Betty. *Symphony Fraternelle*. Brussels: Lumen, 1942.

Diamond, Hanna. *Fleeing Hitler: France 1940*. New York: Oxford University Press, 2008.

———. *Women and the Second World War in France, 1939–48*. New York: Longman, 1999.

Diamont, David. *Le billet vert*. Paris: Renouveau, 1977.

————. *250 combattants de la Résistance témoignent*. Paris: Éditions L'Harmattan, 1991.

————. *Jeune combat: la jeunesse juive dans la Résistance*. Paris: Éditions L'Harmattan, 1993.

Dumoulin, Michel. *Spaak*. Brussels: Éditions Racine, 1999.

Flicke, W. F. *Rote Kapelle: Spionage und Widerstand*. Augsburg, Germany: Weltbild Verlag, 1990.

"(La) Fondation de Rothschild Sous l'Occupation, 1939–1944." Paris: Fondation Rothschild, 2010.

Foot, M. R. D. *SOE in France: An Account of the Work of the British Special Operations Executive in France, 1940–1944*. London: Whitehall History Publishing, 2004.

Frankel, Jonathan, and Dan Diner, eds. *Dark Times, Dire Decisions: Jews and Communism*. New York: Oxford University Press, 2004.

Fredj, Jacques. *Les Juifs de France dans la Shoah*. Paris: Gallimard/Memorial de la Shoah, 2011.

Frickx, Robert, and Raymond Trousson. *Lettres Françaises de Belgique: Dictionnaire des Œuvres*. Paris: Duculot, 1989.

Fry, Varian. *Surrender on Demand*. Boulder, CO: Johnson Books, 1997.

Gensburger, Sarah. *C'Étaient des enfants: Déportation et sauvetage des enfants Juifs à Paris*. Paris: Skira, 2012.

Gildea, Robert. *Fighters in the Shadows*. London: Faber & Faber, 2015.

————. *Marianne in Chains: Daily Life in the Heart of France during the German Occupation*. London: Picador, 2004.

Gilmour, Jane. *Colette's France*. Melbourne: Hardie Grant, 2013.

Goldman, René. *Une femme juive dans les tourmentes du siècle passé: Sophie Schwartz-Micnik*. Paris: AGP, 2006.

Goudeket, Maurice. *Près de Colette*. Paris: Flammarion, 1956.

Guehenno, Jean. *Journal d'un homme de 40 ans*. Paris: Livre Poche, 1964.

Guéno, Jean-Pierre. *Paroles de femmes: La liberté du regard*. Paris: Radio France, 2007.

Guillemot, Marcelle. "Testimony" in "Témoignage de Melle [*sic*] GUILLEMOT, assistant sociale et Directrice de l'Oeuvre du

Temple l'Oratoire du Louvre—La Clairière, 60 ru Greneta, recueilli par Mme GAUDELETTE le 22 février 1946." Archives du Centre de Documentation Juive Contemporaine, Paris, Document CDLXVIII-17.

Gurevitch, Anatoli. *Un certain Monsieur Kent.* Paris: Grasset, 1995.

Gutman, Israel. *Encyclopedia of the Holocaust.* New York: Macmillan Library Reference, 1995.

Haft, Cynthia. *The Bargain and the Bridle: The General Union of the Israelites of France, 1941–1944.* Chicago: Dialog Press, 1983.

Hazan, Katy. *Les Orphelins de la Shoah: Les maisons de l'espoir (1944–1960).* Paris: Les Belles Lettres, 2000.

Hazan, Katy, with Serge Klarsfeld. *Le sauvetage des enfants juifs pendant l'Occupation dans les maisons de l'OSE 1938–1945.* Paris: Somogy Éditions d'Art, 2008.

Helm, Sarah. *A Life in Secrets: Vera Atkins and the Missing Agents of WWII.* New York: Knopf Doubleday Publishing Group, 2008.

Henry, Patrick, ed. *Jewish Resistance Against the Nazis.* Washington, DC: Catholic University of America Press, 2014.

Herzog, Dagmar, ed. *Lessons and Legacies: The Holocaust in International Perspective.* Chicago: Northwestern University Press, 2006.

Howarth, Patrick. *Undercover: The Men and Women of the Special Operations Executive.* London: Routledge, 1980.

Humbert, Agnes. *Resistance: A Woman's Journal of Struggle and Defiance in Occupied France.* Translated by Barbara Mellor. New York: Bloomsbury, 2004.

Hunt, Antonia. *Little Resistance.* London: Leo Cooper, 1982.

Hyman, Paula. *The Jews of Modern France.* Berkeley: University of California Press, 1998.

Jackson, Julian. *The Fall of France: The Nazi Invasion of 1940.* New York: Oxford University Press, 2003.

———. *France: The Dark Years, 1940–1944.* New York: Oxford University Press, 2003.

————. *La Grande Illusion*. London: British Film Institute, 2009.

Joffrin, Laurent. *Les Résistants: Témoignages 1940–1945*. Paris: Omnibus, 2013.

Joly, Laurent. *Les Collabos*. Paris: Éditions les Echappés, 2011.

Josephs, Jeremy. *Swastika over Paris: The Fate of the French Jews*. London: Bloomsbury, 1989.

Kedward, H. R. *Occupied France: Collaboration and Resistance, 1940–1944*. New York: Wiley, 1991.

Klarsfeld, Serge. *French Children of the Holocaust: A Memorial*. Translated by Glorianne Depondt and Howard M. Epstein. New York: New York University Press, 1996.

————. *La Shoah en France*. Volume 3: *Le calendrier de la persécution des Juifs de France, Septembre 1942–Août 1944*. Paris: Fayard, 2001.

————. *Memorial to the Jews Deported from France, 1942–1944*. New York: Beate Klarsfeld Foundation, 1983.

————. *Vichy-Auschwitz: La "solution finale" de la question juive en France*. Paris: Fayard, 1983.

Kosmala, Beate, and Georgi Verbeeck, eds. *Facing the Catastrophe: Jews and Non-Jews in Europe during World War II*. New York: Berg, 2011.

Kramer, Rita. *Flames in the Field: The Story of Four SOE Agents in Occupied France*. New York: Penguin, 2011.

Laffitte, Michel. "The Velodrome d'hiver Round-up: July 16 and 17, 1942." SciencesPo, http://www.sciencespo.fr/mass-violence-war -massacre-resistance/en/document/va-lodrome-da-hiver -round-july-16-and-17-1942.

————. *Un engrenage fatal: L'UGIF face aux realités de la Shoah*. Paris: Éditions Liana Levy, 2003.

Laloum, J. "Les maisons d'enfants de l'UGIF: Le centre de Saint-Mandé," *Revue d'Histoire de la Shoah* 1555 (September–December 1995): 89–90.

Lambert, Raymond-Raoul. *Diary of a Witness, 1940–1943*. Chicago: Ivan R. Dee, 2007.

Laub, Thomas. *After the Fall: German Policy in Occupied France, 1940–1944.* New York: Oxford University Press, 2009.

Lazare, Lucien. *Rescue as Resistance: How Jewish Organizations Fought the Holocaust in France.* Translated by Jeffrey M. Green. New York: Columbia University Press, 1996.

Lederman, Charles. Unpublished memoirs. Collection of Claudie Bassi-Lederman.

Lees, David. "Remembering the Vel d'hiv Roundup." University of Warwick Knowledge Centre, July 2012. www2.warwick.ac.uk /knowledge/arts/roundups.

Legrand, Madeleine (Madeleine Grou-Radenez). *À Fresnes.* Paris: Éditions Stock, 1944.

Leroux, Bruno, Frantz Malassis, and Cecile Vast. "Une dénonciation par l'image de la répression et des crimes nazis. La diffusion des photographies publiées à la Une de Défense de la France du 30 septembre 1943." Fondation de la Résistance, www.fondationre sistance.org/pages/rech_doc/une-denonciation-par-image -repression-des-crimes-nazis-diffusion-des-photographies_photo8 .htm.

"Lettre Pastorale de Monseigneur Saliège du 23 Août 1942." Musée de la Résistance 1940–1945 en ligne, http://museedelaresistanceen ligne.org/media6523-Lettre-pastorale-de-Monseigneur-SaliA.

Levendel, Isaac. *Not the Germans Alone: A Son's Search for the Truth of Vichy.* Chicago: Northwestern University Press, 2001.

Levy, Jean-Pierre. *Mémoires d'un franc-tireur: Itinéraire d'un résistant (1940–1944).* Paris: Éditions Complexe, 2000.

"Limonti, Hugues." Musée de l'Ordre de la Libération, http://www .ordredelaliberation.fr/fr/les-compagnons/598/hugues-limonti.

Lincourt, Michel. *In Search of Elegance: Towards an Architecture of Satisfaction.* Liverpool: Liverpool University Press, 1999.

List-Pakin, Jeanne. "Testimony." Archives du Centre de Documentation Juive Contemporaine, Paris, Document DLXXXVII-7.

Litmanovitch, Sarah. "Juillet 1942, la rafle des juifs dans le 18e, témoignages." Dixhuitinfo.com, March 10, 2010, www.dixhuitinfo .com/societe/histoire/article/juillet-1942-la-rafle-des-juifs.

Lottman, Herbert R. *The Left Bank: Writers, Artists, and Politics from the Popular Front to the Cold War.* Chicago: University of Chicago Press, 1998.

L'Union des Femmes Françaises. *Les Femmes dans la Résistance.* Paris: Éditions du Rocher, 1977.

Lusseyran, Jacques. *And There Was Light: Autobiography of the Blind Hero of the French Resistance.* Translated by Elizabeth R. Cameron. Sandpoint, ID: Morning Light Press, 2006.

"M., René." *La Guerre trop courte: Carnet d'un combattant.* Rio de Janeiro: Americ-Edit, 1942.

Magritte Delvaux Gnoli dans la Collection Claude Spaak. Paris: Galerie Arts, 1972.

Marais, Jean. *Histoires de ma vie.* Paris: Livres de Poche, 1976.

Marcot, François. *Dictionnaire Historique de la Résistance.* Paris: Robert Laffont, 2006.

Marnham, Patrick. *Resistance and Betrayal: The Death and Life of the Greatest Hero of the French Resistance.* New York: Random House, 2002.

Marrus, Michael R., and Robert O. Paxton. *Vichy France and the Jews.* New York: Schocken Books, 1983.

Marshall, Bruce. *The White Rabbit: The Secret Agent the Gestapo Could Not Crack.* London: Cassell, 2002.

Mémorial de la Shoah. *Les Justes de France.* Paris: Mémorial de la Shoah, 2007.

Mergier, Pierre. *Itineraire d'un français libre.* Paris: Librairie Harmattan, 2010.

Meyers, Mathias. "Résistance statt Wehrmacht." Kreisvereinigung Tübingen-Mössingen, July 17, 2012, http://tuebingen.vvn-bda .de/2012/07/17/resistance-statt-wehrmacht.

Milhaud, Fred, and Denise Milhaud. *L'Entraide temporaire: sauvetage d'enfants juifs sous L'occupation.* Paris: Alliance Israelite Universelle, 1984. http://www.europeana.eu/portal/en/record/09305 /C67A0AF1D7E0EB7CC4A923753431A15BEEADBFB6.html.

Miller, Michael B. *Shanghai on the Metro: Spies, Intrigue and the French Between the Wars.* Berkeley: University of California Press, 1994.

Miller, Sarah Lew, and Joyce B. Lazarus. *Hiding in Plain Sight: Eluding the Nazis in Occupied France.* Chicago: Chicago Review Press, 2012.

Mitchell, Allan. *Nazi Paris: The History of an Occupation, 1940–1944.* New York: Berghahn Books, 2008.

Moorehead, Caroline. *A Train in Winter.* New York: HarperPerennial, 2012.

———. *Village of Secrets.* New York: HarperPerennial, 2015.

Muller, Annette. *La petite fille du Vel d'Hiv.* Paris: Hachette Livre, 2012.

Nordling, Raoul. *Sauver Paris.* Paris: Petite Bibliothèque Payot, 2012.

Odic, Charles. *Stepchildren of France.* New York: Roy Publishers, 1945.

Oratoire du Louvre. *Voix chrétiennes dans la tourmente, 1940–1944.* Paris: Imprimerie de France, 1945.

O'Sullivan, Donal. *Dealing with the Devil: Anglo-Soviet Intelligence Cooperation in the Second World War.* New York: Peter Lang, 2010.

Paldiel, Mordecai. *The Path of the Righteous: Gentile Rescuers of Jews during the Holocaust.* Hoboken, NJ: KTAV Publishing House, 1993.

Pannwitz, Heinz. "CARETINA's History of the Sonderkommando Rote Kapelle." EGMA-44213/42334/43172, 38. Central Intelligence Agency library, https://www.cia.gov/library/readingroom /docs/PANNWITZ,%20HEINZ%20%20%20VOL.%202_0041 .pdf.

Paxton, Robert O. *Vichy France: Old Guard and New Order, 1940–1944.* New York: Columbia University Press, 2001.

Perrault, Gilles. *L'Orchestre Rouge.* Paris: Fayard, 1989.

———. *Paris under the Occupation.* Translated by Allison Carter and Maximilian Vos. New York: Vendome Press, 1987.

———. *The Red Orchestra.* New York: Pocket Books, 1970.

Peschanski, Denis. *Des étrangers dans la Résistance*. Paris: Les Éditions de l'Atelier, 2002.

Pierret, Alain. "La Rafle, le film: Le vrai capitaine Pierret raconté par son fils Alain." Dixhuitinfo.com, March 10, 2010, www.dixhuit info.com/culture/cinema/article/la-rafle-le-film-le-vrai -capitaine.

Piketty, Guillaume. *Résister: Les archives intimes des combattants de l'ombre*. Paris: Éditions Textuel, 2011.

Pithers, Ellie. "Who Was the Original Miss Dior?" *Telegraph*, November 12, 2013, http://fashion.telegraph.co.uk/beauty/news -features/TMG10443967/Who-was-the-original-Miss-Dior.html.

Pochna, Marie-France. *Christian Dior: The Man Who Made the World Look New*. New York: Arcade, 1996.

Powell, Jessica. *Literary Paris: A Guide*. New York: Little Bookroom, 2006.

Poznanski, Renée. *Jews in France during World War II*. Translated by Nathan Bracher. Hanover, NH: Brandeis University Press, University Press of New England in association with the United States Holocaust Memorial Museum, 2001.

———. *Propagandes et persécutions: La Résistance et le "problème juif,"* *1940–1944*. Paris: Libraire Arthème Fayard, 2008.

Pryce-Jones, David. *Paris in the Third Reich*. New York: Holt, Rinehart and Winston, 1981.

Rajsfus, Marcel. *Des juifs dans la collaboration*, volumes I and II. Paris: Études et documentations internationales, 1980.

Rayski, Adam. *Il y a soixante ans: La rafle du Vélodrome d'Hiver*. Paris: Marie de Paris, 2002.

———. *Nos illusions perdues*. Paris: Éditions Balland, 1985.

———. "Testimony." Archives du Centre de Documentation Juive Contemporaine, Paris, Document DLXI_84.

———. *The Choice of the Jews under Vichy: Between Submission and Resistance*. South Bend, IN: Notre Dame Press in association with the United States Holocaust Memorial Museum, 2005.

Riding, Alan. *And the Show Went On: Cultural Life in Nazi-Occupied Paris*. New York: Vintage, 2011.

Rosbottom, Ronald. *When Paris Went Dark: The City of Light under German Occuption, 1940–1944*. New York: Little, Brown, 2014.

de Rosnay, Tatiana. *Sarah's Key*. New York: St. Martin's Griffin, 2008.

Rossi, Lauren Faulkner. *Wehrmacht Priests*. Cambridge, MA: Harvard University Press, 2015.

Rubenstein, William D. *The Myth of Rescue*. London: Routledge, 1997.

Schulte, Jan Erik, and Michael Wala, eds. *Widerstand und Auswärtiges Amt: Diplomaten gegen Hitler*. Munich: Seidler, 2013.

Schwarz-Bart, Andre. *The Last of the Just*. New York: Overlook Press, 2000.

Sebba, Anne. *Les Parisiennes: How the Women of Paris Lived, Loved and Died in the 1940s*. London: Weidenfeld & Nicholson, 2016.

de Selva, Martial. *Petite histoire de Belgique*. Brussels: Éditions Couleur Livres, 2005.

Semelin, Jacques. *Persecutions et entraides dans la France occupée: Comment 75% des juifs en France ont echappé à la mort*. Paris: Les Arènes, 2013.

Simenon. *Tout Simenon 23*. Paris: Presses de la Cité, 1992.

Spaak, Claude. *Théatre*, volume 1. Paris: Éditions la Tête de Feuilles, 1973.

Spaak, Isabelle. *Ça ne ce fait pas*. Paris: Éditions des Équateurs, 2004.

Spaak, Janine. *Charles Spaak, mon mari*. Paris: Éditions France-Empire, 1977.

Steegmuller, Francis. *Cocteau*. Boston: Little, Brown & Company, 1970.

Streiff, Gérard. *Un soldat allemand dans la résistance française: Le courage de désobéir*. Paris: Oskar Éditeur, 2011.

Sudholt, Gert. *Das Geheimnis der Roten Kapelle: Das US-Dukument 0/7708*. CIA report.

"Suzanne Spaak Files." Archives du Centre de Documentation Juive Contemporaine, Paris, Document CCXVIII-88a, DLXI(4)-84.

Tarrant, V. E. *The Red Orchestra: The Soviet Spy Network Inside Nazi Europe*. London: Arms & Armour Press, 1995.

Thurman, Judith. *Secrets of the Flesh: A Life of Colette*. New York: Ballantine Books, 1999.

Trepper, Leopold. *The Great Game: Memoirs of the Spy Hitler Couldn't Silence*. New York: McGraw-Hill, 1977.

Trepper, Leopold, with Patrick Rotman. *Le Grand jeu*. Paris: Éditions Albin Michel, 1975.

Unger, Claude-François. *L'adolescent inadapté*. Paris: Presses Universitaires de France, 1957.

Unsworth, Richard P. *A Portrait of Pacifists: Le Chambon, the Holocaust, and the Lives of André and Magda Trocmé*. Syracuse, NY: Syracuse University Press, 2012.

Veillon, Dominique. *Fashion Under the Occupation*. London: Bloomsbury Academic, 2002.

Vercors. *La Bataille du silence: Souvenirs de minuit*. Paris: Presses de la Cité, 1967.

Vercors, James W. Brown, and Lawrence D. Stokes, eds. *Le Silence de la Mer*. London: Bloomsbury Academic, 2002.

Vesper, Karlen. "Ich wollte kein Komplize sein." *Neues Deutschland*, March 6, 2012, www.neues-deutschland.de/artikel/220381.ich -wollte-kein-komplize-sein.html.

Vinen, Richard. *The Unfree French: Life under the Occupation*. New Haven, CT: Yale University Press, 2007.

Vistel, Jacques. "Discours de Monsieur Jacques Vistel, Président de la Fondation de la Résistance" in "Une plaque à la mémoire de Défense de la France à la Sorbonne." Fondation de la Résistance, www.fondationresistance.org/pages/actualites/une-plaque -memoire-defense-france-sorbonne_actu443.htm.

Volk, Patricia. *Shocked: My Mother, Schiaparelli, and Me*. New York: Alfred A. Knopf, 2013.

Watt, Donald Cameron. *How War Came: The Immediate Origins of the Second World War*. New York: Pantheon, 1989.

Weitz, Margaret Collins. *Sisters in the Resistance: How Women Fought to Free France, 1940–1945*. New York: Wiley, 1995.

Whitaker, Mark. *My Long Trip Home.* New York: Simon & Schuster, 2011.

Wieviorka, Olivier. *Une certaine idée de la Résistance.* Paris: L'Universe Historique, 2010.

Wilkinson, James D. *The Intellectual Resistance in Europe.* Cambridge, MA: Harvard University Press, 1981.

Zucotti, Susan. *The Holocaust, the French, and the Jews.* Lincoln: University of Nebraska Press, 1999.

Periodicals

Combat
Défense de la France
Gringoire
J'Accuse
Le Matin
Le Figaro
Le Petit Parisien
Signal
Solidarité
Témoignage Chrétien

Interviews (Personal and E-mail)

Jacques Alexandre
Claudie Bassi-Lederman
Luce "Pilette" Spaak Bennani
Oriane de la Bourdonnaye Guéna
Richard Bruston
Sami Dassa
Larissa Gruszow
Tommy Happé
Patrice Lafaurie

Michèle Meunier
Anthony Palliser
Antoinette Spaak
Paul-Louis "Bazou" Spaak
Mia Verdekerckhove

Films and Recordings

Attention aux enfants! Les Orphelins de la Shoah de Montmorency. Directed by José Ainouz. 2010.

Les Caves du Majestic. Directed by Richard Pottier. Written by Charles Spaak. 1943.

Colette. Directed by Yannick Bellon. 1951.

La Grande Illusion. Directed by Jean Renoir. Written by Charles Spaak. 1937.

Hélène Berr: Une jeune fille dans Paris occupé. Directed by Jérôme Prieur. 2013.

Radio Paris ment and *Messages personnels*. BBC. Jalons, http://fresques.ina.fr/jalons/fiche-media/InaEdu00282/bbc-radio-paris-ment-et-messages-personnels.html.

La Resistance. Directed by Christophe Nick and Félix Olivier. 2008.

16 rue Lamarck, 1938, Paris. Framepool, http://footage.framepool.com/fr/shot/943433765-16-rue-lamarck-hostel-montmartre-entrer.

Sophie (Schwartz) Micnik Oral History Interview. US Holocaust Memorial Museum. 1990. RG-50.146*0003, 1995.A.1281.3.

illustration credits

1. Lucie Spaak collection.
2. Lucie Spaak collection.
3. Lucie Spaak collection.
4. Lucie Spaak collection.
7. Lucie Spaak collection.
9. Lucie Spaak collection.
12. Otto Spronk/CEGES-SOMA.
13. Mémorial de la Shoah.
14. Centre Régional Résistance & Liberté.
15. Larissa Gruszow collection.
16. Claudie Bassi-Lederman collection.
17. Lucie Spaak collection.
18. Mémorial de la Shoah.
20. Mémorial de la Shoah.
21. Richard Bruston collection.
24. Larissa Gruszow collection.
25. Larissa Gruszow collection.
26. Richard Bruston collection.

27. © Tallandier/Bridgeman Images.
28. Mémorial de la Shoah.
30. Oriane Guéna collection.
33. © Imperial War Museums.
35. Jacques Alexandre collection.
38. © Anne Nelson.

index

index

index

index

index

index

index

index

index

about the author

Anne Nelson has reported from three continents as a foreign correspondent and served as the executive director of the Committee to Protect Journalists. She is the author of *Red Orchestra: The Story of the Berlin Underground and the Circle of Friends Who Resisted Hitler; Murder Under Two Flags*; and *The U.S., Puerto Rico, and the Cerro Maravilla Cover-up*, as well as the plays *The Guys* and *Savages* and numerous other publications. Nelson received the Livingston Award for international reporting and a 2005 Guggenheim Fellowship for her work on the German Resistance. She was born in Oklahoma, graduated from Yale University, and has taught at Columbia University since 1995.